BATTLING THE LIFE AND DEATH
FORCES OF SADOMASOCHISM

BATTLING THE LIFE AND DEATH FORCES OF SADOMASOCHISM
Clinical Perspectives

Edited by

Harriet I. Basseches, Paula L. Ellman
and Nancy R. Goodman

Routledge
Taylor & Francis Group

LONDON AND NEW YORK

First published 2013 by Karnac Books Ltd.

Published 2018 by Routledge
2 Park Square, Milton Park, Abingdon, Oxon OX14 4RN
711 Third Avenue, New York, NY10017, USA

Routledge is an imprint of the Taylor & Francis Group, an informa business

British Library Cataloguing in Publication Data

A C.I.P. for this book is available from the British Library

ISBN-13: 9781855758209 (pbk)

Typeset by V Publishing Solutions Pvt Ltd., Chennai, India

CONTENTS

ACKNOWLEDGEMENTS   ix

ABOUT THE EDITORS AND CONTRIBUTORS   xiii

SERIES EDITOR'S PREFACE   xix

CHAPTER ONE
Introduction to sadomasochism in the clinical realm   1
Harriet I. Basseches, Paula L. Ellman and Nancy R. Goodman

CHAPTER TWO
Intersecting forces and development of sadomasochism   15
Paula L. Ellman and Nancy R. Goodman

PART I: CASE PRESENTED BY
PAULA L. ELLMAN AND DISCUSSIONS

CHAPTER THREE
Sadomasochism in work and play with Diane   29
Paula L. Ellman

CHAPTER FOUR
Discussion of the case of Diane   45
Alan Bass

CHAPTER FIVE
Discussion of the case of Diane   63
Jack Novick and Kerry Kelly Novick

CHAPTER SIX
Diane *vs.* reality: unconscious fantasies at impasse?
  discussion of the case of Diane   79
Marianne Robinson

PART II: CASE PRESENTED BY NANCY R. GOODMAN
AND DISCUSSIONS

CHAPTER SEVEN
Sailing with Mr. B through waters of "hurting love"   95
Nancy R. Goodman

CHAPTER EIGHT
Discussion of the case of Mr. B   111
James S. Grotstein

CHAPTER NINE
Discussion of the case of Mr. B   123
Margaret Ann Hanly

CHAPTER TEN
Discussion of the case of Mr. B   137
Terrence McBride

PART III: CASE PRESENTED BY ANDREA GREENMAN
AND DISCUSSIONS

CHAPTER ELEVEN
Eating for emptiness, eating to kill:
  sadomasochism in a woman with bulimia   157
Andrea Greenman

CHAPTER TWELVE
Discussion of the case of Mariah   179
Steven Ellman

CHAPTER THIRTEEN
Discussion of the case of Mariah   197
Shelley Rockwell

CHAPTER FOURTEEN
Trauma, archaic superego, and sadomasochism: discussion
    of the case of Mariah   213
Léon Wurmser

PART IV: CASE PRESENTED BY RICHARD REICHBART
AND DISCUSSIONS

CHAPTER FIFTEEN
The primitive superego of Mr. A: sadistic revenge fantasies,
    arousal and then masochistic remorse   229
Richard Reichbart

CHAPTER SIXTEEN
Discussion of the case of Mr. A   247
Sheldon Bach

CHAPTER SEVENTEEN
Discussion of the case of Mr. A   255
Harriet I. Basseches

CHAPTER EIGHTEEN
Sadomasochism and aggression—clinical theory: discussion
    of the case of Mr. A   273
Leo Rangell

INDEX   289

ACKNOWLEDGEMENTS

We would like to thank all of our contributors who have given to us and our book so generously. You have truly opened the world of sado-masochism to view with honesty and thought. We are grateful to CIPS, The Confederation of Independent Psychoanalytic Societies, for grant-ing us opportunities for our continual professional growth, especially this wonderful book series: The CIPS book series, "The Boundaries of Psychoanalysis". Thanks especially to Rick Perlman for his leadership. We are so thankful to the New York Freudian Society (now the Con-temporary Freudian Society) for coming to Washington to train us in 1985 and to support us in untold ways. Our Washington group of the Contemporary Freudian Society is our mainstay; you join us in our pas-sion for psychoanalysis. Kerry Malawista and Allan Frosch took time to read our first drafts and gave invaluable feedback. Our CIPS telephone study group on Sadomasochism with Diane Dowling, Bonnie Engdahl, Anita Katz, Judy Ann Kaplan, Judith S. Levy, Terrence McBride, and Hadassah Ramin gave us encouragement. Thanks to Beth Kalish-Weiss for writing the biographical material for Leo Rangell.

We thank our publisher, Karnac, for guidance and opportunity.

We are profoundly grateful to our husbands for their unwaver-ing support and love, Robert Basseches, Douglas Chavis, and Louis

Goodman. Also we voice appreciation for the love and support of parents: Mitzie and Joseph Itkin, Muriel and Norton Ellman, Mildred and Robert Rosenthal, and all the children, their partners, and grandchildren: K. B. Basseches and John Holm with Adam Edward, Joshua Basseches and Amy Perry Basseches with Jake and Sophie, and Jessica Basseches; Anna Chavis, Samuel Chavis, and Jennie Chavis; Elizabeth Goodman and David Brown with Ella, Isaiah, and Julian, and Jennifer Goodman and Frederick Yturralde with Kaia and Sophia.

And finally and profoundly, we appreciate each other for continual support, interest, dedication, and mostly, for the openness to the truth of our clinical experience. We have been able to foster honesty with each other since we were first in class together and have studied numerous topics intensively including listening, femininity, 9/11 trauma, and now sadomasochism. We are so grateful for this entire experience.

Special Tribute to Leo Rangell

We want to make a special tribute to Leo Rangell, his friendship with Harriet Basseches, and his chapter in this book. He died on 28 May 2011 at ninety-seven. We are aware that this is one of the last contributions of a vast tome that he wrote. His last correspondence, through email, to Harriet was as follows:

Dear Harriet,

> Sorry for this delay.
> I am writing these days with great difficulties-age-related—a pain in the ass.
> But wanted this to get to you—so here it is, so far.
> That is an amazing duo—our two papers.
> Yes, Harriet, the two together are more than interesting; they are very instructive.
> They might appear to come from different patients, yet both are from the same one.
> That's the way it is, as Walter Cronkite used to say.
> Two explorers in the same cluster of caves are digging in caves side by side which are known and then seen to be connected.
> The two are at close but slightly different levels.
> The tunnel that finally connected the two was the definitive interpretation of castration anxiety in both cases, which liberated the choked-up ego to be able to then rush toward a "cure".

Back come sex and aggression.

Now: your paper is strictly clinical, which is more what was wanted in this book. And by the way, Harriet, your clinical report was awesome. What a clinician! Your flow and thoroughness clinically is MOST impressive.

Mine was more of an overview, and included more of the abstract.

Both are needed.

Especially because this book, as almost all others today, are inquiring about the workings of theory and practice together. How do different theories affect practice?

You answered the question, "what time is it?" by giving the time.

Mine went also into how watches are made!!!???

Both answer the question to the patient, "Do you mean that?" i.e., his various wild rantings and threats: "I will cut your head off (or testicles or penis or anything ...)"

But whether he answers No, or Yes, the meanings to the patient and analyst were metaphoric not literal—in my version and impression ...

I wrote of S-M in its pure or extreme or polarised form. You wrote of "more subtle forms" of S-M, widely present.

And yes, S-M, as fetishism, or as the old latent homosexuality, also exist widely in the general traditional neurotic personality.

On today's scene, it might be that freedom from a threat of sadism, in terrorism, will never again be absent as a possibility.

Only putting both our thoughts together can we present the whole picture of this individual, the patient, this particular self.

I am attaching an update of my paper, with quite a bit added toward the end.

And I am working on the bibliography.

It is perhaps 95% finished at this point but not yet complete or polished.

But is for your (and the other Editors') information at this point.

Love ... Leo

ABOUT THE EDITORS AND CONTRIBUTORS

Editors/Contributors

Harriet I. Basseches, Ph.D., ABPP, FIPA, is a training and supervising analyst in the Contemporary Freudian Society (CFS), formerly the New York Freudian Society, and the IPA (International Psychoanalytical Association), and a member of the CFS Permanent Faculty. She is a diplomate in psychoanalysis certified by the American Board of Psychoanalysis in Psychology (ABPsaP). She has held the following positions: president, the New York Freudian Society; president, the Confederation of Independent Psychoanalytic Societies (CIPS); and trustee of the International Psychoanalytical Association. She has written and presented in the areas of femininity and female psychology, listening, enactment, terror, and sadomasochism. She has a private practice in psychotherapy and psychoanalysis in Washington, DC.

Paula L. Ellman, Ph.D., ABPP, FIPA, is a training and supervising analyst in the Contemporary Freudian Society (CFS) and the IPA. She is the institute director of the Washington Program of the Contemporary Freudian Society, in addition to being on the permanent faculty. She is a diplomate in psychoanalysis certified by the American Board of Psychoanalysis in Psychology (ABPsaP) and assistant professor of psychology at the George Washington University Center for Professional Psychology. She is a Member of the Editorial Board of the CIPS Book series on the Boundaries of Psychoanalysis. She has written and presented in the areas of femininity and female psychology, listening, enactment, terror, and sadomasochism. Her recent publications include: "We're in this too": the effects of 9/11 on transference/countertransference and technique (with N. Goodman, H. Basseches and S. Elmendorf) in N. Goodman & M. Meyers (Eds.) *The Power of Witnessing: Reflections, Reverberations, and Traces of the Holocaust—Trauma Psychoanalysis, and the Living Mind,* (Routledge Press, 2012) and Enactment: Opportunity for symbolising trauma (with N. Goodman) in A. Frosch (Ed.,) *Absolute Truth and Unbearable Psychic Pain: Psychoanalytic Perspectives on Concrete Experience,* (Karnac, 2012). She has a private practice in psychotherapy and psychoanalysis in North Bethesda, Maryland and Washington, DC.

Nancy R. Goodman, Ph.D., FIPA, is a training and supervising analyst and member of the permanent faculty with the Contemporary Freudian Society, Washington DC Program and the IPA. She is interested in unconscious fantasy, witnessing of individual and mass trauma, enactments, and psychoanalysis and film. She is the leader of a CIPS study group on enactments. Her most recent publications include: *The Power of Witnessing: Reflections, Reverberations, and Traces of the Holocaust—Trauma Psychoanalysis, and the Living Mind* (co-editor/writer with Marilyn B. Meyers, Routledge Press, 2012), Enactment: Opportunity for symbolising trauma (Ellman & Goodman, 2012) in A. Frosch (Ed.,) *Absolute Truth and Unbearable Psychic Pain: Psychoanalytic Perspectives on Concrete Experience,* (Karnac, 2012), and editor of *Psychoanalysis: Listening to Understand—Selected Papers of Arlene Kramer Richards,* (IP Books, 2013). She maintains a psychoanalytic practice in Bethesda, MD.

Contributors

Sheldon Bach, Ph.D., FIPA, is adjunct clinical professor of psychology at the NYU Postdoctoral Program in Psychoanalysis, and a training and supervising analyst at the Institute for Psychoanalytic Training and Research and at the Contemporary Freudian Society. He is the author of numerous articles and four books: *The Language of Perversion and the Language of Love; Getting from Here to There: Analytic Love, Analytic Process; Narcissistic States and the Therapeutic Process;* and *The How-To Book for Students of Psychoanalysis and Psychotherapy.* In 2006 he received the Heinz Hartmann Award for outstanding contributions to psychoanalysis.

Alan Bass, Ph.D., FIPA, is a training and supervising analyst and faculty member at IPTAR and the Contemporary Freudian Society. The author of two books (*Difference and Disavowal: The Trauma of Eros* and *Interpretation and Difference: The Strangeness of Care*, both published by Stanford University Press) and many articles. He also teaches psychoanalysis in the graduate philosophy department of the New School for Social Research. He is the translator of four books by Jacques Derrida.

Steven J. Ellman, Ph.D., FIPA, is professor emeritus City University of NY. He is a training and supervising analyst at IPTAR where he was program chair and twice president. He was the first president of the Confederation of Independent Psychoanalytic Societies (CIPS) and was on the executive council of the International Psychoanalytic Association. He has published more than seventy papers on psychoanalysis, sleep and dreams, and the neurophysiology of motivation and held many editorial positions on psychoanalytic journals. He has authored and edited seven books including *When Theories Touch; A Historical and Theoretical Integration of Psychoanalytic Thought* (the first CIPS series book); *Enactment: Toward a New Approach to the Therapeutic Relationship* (co-editor, Michael Moskowitz); *The Mind in Sleep* (with Antrobus); and *Freud's Technique Papers: A Contemporary Perspective.*

Andrea Greenman, Ph.D., FIPA, is a graduate of New York University's postdoctoral program in psychotherapy and psychoanalysis, where she is currently a supervisor and member of the faculty. She is a training and supervising analyst at the Contemporary Freudian Society, where she is also a member of the board of directors and past chair of the Psychotherapy Training Program. She is a member, supervisor, and faculty at IPTAR, and a graduate of IPTAR's Socioanalytic Training Program. In addition, Dr. Greenman is clinical adjunct faculty in the clinical psychology doctoral programs at CUNY and LIU. She is a fellow of the International Psychoanalytic Association and in private practice on the Upper West Side of New York.

James S. Grotstein, M.D., FIPA, is clinical professor of psychiatry at the David Geffen School of Medicine, UCLA, and training and supervising analyst at the New Center for Psychoanalysis and the Psychoanalytic Center of California, Los Angeles. He is a member of the editorial board of the *International Journal of Psychoanalysis* and is past North American vice-president of the International Psychoanalytic Association. He has published over 250 papers including, "The Seventh Servant: The Implication of the Truth Drive in Bion's Theory of 'O'" (*International Journal of Psychoanalysis*), "Projective Transidentification: An Extension of the Concept of Projective Identification" (*International Journal of Psychoanalysis*), and most recently "Dreaming as a 'Curtain of Illusion': Revisiting the 'Royal Road' with Bion as our Guide" (*International Journal of Psychoanalysis*). He is the author of many books, including, *Who is the Dreamer Who Dreams the Dream: A Study of Psychic Presences* (2000) and *A Beam of Intense Darkness: Wilfred Bion's Legacy to Psychoanalysis* (Karnac 2007). His most recent book is a two volume work on psychoanalytic technique, "*... But at the Same Time and on Another Level ...*" *Psychoanalytic Theory and Technique in the Kleinian/Bionian Mode, Volumes I and II* (Karnac 2009). In 2011, the IPA 47th Annual Congress in Mexico City featured a presentation and panel honoring his life's work. He is in the private practice of psychoanalysis in West Los Angeles.

Margaret Ann Fitzpatrick Hanly, Ph.D., FIPA, is a training and supervising analyst in the Toronto Institute of Psychoanalysis, IPA. She is in private practice in psychoanalysis and psychoanalytic psychotherapy in Toronto, Canada, president of the Canadian Psychoanalytic Society, associate-director of the Toronto Institute of Psychoanalysis, member of the International Psychoanalytical Association Committee on Clinical Observation, chair of the NAPsaC Working Party Steering Committee. She is on the executive editorial board of the *Psychoanalytic Quarterly* and on the editorial board of the *Canadian Journal of Psychoanalysis*. Among her publications are "Keats's Oral Imagination: 'Tis not through envy'" (*Psychoanalytic Quarterly*, 1986); "Sado-masochism in Charlotte Bronte's *Jane Eyre*: 'A Ridge of Lighted Heath'" (*International Journal of Psychoanalysis*, 1993); Editor, *Essential Papers on Masochism* (New York University Press, 1995); "Narrative, Now and Then: A Critical Realist Approach" (*International Journal of Psychoanalysis*, 1996); "Creativity and oedipal fantasy in Austen's *Emma*" (*International Journal of Psychoanalysis*, 2003), "Masochistic Character and Psychic Change in Austen's *Mansfield Park*, (*International Journal of Psychoanalysis*, 2005); "Object Loss, renewed Mourning and Psychic Change in Jane Austen's *Persuasion*, (*International Journal of Psychoanalysis*, 2007); "Aesthetic Ambiguity and Sibling Jealousy in Austen's *Pride and Prejudice*" (*Psychoanalytic Quarterly*, 2009).

Terrence McBride, Psy.D., FIPA, is a training and supervising analyst and faculty member at the Los Angeles Institute and Society for Psychoanalytic Studies (LAISPS) and past president and director of training. He has served on the board and is vice president of the Confederation of Independent Psychoanalytic Societies (CIPS). He is in private practice in West Los Angeles and Hollywood, California.

Jack Novick, Ph.D., FIPA, and **Kerry Kelly Novick,** FIPA, are child, adolescent, and adult psychoanalysts on the faculties of numerous psychoanalytic institutes around the country. They are both training and supervising analysts of the International Psychoanalytical Association. They trained with Anna Freud in London, England, and, in addition to their clinical work, have been active in teaching, research, professional organisations, and the community. They joined other colleagues to found the award-winning non-profit Allen Creek Preschool in Ann Arbor and the international Alliance for Psychoanalytic Schools. Jack and Kerry Novick have written extensively since the 1960s, with many articles published in major professional journals. They have published four books, including *Fearful Symmetry: The Development and Treatment of Sadomasochism.* Several have been translated into Italian, German, and Finnish.

Leo Rangell, M.D., FIPA, (1913–2011) was, from 1995, honorary president of the International Psychoanalytical Association. He served twice as president of both the American Psychoanalytic and the International Associations and was clinical professor of psychiatry at the University of California, Los Angeles and San Francisco. He is the author of nearly 500 publications in psychoanalysis and related mental health sciences, including his most recent highly acclaimed text, *The Road to Unity in Psychoanalytic Theory* (2007). In 2011, shortly before his death, he was awarded the first honorary presidency of the American Psychoanalytic Association.

Richard Reichbart, Ph.D., FIPA, is president-elect and training and supervising analyst of the Institute for Psychoanalytic Training and Research (IPTAR) in New York City. He is also past president of the New Jersey Psychoanalytic Society, and training and supervising analyst at the Center for Psychotherapy and Psychoanalysis of New Jersey (CPPNJ). He is a board member of the China American Psychoanalytic Alliance (CAPA), a member of the American Psychoanalytic

Association (APsaA), and a fellow of the International Psychoanalytic Association (IPA). He has published numerous psychoanalytic papers. He maintains a private practice in Ridgewood, NJ.

Shelley Rockwell, Ph.D., FIPA, is a training and supervising analyst with the Contemporary Freudian Society and in private practice in Washington DC. She has taught, written, and presented on contemporary Kleinian theory and on the relationship between psychoanalysis and literature.

Marianne Robinson, Ph.D., LCSW, FIPA, is a training and supervising psychoanalyst, a founding member of Northwestern Psychoanalytic Society and a full member of Psychoanalytic Center of California. She practices in Seattle. Her thinking is compatible with that of Klein, Bion, Tustin, and with many who develop their ideas. Her research focuses on investigating and understanding the earliest physical, emotional, and mental experiences as they manifest in the clinical situation and she has presented and published on these subjects including A binocular view of adhesion: From prenatal contiguity to postnatal appetite. In *Primitive Mental States*, J. Van Buren & S. Alhanati (eds.), Routledge, 2010, and Infant observation: Catastrophic change under a microscope, Bion in Boston International Conference, Boston July 23–26. In *Growth and Turbulence in the Container/Contained—Bion's Continuing Legacy*, H. Levine & L. Brown (eds.) Routledge, 2013.

Léon Wurmser, M.D., Ph.D. h.c. (honorary degree in philosophy, Humboldt University, Berlin), FIPA, is a psychoanalyst and former clinical professor of psychiatry, University of West Virginia, with regular and extensive teaching in Europe. He is the author of *The Hidden Dimension* (1978); *The Mask of Shame* (1981); *Flight from Conscience* (1987, in German); *The Riddle of Masochism* (1993, in German); *Magic Transformation and Tragic Transformation* (1999, in German); *The Power of the Inner Judge* (2000); *Values and Ideas of Judaism in Psychoanalytic View* (2001, in German); *Torment Me, but Don't Abandon Me* (2007); *Shame and the Evil Eye* (in German, 2011) and co-author with Heidrun Jarass of *Jealousy and Envy—New Views on Two Powerful Emotions* (2007), *a monograph in Psychoanalytic Inquiry Book Series*, and *Nothing Good is Allowed to Stand* (2012), in the same series. He is a training and supervising analyst for the Contemporary Freudian Society, formerly the New York Freudian Society, and recipient of the Egnér Foundation and the *Journal of the American Psychoanalytic Association* prizes.

SERIES EDITOR'S PREFACE

Fredric Perlman

It is my great pleasure to offer these prefatory notes to this volume, *Battling the Life and Death Forces of Sadomasochism: Clinical Perspectives*, the sixth installment in the CIPS Book Series on the *Boundaries of Psychoanalysis*. My delight is twofold. First, this book is a treasure, and I most heartily and happily congratulate the editors, Harriet Basseches, Paula Ellman, and Nancy Goodman, and each of the terrific contributors who have brought this wonderful effort to life. Second, and of particular importance to so many of us at CIPS, this book fulfills a core purpose of our confederation of psychoanalytic societies: to promote and protect the theoretical pluralism of our community while, at the same time, capitalizing on our diversity of thought by creating opportunities for probing clinical dialogue across societies and schools of thought.

Since its inception in 1992, CIPS has endeavored to create and nurture such dialogues through an expanding program of clinical conferences, ongoing study groups, and writing projects formed in conjunction with this book series. Each of these endeavors was intended to encourage and enable our members to transcend insular parochialisms of psychoanalytic thought and so, over time, to transform our coalition of separate component psychoanalytic societies into a multi-lingual, multi-cultural professional community. The experience of the past twenty years has indeed demonstrated the value of this effort. This book, like its predecessors in the CIPS Book Series, was born in the clinical dialogues, both planned and spontaneous, that spring to life within the formal programs and informal collegial networks that CIPS has promoted.

As Robert Wallerstein observed a quarter of a century ago, all psychoanalysts, no matter their orientation, share a common body of clinical experience shaped by the real-life psychologies of our real-life patients and the common unifying purpose towards which we all strive: to listen, to understand, to illuminate rather than persuade. The clinical encounter, Wallerstein wrote, is our common ground, the basis for our collaborative efforts across the country and around the world. But this common ground is readily lost when we talk in specialized terminologies or substitute technical terms for everyday descriptive language. The promise of clinical experience as a common ground for analysts in a pluralistic theoretical universe rests on a commitment to phenomenology, on a dialogue that begins with descriptions of the clinical encounter rather than theoretical abstractions disconnected from empirical referents.

Although CIPS has not, to my knowledge, ever promulgated any formal rules to regulate our dialogue, a commitment to descriptive clinical reporting is an informal convention, promoted by common sense, good will, and the spontaneously generated culture of our conferences and study groups. I recall with some amusement my first experience in a small-group case discussion at one of our clinical conferences that was held in Los Angeles. I had presented a difficult patient with pronounced sadomasochistic character pathology, and toward the end of my presentation, referred to the "masochistic countertransference" in which I found myself as I was repeatedly pummeled by the patient's incessant complaints. I was informed by none other than the wise and wonderful Hedda Bolgar that such technical lingo conceals more than it conveys, and that it was incumbent upon me, in keeping with our clinical tradition, to spell out in simple terms what I was feeling toward this patient. And, oh, how right she was!

In keeping with the tradition of CIPS clinical conferences and study groups, this volume is fundamentally a clinical enterprise. The volume was planned by its three editors/writers, who then invited CIPS members from different societies and different schools of thought to join them in the clinical exploration of sadomasochism. It is organized around four detailed clinical reports, all written in plain English to convey the actualities of the clinical encounter in experience-near terms. Every clinical report is followed by three probing discussions, each of which examines the clinical data from a different theoretical or technical perspective. The result is a stimulating series of encounters with challenging patients, dedicated analysts, and esteemed collaborators whose unique points of view bring the four cases to life in novel ways. Each illuminates hidden clinical features like changing light settings that reveal different aspects of a theatrical set or the faces of the actors appearing within it.

Any book on sadomasochism is apt to be unsettling and this book is no exception. How could it be otherwise? As Freud and others have long observed, sadomasochism challenges our theory, highlighting unresolved questions about the nature of the drives, the roots and genesis of aggression, the complex relationship between aggression and sexuality, between love and hate, and the reciprocal influences of sadomasochistic sexual fantasies and sadomasochistic object relations. Sadomasochistic phenomena also challenge our clinical technique and, at times, our clinical identities. When sadomasochistic fantasies are central to object relations, perverse destructiveness can transform the analytic situation into an arena for the persistent enactment of sadomasochistic scenarios, paralyzing or overwhelming the analyst. Every utterance can be perversely exploited to fuel exciting sadomasochistic fantasies that shape insistent definitions of the psychoanalytic situation. At times, work with such patients moves us to the outer limits of our capacities as analysts, indeed, to the boundary of our clinical enterprise.

Few analysts will read the clinical accounts at the core of this book without experiencing occasional eruptions of unbidden emotion, analogous to countertransference. While readers will, of course, differ in their readiness to "enter" the situations that are described herein, I think anyone who imagines himself or herself working with these four patients will experience aggravation, indignation and hostility—or in another moment—depression, deflation, and detachment from the patient and the treatment. For some readers, this clinical material is bound to evoke disturbing memories of difficult cases and, perhaps, the dim rumble of self-doubt about treatments whose outcomes might have been better. As I read through each case, I repeatedly found myself recalling one patient or another, imagining "do-overs" in fantasy to master past challenges failed in reality. Such disquiet may be the unavoidable concomitant of an expanding understanding for any increment of insight is apt to elicit recollections of moments whose potential might have been better fulfilled—if we only had known then what we are coming to know now. This book is filled with such insights, novel ideas that can elicit regrets or stir up wishes for second chances to better redeem the promise of treatment.

However disturbing, the disquiets of this book are well worth enduring. The readings that follow this preface demonstrate not only the complex and dispiriting challenges we encounter when we treat such provocative and destructive patients, but also the enduring value of our effort and the potential efficacy of our methods. For any reader who has felt alone and overwhelmed by patients such as those described in this book, these four cases and the discussions that accompany them will offer not only the comfort of a wider collegiality but much clinical wisdom. The four cases and twelve discussions constituting this book are all hopeful and inspiring. They demonstrate that despite the confusion, hurt, and tension these patients can arouse—despite the very real challenges to the analyst's work ego and sense of identity—there is good reason to labor on with a measure of confidence in the psychoanalytic enterprise and the long-term promise it holds, even for patients whose pathology compels them to dismiss and denigrate our efforts. The voice of the intellect is soft, Freud told us, but it is persistent. The steady pursuit of understanding, perseverance in our psychoanalytic vocation, is vindicated by the clinical experiences described in these pages.

I cannot close this short preface without a pause, a shared moment devoted to the memory of our much esteemed and much loved colleague, Leo Rangell. Leo Rangell's chapter, a discussion of Richard Reichbart's case report, is his final published word. Those who knew Leo personally will read his words and hear his voice, ever strong and spirited. Leo was a person of enormous stature in psychoanalysis, a master theoretician, teacher, and stalwart leader of the psychoanalytic movement for many years. The CIPS community honored him, learned from him, enjoyed his company, and took great delight in his stories and his playful sense of humor. Leo was endlessly vigorous in his engagement with psychoanalysis, always ready to take up new challenges. Our last conversation, which took place shortly before his death, was a discussion of an idea for a new book on the subject of personal integrity, a topic to which Leo had come to devote a great deal of attention in recent decades. Leo's death leaves a vacuum in the psychoanalytic world, and an ache in the hearts of those who knew and loved him. I was privileged, enormously privileged, to know Leo as a thinker, a mentor, and a friend for all seasons. I wish he were here now to enjoy the publication of this volume, a volume to which he was eager to contribute, and of which he would be quite rightly proud.

CHAPTER ONE

Introduction to sadomasochism in the clinical realm

Harriet I. Basseches, Paula L. Ellman and Nancy R. Goodman

This book examines the forces of sadomasochism in the clinical domain where transference and countertransference reside. This is a clinically centred book in which psychoanalysts write in depth about cases where sadomasochism is present for analysand and analyst. Four cases present the unfolding analytic exchange where life and death forces collide. Psychoanalysts from varying schools of thought provide clinical material and discussions on each case illuminating the complex phenomena that often include lifelong perversions and painful narcissistic difficulties. Through the four case presentations and each of their three discussions, psychoanalytic therapists will find maps for guiding their own work with sadomasochistic processes. Cases where sadomasochism is prominent abound with dramas containing control and denigration, domination and submission. Often there is history of overstimulation and under-stimulation from infancy and childhood.

Since Freud first introduced infantile psychosexual development and the concepts of component instincts, both passive and active, psychoanalysts have been exploring sadomasochism in its various forms (Freud, 1905). The belief that togetherness must involve pain, creates a life and death struggle that is imbued with powerful instinctual

1

gratification. Unconscious sexualised scenes, both dyadic and triadic, carry humiliation and conquest. When these forces are brought to treatment, the analyst's affective responses to negations and attacks, the countertransferences, provide opportunities to recognise conflicts and repetitions, and to move them into a symbolising process. Rather than embroilment in a negative therapeutic reaction, the treatment process is freed to proceed and deepen. In this chapter, we describe the way our interest in sadomasochism in the mind developed from our clinical work and discussions with each other over many years. We present our evolving thinking about the factors contributing to the dynamics of sadomasochism as they present clinically.

A scene

Imagine that there are two people—a man and a woman or even an analyst and an analysand. In this scene, there might be a third person, a witness, an observer. The exchange could sound like a fight, a power struggle over who controls whom, who dominates whom, who wins, who suffers, and who submits. Or it could seem like the sounds of exciting violent love-making. Pain and denigration are necessary ingredients of togetherness leading to intense orgiastic sexual contact, then renewal of separateness. Whatever the subject matter of the exchange, the quality of the relationship is of one person hurting the other, even each hurting the other in turn. The third, if present could feel helpless, painfully overstimulated, anxious, invisible, as if the mutual absorption of the interacting duo excludes or possibly even annihilates. In their connection the couple ignore and destroy conventional boundaries. Important to our understanding of the sadomasochistic transference and countertransference is the internal representation in each participant. The observer analyst, the third, may at times become overwhelmed. Or analytic reflection may manage to remain active. The scene captures feelings of aliveness and deadness. It is compelling. We have heard the story many times.

Sadomasochism plays out on the theatrical stage, in literary sagas, and in the consultation room. Marquis de Sade wrote many scenes of the erotic form of sadomasochism from his prison cell. The words "sadism" and "sadist" are derived from his name. Krafft-Ebing (1886) coined the term "masochism" based on Leopold von Sacher Masoch's descriptions of his erotic life in his novella, *Venus in Furs* (1870). Recently, in a theatrical adaptation by David Ives (2011), a man and a woman prompt and provoke each other to enact a sadomasochistic way of relating that is both frightening and exciting. The individuals in the couple shift roles continually, recasting themselves, each as dominating, dominated, humiliating, humiliated, master, and slave. They successfully appear to redefine the feminine and the masculine, and imply a triumph over reality, that is, enacting a perversion. Edward Albee (1962), another playwright, powerfully captured the painful and sadomasochistic interaction between George and Martha in *Who's Afraid of Virginia Wolf?* The popularity of these plays suggests both the timelessness and appeal of the topic. It is a subject that continues to challenge and perplex psychoanalysts ever since Freud originally chose to write about it. Freud (1905, 1919, 1924, 1927, 1937, 1940). developed his ideas, and many analysts since have reviewed the topic (for example JAPA psychoanalytic panels: 1981, 1984, 1991). Some analysts emphasise the sadistic aspect, others the masochistic, and still others the perverse. The vastness of the psychoanalytic literature as well as the literature of public discourse attest to the compelling nature of the subject. Perhaps its profound linkage to sexuality and aggression, and its pervasiveness in so many aspects of life activities, may help to explain the fascination and universality of this topic.

The fuel for generating this volume: how we arrived here

We have shared our clinical work with one another for over thirty years. As we brought our most despairing cases to each other, we found a trend in the nature of the clinical challenges we were each facing. With certain patients we felt deadened, ineffective, overstimulated, and guilty. These are the patients about whom we prefer not to speak. These are the patients that we are locked in with, believing that the work is at a standstill and not knowing how to free ourselves. With many, we feel anxious or sleepy, dead and invisible. "The analysis seems impossible." In our study group we came to identify as sadomasochism the hold that these patients were having on us and our analysing capacities. Each of us felt tempted by despair. Were we incompetent, or were our patients unanalysable? Thinking together, we came to realise that there was masochism and sadism at work. We yearned for knowledge. We immersed ourselves in the literature on sadomasochism discovering invaluable ideas about symptoms, dynamics, and efforts at technical strategies. In fact many of the discussants in this book write about sadomasochism, perversion, disavowal, narcissism, and shame. Reading and thinking together provided the grounding for us, anchoring us from feeling swept away.

Transference/countertransference is the playing ground for these sadomasochistic patients' core issues—their hatred, their need, their contempt, their terrors, their addictive arousal, their degrading and degraded selves. As we started to bring to one another the feelings and fantasies we were secretly harboring in our countertransferences, we found greater access to the transferences of our patients. Our process permitted us to create movement in our analytic work and to make contact with our patients' minds. Unrecognised sadomasochism often threatens treatment with negative therapeutic reactions. Once we identified our deadness of mind, we found meaning and symbolisation, bringing life back to the analyst's mind and to the analytic process itself. In other words, centring on the transference and countertransference experience encouraged the battle to continue rather than the treatment be destroyed. We are tremendously grateful for having a place with each other where we are free to expose honestly the workings of our own psyches and our listening capacities (Goodman, Basseches, Ellman, et al., 1993), and discover those of our patients.

With this understanding in mind, we decided to write a clinical book, a book focused on what happens in the consultation room. We decided on a format in which the case could become known to the reader, a complete case write-up with clear delineation of the contours of the experience. A full clinical case presentation allows more in-depth access to the mind of the analyst, the mind of the patient, and the unfolding analytic process. Not only are we offering a clinical volume, but one which gathers together a collection of four clinical cases into one compendium—a window into the duet of two psyches in four different dyads. Each case remains close to the experience of sadomasochism between the analyst and analysand. This format brings about an enlivening dialogue honouring the way psychic communication unfolds in the dyad of treatment. Each case has the attention of three discussants. We asked all discussants to stay close to the experience as written by the analysts who held the stories of sadomasochism. Our instructions were: "This is not supervision—this is an opportunity to associate freely and comment, to show the best of psychoanalytic dialogue." Engaging our psychoanalytic community through discussions expands understanding of the sadomasochistic paradigm: traumas, desires and their conflicts, aggression and hatred, perversions and fragilities of narcissistic vulnerabilities.

Sadomasochism

A life and death struggle is at the core of sadomasochism. The elements of the erotic sadomasochism, such as humiliation, domination, submission, merger, intense arousal, and ultimately orgasm, appear as intrapsychic conflict and in object relations representations. There is layering in the psychic organisation such that the affects present in this sexual realm also relate, equivalently, to wishes, fantasies, and compromise formations. There can be character organisation as well, based on moral masochism and moral sadism, that is, where the erotic seems muted or appears nonexistent. Freud first taught us that sadomasochism is found in each child's developmental makeup (1905). Other analysts suggest that sadomasochism only emerges in the face of sexual trauma forced on a child by an abusing adult. These questions lead psychoanalysts to explore the mysteries of sadomasochism, trying to identify its sources and roles. As we discussed sadomasochism in our study group we often found a sense of "too much"—too much need, too much arousal, too much humiliation, too much dominance and submission. The mind searches for a way to manage this "toomuchness" and constructs internal images of a scene entailing "the battle of life and death forces".

By life and death struggle, we refer to forces within each individual and in the relationship that are intent on destruction (death), and at the same time, preservation (life). We recognise both the preserving life-saving aspects of these constructions, and the destructive potential, as we think and write here about sadomasochism in the mind. Life instincts refer to pleasures and libidinal wishes. Death instincts refer to destruction, aggression, and repetition. Unconscious fantasy compromises from all phases of development and vicissitudes of conflict and trauma are found in sadomasochism. These forces coalesce around internal representations of a relationship where someone is hurting and dominating the other with the correlate of someone being hurt and dominated—a coupling that can easily reverse. There is a co-existence of pleasure and pain, and sexual perversity may be present.

In the case material in this book sadomasochism is not only present but often at the centre of the transference-countertransference dynamics taking place in the psychoanalytic treatments. Most of these patients do not overtly enact sexual sadomasochistic scenes. Nevertheless, all of these patients do have sadomasochistic relationship images in their psyches—"psychic sadomasochism"—and enact them with others including their analysts (Basseches, 1998; Ellman, 1998; Goodman,

1998). In fact the keeping of the frame for both patient and analyst can be experienced as a sadomasochistic act. The analyst can be felt as torturing the analysand by inviting the intimacy of the analytic dialogue while also maintaining the time of the session, beginning and ending, and expecting payment. Conflicts of aggression and hate, and libido and love, are arranged in sadomasochistic patterns in which pain in some form is present. Our patients so yearn for life—to connect, to attach, to arouse and be aroused—but at the same time wish to destroy us and themselves. Sadomasochism may be the best effort to find a way to connect to the object, rather than retreat to a narcissistic, isolated world. It may be the only way to hold together states of terror and inner convictions that all life forces, if detected, will invite both superego retaliation and re-traumisation from early narcissistic injuries and infant traumata. This type of attachment is also a way of sustaining distance and brings fragility to the formation of a therapeutic alliance. An episode of sadistic attack or masochistic suffering so easily can push the analytic couple apart and require repair for the alliance to reconvene.

As a psychoanalysis deepens, the battle of life and death forces intensifies and repetition compulsions take hold. There is something about these sadomasochistic repetitions that is most troubling as they often lead the patient or analyst to withdraw, claiming therapeutic partnership impossible. Freud wrote: "We started out from the great opposition between the life and death instincts" (1920, p. 53). We see in these patients that when the instincts are in such battle, the libido is affixed and the object cathected in a gripping way with the binding force of active and passive desires to possess and be possessed, to consume and be consumed, triumph over or submit, and even destroy or be destroyed. Masochist and sadist are embedded in one another, each yearning for and fighting against the symbiotic merger. Here the strength of opposing forces introduces the question of survival of the self, other, and the analytic process.

The clinical presence of sadomasochism in the mind: introduction of cases

All of the cases in this book reveal the dynamics of sadomasochism that exist in the patient's mind, the analyst's mind, and the analytic interchange. The activity of sadomasochism is present in differing degrees across the cases. Yet, each one is a living example of "psychic sadomasochism" in which the patient draws in the analyst to become a controlling or submitting presence. When sadomasochism enters the transference-countertransference in this way, despair arises, often making analyst and analysand doubt the viability of treatment. There are moments of being overwhelmed, doubtful, and attacking of the treatment process. Alternatively there may be an illusion of merger involving a saviour fantasy. The reader, too, is likely to feel the pull for submission, dominance, and destruction as the life and death battleground is vividly portrayed. These analysts and commentators have written with a willingness to know and experience the scripts of sadomasochism. The overall intent of the cases and discussions is to underscore the mysteries of sadomasochism, bringing them into view in a compelling way. Readers will be better able to acknowledge sadomasochism in their patients, in themselves, and in the material and enactments taking place in their treatments.

The discussions provide reflective space where analysts of differing theoretical backgrounds bring understanding to what is transpiring in the analyses. Although there are certainly common themes amongst their presentations, each describes his or her ideas of what brought these patients to their troubles. They find sources for the clinical presentation of sadomasochism in the history of trauma and narcissistic issues. Also ideas about self-cohesion, and defenses against anxieties of preoedipal and oedipal conflicts figure prominently. The felt desire to understand, to help maintain life forces over death forces, is present in each commentary. The treatments presented, and the informative discussions, bring articulation to this often mysterious destructive constellation.

We acknowledge the value of bringing to light these heart-wrenching psychic realities, thereby loosening the hold of sadomasochism and freeing the individuals who have been bound by it. Remarkably, patients and analysts begin to symbolise and dream, and renew their alive analysing instrument.

Commentary on the cases and discussions

The writers of the cases and the discussants come from a variety of orientations to psychoanalytic knowledge. They focus on the presence of sadomasochism in the ongoing clinical realm as it emerges and grips the analytic process. A reader might be somewhat surprised by the ways that one can see overlap and elements of agreement among the discussions even as they each find unique aspects to explore. It seems promising for psychoanalysis to think that the diversity of points of view can also be converging in their clinical understanding. Many note the way that the relating flips between sadism and masochism, under-scoring the pairing of the two positions.

All case presenters and commentators find intrapsychic and interper-sonal object relationships in the sadomasochism of the treatments. Dis-cussants' ideas fall into several main categories: (1) their understanding of sadomasochism in psychic life from a historical/theoretical perspec-tive and a phenomenological perspective; (2) their creative ideas about the minds of the patients, moment to moment and in a "big picture" way, and especially the defensive use and meanings of the behaviors and interactions; and (3) a range of relevant suggestions about analytic technique and the working analytic couple. There is an aliveness in addressing the topic that runs through all the cases and the discussions, giving renewed vigour to thinking about bearing the unbearable, by both therapist and patient when sadomasochism is prominent. Here we capture summaries of the cases and the ideas that the discussants bring to the material.

Dr. Paula Ellman describes the case of Diane—Sadomasochism in work and play with Diane (Chapter Three)—bringing forth the agony of Diane and the intensity of sadomasochism in the transference and countertransference. As Diane describes the suffering in her soma, her helplessness and her need and denigration of her analyst, Dr. Ellman reveals her psychic responses to her patient. The countertransference pull is to identify masochistically with the devalued object and also succumb to feeling helpless. As the patient describes sexual contacts of passion and shame she makes her analyst ashamed of being unable to enliven her patient's mind. Tracking the process shows the enactment of a sadomasochistic pair. The analyst's reflections of her sadistic and masochistic felt reactions brings about contact with and understanding of the internal experience of her patient.

The discussions of Dr. Paula Ellman's case are written by Alan Bass, Jack and Kerry Novick, and Marianne Robinson. Bass admires the full case report as the "best basis for thinking about the integration of theory and practice." He uses a dream as his starting place, suggesting that it is an "atypical moment". He informs us that the inflicting of pain on the body is "an unconscious attack on the mother's body". Using Freudian and Kleinian ideas he takes us into the mind, the internal world that gives some breathing space from the constant psychic beatings taking place. He thinks of the analyst's suffering as the needed receptivity to let the patient "inside" and reminds us of the importance for psychoanalysts to have tolerance for all forms of sexuality and the place that pain can have in stimulation and sexual arousal. Interestingly, the other two discussants also focus on that same dream, each with some unique kernel of added insight. The Novicks focus on the end of the dream—"and then I [the patient] walk out"—and suggest that in her own mind the patient has just committed a "heinous crime"—that of picturing herself as separating from the mother/analyst, creating "separation guilt" and thus deserving severe punishment. They characterise sadomasochistic relationships as fraught with struggles over power and defensive omnipotent beliefs and fantasies. What they call the open system is attuned to reality, self-regulation, and conflict resolution while the closed system organises around omnipotence, hostility, aggression, and self-destruction. They are trying to elaborate what Diane's "beating fantasy" is and how it comes into play in her over-training and hurting of herself. Robinson brings Kleinian ideas to the same element of the dream, showing how the attempt at a depressive position stance is in fact only omnipotent repair. "And then I walk out" for her means that the patient unconsciously believes that "it is possible to leave her 'bad' painful parts in her analyst." She brings ideas of manic defenses (Klein) and second (armoured) skin (Bick) to her understanding of Diane and the here and now with the analyst. Life forces are avoided and basic defenses of splitting and projection are active.

Dr. Nancy Goodman writes about the case of Mr. B—Sailing with Mr. B through waters of hurting love (Chapter Seven)—where the choice for the analyst and patient seems to be to exist or not to exist. Mr. B's struggle is about autonomy, fantasies of merger, and an unconscious belief in what Goodman calls "hurting love". Hurting love carries evidence of the inevitability of overstimulation, oral, anal, and genital, or understimulation, never being recognised nor responded to. As the transference and countertransference tensions increase, symbolisation emerges through dreams and narrative.

The discussants, James Grotstein, Margaret Ann Hanly, and Terrence McBride write about aspects of the working dyad. Grotstein speaks to the love-hate affair of sadomasochism and the intersubjective "group dream" co-constructed by analyst and analysand. He has the intriguing idea that sadomasochism may be found in analytic work because of the inevitable frustrations of the frame combined with the intensity of feelings leading to arousal of "hurting love". He defines "psychoanalytic sex" as the exploration and discovery of the meaning of one's sexual capacity and unconscious sexual history. Mr. B is unconsciously mandated to repeat affects with his analyst as a "passion play" in which Goodman must feel the pain. Dr. Hanly notes the central importance of annihilation anxiety and the patient's use of sadomasochistic relationships to keep it at bay. Hanly suggests that the analytic process requires of the analyst a form of submission to the control of the patient. She notes the importance of the interpretation of traumatic overstimulation and its link to his sadism. She brings focus to the termination phase and its transformational process as the traumatic infantile experiences and resulting perverse fantasies become symbolised. McBride notes the prevalence of issues of power and control in the analysis—who hurts whom, who attacks whom, who annihilates whom. He describes the oscillation in the transference and countertransference from masochism to sadism and converted helplessness into triumph, mastery, and revenge. He points out that the effect of deadness on the analyst reflects Mr. B's covert sadistic nature; and yet, at the same time, Mr. B shows his need for connectedness with the mother/analyst.

Dr. Andrea Greenman presents a case—Eating for emptiness, eating to kill: Sadomasochism in a woman with bulima (Chapter Eleven)—where bulimia captures the sadomasochism. Fears of annihilation and dissolution, and their sadomasochistic defences, play out in the exchanges of the analytic dyad. Early trauma is central to the origins of Mariah's narcissistic orientation that include fantasies of destructive oral voraciousness. In the transference/countertransference arena analyst and patient recreate the helpless vulnerability that gives rise to wishes to attack, fears of penetration, and efforts to vacate oneself to avert the sadistic self.

Three discussants, Steven Ellman, Shelley Rockwell, and Léon Wurmser, all highlight the "breaks" that Greenman's patient, Mariah, takes from the analysis. For Ellman the breaks are Mariah's need to punish Greenman for existing independently (that is, having her own thoughts, going away on weekends, having other patients, etc.), and take revenge, as well as retreat, from a situation where her sense of self is consistently threatened. Further, he suggests that it is hard for her to accept contact as well as, paradoxically, any type of separation, lacking sufficient object constancy. Using different language, Rockwell weaves thoughts about the breaks throughout her discussion. She sees the physical breaks as one manifestation of the patient's efforts to show contempt for and create distance from the analyst along with the wish to diminish the analyst into whom she has projected the unwelcome self aspects. Rockwell describes the patient's pathological introjections of mother, father, and the parental couple that lead to the formation of pathological "identificates". Wurmser notes the way in which the patient denies any feeling about absences. He links the breaks with shame. He understands the painful shame to be a response not only to closeness, but more, to intense feelings of any kind including dependency. The patient experiences the analyst's interpretations as penetrating, resulting in shame and the arousal of overwhelming sadomasochistic fantasies.

Dr. Richard Reichbart's case—The primitive superego of Mr. A: Sadistic revenge fantasies, arousal and then masochistic remorse (Chapter Fifteen)—offers a strong emphasis on the developmental sequence. Much of the sadomasochistic phenomena are presented in displacement in the form of sexualised overstimulating exchanges and fantasies, thus situating the analyst often as witness. The demand on the analyst/object is heavily weighted towards a position of tolerance, listening, and benign acceptance. From this position Reichbart shows how the patient emerges from his isolating, inhibited defensive shell, leading to the easing of the sadomasochistic flavour of his form of relating.

The discussants, Sheldon Bach, Harriet Basseches, and Leo Rangell, emphasise different elements influencing the sadomasochism in this case. Bach highlights the narcissistic roots in this case. He expresses sympathy for the reaction of boredom of the analyst as being a form of self-defence and the only way to stay alive or not give up in a difficult treatment. He notes the patient's amnesia for childhood memories as coming from a state of cumulative trauma, leading to difficulties in forming a reliable memory history and a well-regulated self. He sees the patient as initially responding with overwhelming fears of annihilation and later able to share his sadomasochistic fantasies because of the establishment of analytic trust. Basseches emphasises early developmental factors that lead to a faulty oedipal solution and presage the patient's adolescent sadomasochistic crisis. She predominantly follows a Freudian (Sigmund *and* Anna) developmental approach to understanding the case. Further, she analyses sadomasochism in the treatment in terms of both content and process to flesh out the underlying unconscious fantasy. Rangell sees sadomasochism as representing a form of aggression. He sees the suffering as a severe neurotic problem centreing on a fear of homosexuality. This, he explains, is caused by his identification with the mother, leading to identity confusion and debilitating castration anxiety. He sees the sadomasochistic fantasies as a defensive testing of the analyst. In de-emphasising the sadomasochistic fantasies of Reichbart's patient, he also minimises his primitiveness and isolation.

In the cases and discussions we find preoedipal and oedipal issues and their associated unconscious fantasies. The sadomasochistic object relationship in the service of maintaining the tie to the early mother is the centre of some discussions. Annihilation fears and survival are mentioned, especially in the use of narcissistic defences. Aggression and the role of the harsh superego, as well as perverse attitudes, receive attention. Punishment for oedipal wishes and fears of castration, with consequent regression to anal and oral fixation points, are the foci of others. The role of the beating fantasy with concomitant aggression and arousal is often mentioned. Others bring in the trauma of soul blind and soul murder parental abuse to the intensity of the sadomasochistic phenomena. Trauma can be sexualised and erotic life can be associated with trauma. Several discussants put forth the idea that it is ill-advised to make early transference interpretations, or even clarifications, when working with the sadomasochism of traumatised and narcissistic individuals. Before such interpretive work can be helpful, there must be a building up of analytic trust, and the forming of a working alliance.

Another point of coalescence among discussants is the idea that countertransference needs to be considered in a nuanced way, to include the analyst's conflicts relating to sadomasochism, the affects in response to the enacted sadomasochism, and the patient's projections active in the analyst's mind. The discussants address how to work with the many forms of countertransference; for example, the idea that the analyst must tolerate torture, both active and passive.

There are many instances when sadomasochism presents as though it were a matter of aggressivised sexuality when in fact the sexualised content may be in the service of many other motives, particularly defending against and expressing narcissistic issues. Nevertheless, sexuality plays its role in sadomasochism, even if muted. We have an awareness of the way in which sadomasochism functions as the best adaptation the individual can make. We underscore the importance of remembering that it can be a compromise formation with multiple determinants.

In analytic work, the discovery of the sadomasochism in the transference/countertransference can save an analysis from destruction by opening up not only understanding but possibility; knowledge is an antidote to negative therapeutic reaction. We emphasise the extent to which we found that studying the gamut of transference and counter-transference aspects in these cases strengthened our analytic listening and ability to tolerate the intolerable. Understanding and metabolising the feelings and meanings evoked in the unconscious of the analyst, as well as in the unconscious of the patient, allows for work with sado-masochism. Realising the vital role of the pleasurable addictive qual-ity of sadomasochism helps to facilitate a transformational symbolising process. Whether pervasive and all-encompassing or barely noticeable, sadomasochism is ubiquitous.

References

Albee, E. (1962). *Who's Afraid of Virginia Wolf?* London: Vintage, 2001. (Premiered at the Broadway Billy Rose Theatre, 13 October 1962.)

Basseches, H. I. (1998). Enactment: What is it and whose is it? S. J. Ellman & M. Moskowitz (Eds.) *Enactment: Toward a New Approach to the Therapeutic Relationship*. New York: Jason Aronson.

Ellman, P. L. (1998). Is enactment a useful concept? In: S. J. Ellman & M. Moskowitz (Eds.) *Enactment: Toward a New Approach to the Therapeutic Relationship*. New York: Jason Aronson.

Freud, S. (1905). Three essays on the theory of sexuality. *S.E., 7*: 123–246. London: Hogarth.

Freud, S. (1919). "A child is being beaten": A contribution to the study of the origin of sexual perversions. *S. E., 17*: 175–204. London: Hogarth.

Freud, S. (1920). Beyond the pleasure principle. *S. E., 18*. London: Hogarth.

Freud, S. (1924). The economic problem of masochism. *S. E., 19*: 155–172. London: Hogarth.

Freud, S. (1927). Fetishism. *S. E., 21*: 147–158. London: Hogarth.

Freud, S. (1937). Analysis terminable and interminable. *S. E., 23*: 255–270. London: Hogarth.

Freud, S. (1940). Splitting of the ego in the process of defence. *S. E., 23*: 271–279. London: Hogarth.

Goodman, N. R. (1998). The fixity of action in character enactments. In: S. J. Ellman & M. Moskowitz (Eds.) *Enactment: Toward a New Approach to the Therapeutic Relationship*. New York: Jason Aronson.

Goodman, N. R., Basseches, H. I., Ellman, P. L., Elmendorf, S., Fritsch, E., Helm, F. & Rockwell, S. (1993). Panel presentation: "In the mind of the psychoanalyst: The moment before speaking", International Psychoanalytical Association Congress, Amsterdam, 29 July 1993.

Ives, D. (2011). *Venus and Furs*. Evanston, IL: Northwestern University Press, 2012. (Opened off-Broadway at the Classic Stage Company on 13 January 2010 and on Broadway at the Samuel J. Friedman theatre on 13 October 2011).

Journal of the American Psychoanalytic Association, Panel (1981). Cooper, A. M. & Fischer N. Masochism: Current Concepts, 29: 673–658; Panel (1984), Rothstein, A. & Caston, J. The relation between masochism and depression, 32: 603–614; Panel (1991) Sacks, M. H. Sadism and masochism in character disorder and resistance, 39: 215–226.

Krafft-Ebing, R. von, (1886, first edition). *Psychopathia Sexualis*. (1922, Translation)

Sacher Masoch, Leopold von (1870). *Novella Venus and Furs, in Love*, (Volume 1).

CHAPTER TWO

Intersecting forces and development of sadomasochism

Paula L. Ellman and Nancy R. Goodman

Sadomasochism in our clinical work arises from intersecting forces of developmental phase fantasies, conflicts, and traumas. There is a fixity to the sadomasochistic way of relating that lives in the patient's mind and captures the analyst and patient exchange. Perspectives on the developmental position of sadomasochism and the formative effect of trauma figure into efforts to understand the intractable hold that sadomasochism has on the analytic dyad. Interacting forces of narcissism, anality, trauma, and perversion fuel the battle arising from all stages of development with their accompanying unconscious fantasies and object relations. Narcissistic vulnerabilities related to trauma and psychic helplessness play a major role in creating fertile ground for the growth of sadomasochism. Additionally, individuals seek sexual gratifications through dominance and submission. While the oral and genital/oedipal stages of development are discernible in sadomasochism, the anal phase of development gives sadomasochism its shape in the mind and in interactions with others. The centrality of anality is due to its important organising function in psychic activity. Here we find unconscious fantasies related to inside and outside, autonomy, control, submission, and conquest. At this time of development, both disavowal and perversion contribute to sadomasochism in the arena of fantasies about spaces within the body and mind, and between self and other. Differences of all kinds may not be tolerated and sadomasochism can be used to either manage or obliterate them. We bring a focus on the anal phase of development followed by discussions of orality and narcissism, trauma, the oedipal, and lastly, consideration of the place of disavowal and perversion.

Anality

We find in the clinical material and in the literature that the anal stage, the time of body mastery and self-other differentiation, is where sadomasochism organises and then burgeons. Psychoanalysts from all schools of thought find links to anality in the basic functioning of sadomasochism (Bach, 1994, 2002; Chasseguet-Smirgel, 1984a, 1991; Meltzer, 1973, 1992; Novick, J. & Novick, K. K., 1996; Shengold, 1988, 1989; Wurmser, 2007). In their understanding of the historic place of Freud's thinking about sadomasochism, La Planche and Pontalis (1973) state the following:

> Freud described the part played by sadism and masochism in the various libidinal organizations of childhood development. First and most importantly, he recognized their action in the anal-sadistic organization; but they are present in the other stages too. ...
> (p. 403)

Many characteristics defined by anal functioning were identified by Freud (1905, 1908, 1909) and Abraham (1923) in their descriptions of the anal character who hordes, is parsimonious, and hides in an array of behaviours attempting to keep others under control. Both helplessness and grandiosity accompany the building of the anal character. Shengold (1989) writes of the fluctuations from deadness, "a self hypnotic state" and the elation of having all for oneself, as the defining features of the person traveling this anal pathway.

In our work with our patients, painful power struggles engage us in anally oriented exchanges. We are often pulled into a battle for control. Our analytic function is threatened by our patients' wishes to possess us, degrade us, dominate us, and likewise to have us possess them, degrade them, dominate them or to be rid of us, never let us go, have us cling to them or look to eliminate them. We see the linkage between anality and sadomasochism; both hold opposing impulses of expulsion and retention, destruction and control. Analysts may feel they are losing hold of their analytic mind and worth. "I am worthless, incompetent, and want to fight to prove my value and rightful place." When the analyst feels the pull towards this masochism and sadism, space for thought is on the verge of collapse. Sadomasochism begins to destroy differentiation; symbolisation is hampered. There are not two. The relationship of object and subject and who owns the body becomes prominent.

Fantasies about the anal space are projected onto representations of all kinds of spaces: internal bodily spaces, psychic space, space between objects, and the space of the treatment. Meltzer (1992) identifies "life in the maternal rectum" as the claustrum where sadomasochism reigns, where feelings are filled with violence and seek to pervert and to addict. In the clinical sphere the analysis itself can become a claustrum and the position of sadist and masochist fluctuates between analyst and patient. In his *Three Essays* (1905), Freud states: "A sadist is always at the same time a masochist" (p. 159). We find that these patterns of sado-masochism present in the form of shifting character enactments in the transference-countertransference arena (Ellman, 1998; Goodman, 1998; Ellman & Goodman, 2012). In the analysis, words can then be experi-enced as actions: "When I speak to my patients I feel like I am forcing my thoughts into them—penetrating them. My patient's words keep me out, or are weapons penetrating me and destroying my capacity to think." Early narcissistic threats to not being loved as separate from the needs of parents are awakened and take on traces of anal imagery as development unfolds.

The actual and symbolic meaning of a working anal sphincter is the psychic and somatic location between inner and outer. The sphincter is the place of interface between the internal self and the external world, the place where differentiation becomes possible. Dysregulation can become manifest when earlier impingements and psychic helplessness occurred.

The sphincter in the sadomasochistic mind enters the consulting room and we experience it in the enactments where the patient looks to hold on, to hold back, to thwart and fault us, to deaden forward movement, to keep it all for the self, to flood, to evacuate all that is internal including cathected representations of others. We see fluctua-tions between deadness and the elation of having all for oneself. Often there is a core fantasy of evacuating the relationship itself or of being evacuated, accompanying the wish to dissolve object relatedness or the wish for re-birth. The metaphoric dysfunctional sphincter makes for the dysregulation of the sadomasochist, who struggles to manage the over- and under-stimulation of what is outside and what is inside the mind and body.

The oral: trauma and narcissism

The early interactions between infant and mother of feeding, holding, reciprocity, and containment produce abundant occasions for narcissistic injuries, traumas, envy, and experiences of heightened aggressivity, hate, and love. Through the infant's efforts to make contact, there are moments that either satisfy or alternatively frustrate, thereby arousing fears and wishes to merge, withdraw, or attack with fantasies of destroying or being destroyed. Centreed in these early infant-mother interactions, feelings oscillate between need and satisfaction, between fullness and emptiness, between grandiosity and invisibility. Narcissistic wounds from insecurities of attachment, absences in reciprocity, holding (Winnicott, 1953, 1971) and containment (Bion, 1967) create ruptures that can fuel the development of sadomasochism. An internal landscape filled with unmanageable tensions easily gives way to depending on sadomasochism for making contact in pain and bringing about the illusion of the grandiose merger (Bach, 1994, 2002). According to Klein (1946), the aim of the infantile sadism is to gain possession of the contents of the mother's body and to destroy her by means of every weapon that sadism can command. Efforts are to injure and to possess (Rosenfeld, 1971, 1988). There may be the presence of a fantasy of disappearing inside the analyst/mother's body (Grotstein, this volume, Chapter Eight). This fantasy of invasion and incorporation can also become the basis for an identification of one's own body with that of the object, having the effect of arousing hatred for the contents of one's own body (Chasseguet-Smirgel, 1984b).

The illusion of oneness is the psychic counter-force to ward off murderousness and annihilation fear. Fear of annihilation speaks to the terror of dissolving, falling apart, losing a sense of self, and dissolution of one's internal structure (Hurvich, 2003, 2011). Castration/female genital anxieties speak to the fears of attack on one's body, bodily harm, and loss of potency and procreation. Sadomasochism is often used to ward off these anxieties. It is better to be in desperate pain with another, passively or actively, than to be forgotten or to know the terror in one's mind.

The dysregulation from early life trauma and drive-associated affects (oral, anal, or genital) can carry a sense of "toomuchness" that shows up as shame. Wurmser (2007) stresses and elaborates the place of shame in the mind when traumatisation has entered psychic organisation. He highlights the attempts at mastery that belong to sadomasochistic solutions. Anything—being demeaned, beaten, psychically torn apart—is better than enduring uncontrollable shame and suffering abandonment. According to Blos (1991), at times sadomasochism functions against re-experiencing and remembering painful affects. Sadomasochism serves to preserve the wish that past traumas can be reversed. "... somewhere, someway, some day, what happened can be undone. ... This fantasied hope of reversibility is sustainable only so long as the sadomasochism position is maintained ..." (p. 421).

Narcissistic trauma occurring in this early phase of development becomes fuel for the life and death struggle of sadomasochism. The early attachment to "the mother of pain" (Bach, 1994, 2002) is affirmed over and over, becoming unbreakable and indestructible. This attachment must be searched for and found in treatment. With our patients, we then experience their pursuit of oneness, togetherness/merger, the object hunger and the denigration of the analyst as separate. Paradoxically, wishes for merger can, at the same time, lead to annihilation terror/panic associated with obliteration of oneself.

The tangle of sadomasochism becomes a familiar way of making contact, that is, to feel, to hurt, and to wish for grandiose solutions. In treatment the analyst is drawn into these landscapes in a variety of ways. In the masochistic position, the analyst invites attack as if declaring: "If your only way to be with me is to humiliate me and arouse me, I will do that to show I care and want contact with your mind." Or, in the sadistic position the analyst may carry the rage at being perversely used and become silent, numb, withholding, and use a tone of derogation. In the reflective position, both analyst and patient return to a psychic space where more play and creative interplay can develop.

The genital/oedipal

Oedipal desires highlight the existence of three. Two are entwined with excitement—with sexual intercourse. One is the onlooker. The primal scene, whether an actual experience or solely internally constructed, enters the psyche. Envious needs may include the desire to claim one member of the dyad or the desire to be one of the two, or both. The traumas of too much excitement, too much terror, and too much shameful helplessness can lead to a representation of sadomasochistic excitement. The excruciating pain of the oedipal longings and frustrations, the terrible arousal and need, can feel uncontainable. Analyst and patient may painfully feel left out and diminished by the other. Dominance and submission easily become part of attempts to manage the intense affects stirred by the triad of the oedipal. The pain, arousal, and helplessness lead regressively to affinity for the internal dyadic representation of a sadomasochistic couple for whom the sexual scene must include pain. There can be an intense desire to reverse the primal scene, to undo what made one feel helpless (Kernberg, 1991). The perverse takes control. The perversion is in the idea of feeling pleasure by bringing pain, destruction and humiliation. "The only way I can feel omnipotent and powerful is to leave you out, annihilate your significance to me or even to prove that I can over-arouse or hurt you."

Freud (1919) wrote of the beating fantasy as central to the understanding of sadomasochism. The beating fantasy calls on the oedipal time, where punishment and fear of retaliation for sexual pleasure is central. Evolving from the oedipal phase and the development of the superego, there must be pain and the pain permits and makes sexual pleasure possible. The beating fantasy may appear in many compromises of the mind (Novick, J. & Novick, K. K., 1996). For instance, the beating fantasy can substitute for the withdrawal of cathexis from the traumatising object (Novick, J. & Novick, K. K., 1987). Welldon (2002) identifies the mother who beats her child as evidence of female perversion, reminding us of the likely presence of transgenerational traumas. When the mother projects her unwanted affects into the child, leading to beatings, the child grows up with these painful externalisations. Instead of withdrawing into a narcissistic retreat, there is a turn towards the beating fantasy. The unconscious beating fantasy of sadomasochism captures the orientation towards pain in the relationship. The pain becomes the way of attaching to the other. Links are formed early in life between experiences of unpleasure and the phase-related developmental needs. These are carried forward to adult adaptations and present to the analyst as pressures for particular strains of engagement. The strains intermingle pleasure with pain, separateness with oneness, creation with destruction, life with death.

Perversion and disavowal of difference

Analysts have increasingly expanded the definition of perversion to include an erotised form of hate (Stoller, 1975), an effort to destroy reality (Chasseguet-Smirgel, 1991), and the disavowal of difference (Bass, 2000). Chasseguet-Smirgel (1991) asserts that she has "never encountered a case of perversion that is devoid of sadomasochistic elements, even though their presence in the clinical picture may be very discrete" (p. 399). Richards (2013) finds that there is always the presence of domination in perverse relating. When sadomasochism is the most powerful organisational piece of the personality, it may shift from its integrated place in the structure of the psyche, to enter the domain of perversion. By perversion we mean perverse elements in the mind rather than full-blown sexual perversion.

Perversity is expressed through the mechanism of disavowal. Disavowal in the transference/countertransference may function to communicate, "You are there but you are not there, I see you and I never see you". Terror lurks when difference is perceived. A collapse of space takes place in the sadomasochistic scene; self and object are interchangeable. Generational difference no longer exists. Sexual difference is unrecognised. Chasseguet-Smirgel's (1991) well-known thesis is that perversion represents the replacement of the reality of the difference between the sexes and the generations with idealised anal fantasies. "The Sadian universe is invoked and is a place of confusion, chaos, mixture, inverted and abolished values" (p. 403).

We experience with our patients their efforts at disavowal of our existence as the analyst. There is an effort to dismiss the analytic function. The attempt to eliminate the separateness of the analyst closes the psychic space of the treatment and of the individual minds of both analysand and analyst. Goodman (2008) puts forth the idea that the representation of a sadomasochistic object relationship "functions similarly to a fetish in that it is meant to keep away the disorganizing terror of difference" (p. 2). According to Chasseguet-Smirgel (1991), fetishism exemplifies the perverse compromise, as it is the result of the replacement of differentiation with fantasy-laden concrete things, whose basic aim is to attack the reality of the "law of differentiation" and the reality-based capacity to think about difference. Autonomy is escaped by being embroiled in hostile, aggressive erotised contact approaching merger (Coen, 1988). In the merger, there is a powerful pull to stasis, to remain unmovable, and to enact continually the sadomasochistic relationship.

In our work with sadomasochism, we see the patient's pleasure from endless repetitions expressing their wish to avoid mental differentiation and separation. According to Meltzer (1973) patients are driven to bind self and other in "addictive passivity". "… The patient is… sadistic towards the analyst… and is sadistic towards … part of the self which is masochistically caught up …" (p. 133). "No ordinary pleasure, genital, sexual or other, offered such delight as this type of terrible and exciting self-annihilation which annihilates also the object" (Joseph, 1982, p. 451). Here is the intermingling of pleasure and pain.

The question remains open: will life or death win out? To preserve life, we observe our temptation in the countertransference to give way to the perverse addictive pressures of our patients. We have come to know the aggressive exchanges between ourselves and our patients and how they can carry a sexual current. Celenza (2000) reminds us not to overlook the presence of sexual desires belonging to sadomasochism. The repetition of our patients' attacks, their failures, unhappiness, and guilt, carry sexual excitement and pull us into their misery with them and trap us both. In this perverse entrapment is the sexual pleasure, perhaps for both patient and analyst, and may be the only available pleasure as life forces fend off death forces. With the sadomasochistic elimination of difference, concreteness takes hold; our analytic process that we so value and depend upon appears to be hijacked. We struggle with the sense that we are losing our capacity to think. Here, we are speaking of the way in which the narcissistic process of destruction and desymbolisation destroys psychic space (Bass, 2000; Freedman & Berzofsky, 1995). Minimal psychic space is necessary for symbolisation (Ellman & Goodman, 2012). A degree of internalisation of differentiation is needed for a symbol not to be equated with what is symbolised, for there to be an "as if" metaphoric meaning (Bass, 2000). Our analytic work becomes flat, repetitive, stuck, and replete with aggression and counter-aggression that is often sexualised. Here is our despair in the experience of the deadening of our work with these patients. The analyst takes note that sadomasochism with all its pains and pleasures is present. Recognising and making efforts to understand the countertransference allows for a window into "psychic sadomasochism". The analyst must be aware that she too is holding onto the sadomasochistic relationship as the only viable connection to her patient, and that she too is disavowing the recognition of difference. Symbolising opens inroads for alternatives to the ultimate enactment of sadomasochism, the negative therapeutic reaction. In conclusion, the influences of the oral, anal, and oedipal configurations, and trauma, each in turn and in combination affect the development of sadomasochism in the mind with a sense of there being no alternative. Sadomasochism arises from the intersecting forces of conflict, trauma and adaptation. The recognition of "psychic sadomasochism" opens the transference/countertransference arena where meaning can be discovered and movement out of the sadomasochistic hold is possible.

References

Abraham, K. (1923). Contributions to the theory of the anal character. In: *Selected Papers of Karl Abraham*. Basic Books: New York, 1927.

Bach, S. (2002). Sadomasochism in clinical practice and everyday life. *Journal of Clinical Psychology*, 11: 225–235.

Bach, S. (1994). *The Language of Perversion and the Language of Love*. Northvale, NJ: Jason Aronson.

Bass, A. (2000). *Difference and Disavowal: The Trauma of Eros*. Stanford: Stanford University Press.

Bion, W. R. (1967). *Second Thoughts: Selected Papers on Psychoanalysis*. New York: Jason Aronson.

Blos, P., Jr. (1991). Sadomasochism and the Defense Against Recall of Painful Affect. *Journal of the American Psychoanalytic Association*, 39: 417–430.

Celenza, A. (2000). Sadomasochistic relating: What's sex got to do with it? *Psychoanalytic Quarterly*, 69, 3: 527–543.

Chasseguet-Smirgel, J. (1984a). *Creativity and Perversion*. Norton: New York.

Chasseguet-Smirgel, J. (1984b). Thoughts on the Concept of Reparation and the Hierarchy of Creative Acts. *International Review of Psychoanalysis*, 11: 399–406.

Chasseguet-Smirgel, J. (1991). Sadomasochism in the Perversions: Some Thoughts on the Destruction of Reality. *Journal of the American Psychoanalytic Association*, 39: 399–415.

Coen, S. J. (1988). Sadomasochistic Excitement: character disorder and perversion. In: R. A. Glick & D. I. Meyers (Eds.), *Masochism, Current Psychoanalytic Perspectives*, 1988. Hillsdale, NJ: Analytic Press.

Ellman, P. L. (1998). Is Enactment a Useful Concept? In: S. J. Ellman & M. Moskowitz (Eds.), *Enactment: Toward a New Approach to the Therapeutic Relationship*. Northvale, NJ: Jason Aronson.

Ellman, P. L. and Goodman, N. R. (2012). Enactment: Opportunity for symbolising trauma. In: A. Frosch (Ed), *Absolute Truth and Unbearable Psychic Pain: Psychoanalytic Perspectives on Concrete Experience*. CIPS series on the boundaries of psychoanalysis. London: Karnac.

Freedman, N. & Berzofsky, M. (1995). Shape of the communicated transference in difficult and not so difficult patients: symbolized and desymbolized transference. *Psychoanalytic Psychology*, 12: 363–374.

Freud, S. (1905). Three essays on the theory of sexuality. *S. E.*, 7: 125–243. London: Hogarth.

Freud, S. (1908). Character and anal eroticism. *S. E.*, 9. London: Hogarth.

Freud, S. (1909). Notes upon a case of obsessional neurosis. *S. E.*, 10: 155–318. London: Hogarth.

Freud, S. (1919). A child is being beaten. *S. E.*, 17: 175–204. London: Hogarth.

Goodman, N. R. (1998). The fixity of action in character enactments: Finding a developmental regression. In: S. J. Ellman & M.l Moskowitz (Eds.), *Enactment: Toward a New Approach to the Therapeutic Relationship*. Northvale, NJ: Jason Aronson.

Goodman, N. R. (2008). Love that hurts when sadomasochism organizes the psyche. Paper Presentation, Tampa Bay Psychoanalytic Society, Tampa, FL.

Hurvich, M. (2003). The place of annihilation anxieties in psychoanalytic theory. *Journal of American Psychoanalytical Association*, 51: 579–616.

Hurvich, M. (2011). *Another Kind of Evidence*. London: Karnac.

Joseph, B. (1982). Addiction to near-death. *International Journal of Psychoanalysis*, 63: 449–456.

Kernberg, O. F. (1991). Sadomasochism, sexual excitement and perversion. *Journal of American Psychoanalytical Association*, 39: 333–362.

Klein, M. (1946). Notes on some schizoid mechanisms. In: *Developments in Psycho-Analysis*. London: Hogarth, 1952.

Laplanche, J. & Pontalis, J. B. (1973). *The Language of Psycho-Analysis* (Translated by Donald Nicholson-Smith). New York: W. W. Norton & Company.

Meltzer, D. (1973). *Sexual States of Mind*. Perthshire: Clunie Press.

Meltzer, D. (1992). *The Claustrum: An Investigation of Claustrophobic Phenomena*. London: Stylus Publishing.

Novick, K. K. & Novick, J. (1987). The Essence of masochism. *PSC*, 42: 353–384.

Novick, J. & Novick, K. K. (1996). *Fearful Symmetry: The Development and Treatment of Sadomasochism*. Northvale, NJ: Jason Aronson.

Richards, A. K. (2013). Introduction to Perversion Section. In: N. R. Goodman (Ed.), *Psychoanalysis: Listening to Understand*, Selected Papers of Arlene Kramer Richards, pp. 143–147. New York: IP Press.

Rosenfeld, H. (1971). A clinical approach to the psychoanalytic theory of the life and death instinct: An investigation into the aggressive aspects of Narcissism. *International Journal of Psychoanalysis*, 52: 169–178.

Rosenfeld, H. A. (1988). On masochism: A clinical and theoretical approach. In: R. A. Glick & D. I Meyers (Eds.), *Masochism, Current Psychoanalytic Perspectives*, 1988. Hillsdale, NJ: Analytic Press.

Shengold, L. (1988). *Halo in the Sky: Observations on Anality and Defense.* New York: Guilford Press.

Shengold, L. (1989). *Soul Murder, The Effects of Childhood Abuse and Deprivation.* New Haven: Yale University Press.

Stoller, R. (1975). *Perversion: The Erotic Form of Hatred.* London: Pantheon Books.

Welldon, E. (2002). *Sadomasochism Ideas in Psychoanalysis.* London: Icon Books.

Winnicott, D. W. (1953). Transitional objects and transitional phenomena— a study of the first not-me possession. *International Journal of Psycho-Analysis*, 34: 89–97.

Winnicott, D. W. (1971). *Playing and Reality.* London: Tavistock Publications.

Wurmser, L. (2007). *Torment Me, But Don't Abandon Me: Psychoanalysis of the Severe Neurosis in a New Key.* Northvale, NJ: Jason Aronson.

PART I

CASE PRESENTED BY
PAULA L. ELLMAN AND DISCUSSIONS

CHAPTER THREE

Sadomasochism in work and play with Diane

Paula L. Ellman

"My only interest is in being freed of my pain; my body screams at me all day in pain. There is worsening of pain in my toe and ankle. Nonetheless, you did not pursue competently the question of my early sexual abuse by my father. You were not on my case adequately. How can you help anyone when you have patients leaving and another one coming, one right after the other? You cannot help me ..."

[I revisit from my years of working with Diane my tortured feelings of failing her, having nothing to offer her—not being good enough, and my anger at her not appreciating me for my efforts.]

"With my girlfriend, I wanted to celebrate the inauguration. But because of her relatives, she needs to believe Bush is great so she reacts with her limited small-minded demeaning remarks about Obama. She and I have been over that so many times. I don't think I want to invite her to visit again. It is just not worth it ... I continue to try to speak with my mother about the past, about our family's early problems, but she is no longer willing to look back and discuss what has happened in the past. That may be the end of that. It may make sense to just live alone (tearful)—that is far preferable over this crap ..."

[I feel for her pain, her profound disappointment in people and her isolation, but also for my own pain of feeling so inadequate, as if I am lacking, with little to offer in the psychoanalysis.]

When Diane becomes aware of the presence of the other's needs, she believes there is no room for her own. She sees that I have patients other than her; she hears her mother's wish to protect herself from being riddled with regret; she experiences her girlfriend's loyalty to her family—and with these moments of feeling left out, Diane is enraged and finds comfort in rejecting the offending others and remaining alone.

For Diane, any sign of separateness of the other is not tolerable. Diane's struggle with herself and in her relationships is rooted in her sadomasochism. "The [sadomasochist's] hatred is aimed at reality in general and this is essentially composed of differences ... between the appearance of the need (or wish) and its satisfaction ..." (Chasseguet-Smirgel, 1991, p. 400). Therefore, the need-satisfying object is not well differentiated from the self. Diane cannot bear experiencing the difference between her need—what she wants—and its satisfaction. Frustration for her proves to be unbearable. Her girlfriend, her mother, and I frustrate her wishes and her sadomasochism floods her inner life and object world.

Diane, a forty-year-old single woman, is a top academic in a prominent educational institution. She was raised in a working class Irish Catholic family. She is the sixth of seven children (with an oldest brother, four older sisters, and one younger brother.) Diane's eldest brother was most valued by both parents, especially by her father. Her father and eldest brother were in a mutually idealising relationship that included alcohol, athletics, and what Diane experienced as a strutting of their masculinity. Diane remembers her seething hatred at witnessing her father in his chair watching TV, and with his hand in his pants, scratching his genitals in an exhibitionistic way.

For Diane, being a woman in the heterosexual world meant being in relationship to a man where she is denigrated and the man highly valued. Diane's family's church culture honoured the male. Diane longed to be "an altar boy" like her older brother, and bring pride to her parents; however this was reserved for males. It seemed that being the son was the only way to bring pride to her parents. On his death-bed, Diane's father proclaimed how his eldest son surpassed all in his career success, when in fact there is no doubt that Diane reached a career pinnacle far beyond anyone else in her family. Even when Diane enjoyed the dominant phallic position in relationship to her work subordinates, she felt that her accomplishments went unrecognised by her father. Diane basked in her sense of being her mother's favourite, but she was acutely aware of her place as one of four daughters relied on for household chores. She felt that her mother tried to provide adequately for her family in spite of being overwhelmed with the demands of seven children, yet she also felt that her mother lavished too much attention on her father and eldest brother in a way that disgusted her. She remembers her intolerance for her mother attending to her father's needs and seeming so easily to accept his crude masturbatory exhibitionism.

In high school sexuality was associated with dirt or dirty activity. Diane wanted to avert exchanges with boys. She hated their pushing up against her, their out-of-control urges, and her feeling like dirt. Her associations to Catholic proscriptions include being "like dirt" by engaging sexually; she is dirt as "the hole" for the guy, "nothing but a hole for him". Diane remembers her mother's prohibition against masturbation, despite her acceptance of Diane's father's exhibitionistic "genital scratching". She kept her hands away from her body; her sexual urges were prohibited. She thought that her vaginal wetness was urine and "coached" herself to sit on the toilet for a prolonged time to try to empty her bladder and do away with the wetness.

From early childhood, Diane excelled at athletics and successfully competed on boys' teams, often outplaying the boys. She felt intent on surpassing her older brother, athletically. As a young adolescent she independently established a rigorous practice schedule to perfect her tennis. Every afternoon, she hit no fewer than 500 tennis balls on her own. The results of her extreme effort and talent launched her into professional national championships, despite missing the private coaching that she envied other young athletes receiving. She earned a full athletic scholarship to a top university. Later, just as with athletics, Diane drove herself in her career with a rigorous work schedule.

In her late twenties Diane "came out" with her homosexuality. Neither parent accepted her lesbianism; both treated her with contempt. Diane remembers her painful aloneness, feeling cast out by her parents. Soon after, Diane's father suffered complications from alcoholism and developed cancer, proving to be fatal.

Diane came to psychoanalysis unhappy in her relationship with a woman who was a victim of sexual abuse. Diane felt frustrated by her partner's unavailability for intimacy. Diane has had few satisfying relationships with women or men. She believes that she carries the weight of others' needs with little room for her own. Most glaring in Diane's clinical presentation was the massive physical disability of her lower limbs that had developed within the years preceding her entry to therapy, rendering her unable to participate in the athletic lifestyle she had previously embraced; in fact, she was barely able to walk. With many possible medical diagnoses, no treatment was definitive. Diane believed that she had inadvertently made demanding choices which were, by nature, "being the best she can be", resulting in her current disabled state. The bone structure and musculature in both feet deteriorated due to unusual complications of overuse, making even walking painful. Diane was crippled for a prolonged period of time. Actually, she may have "worked herself to the bone" by virtue of her lifelong unconscious motivation to overlook discomfort in order to pursue the high and hard road. "Working herself to the bone" appears to have been her compromise formation related to her unconscious guilt around becoming sexually active both in her homosexuality and in her finding pleasure in her own body. The analysis would bring to light more about the unconscious fantasies that Diane enacted in her life.

The early phase of Diane's analysis was about her search for a psychological inroad to relieve her chronic pain. She had a specific interest in the mind-body paradigm and read many books on this topic. One arena of development that she was interested in was based on the idea that chronic pain was frequently the result of the presence of unconscious rage related to early life experience, and the way to healing chronic pain was to access and express this rage. Diane was receptive to the recommendation for psychoanalysis since it fit with her notion of a cure for bodily pain that is built on the premise of understanding the unconscious and for her, her unconscious rage.

Diane wanted my assurance that psychoanalysis would bring her a physical cure. She spoke her associations, to family, work, friends, early memories, with pressure and expectation that this would relieve her physical pain. When relief did not come readily, she was angry with me and pursued other remedies: physical therapy, massage, Reiki, Tai Chi, Chi-gong, psychics, etc. While I could not promise healing, I did indicate that I believed that there was much she was troubled about and that psychoanalysis would be a vehicle towards understanding the turmoil she suffered in her relationships and sense of self. Nonetheless, I, too, became invested in her cure from pain and participated in the same phenomenon, in the countertransference, of feeling that I was not working hard enough and was coming up short (clitoris vs. penis). I continued to consider how this countertransference could be expressing aspects of Diane's experience of herself, and, in particular, the femaleness of her body such that there could never be sufficiently hard enough work to alter it.

Diane expects only the best of herself as she prizes her competence and effectiveness. She tortures herself with blame for the crippling horror she is living. She serves as the provider/caretaker for her distracted over-committed disorganised partners. Diane likes the idea that she is the one in control, the expert, the one "on top", but believes that this idea has some association with an early undefined memory of having her genitals inappropriately touched by an older man when she was a young child. The thought of a penis penetrating her seems pleasurable, but she is disgusted by the thought of submitting to the sexual urges of a man. With the man's penetration comes giving herself up to someone with whom she feels enraged.

Recently, a female partner challenged Diane with awareness of her own emotional constriction and sexual inhibitions. Her partner's demands for open honest exchanges were unrelenting, verging on sadistic, thereby reminding Diane of her own inner demanding voice. Her partner's apparent comfort with her own sexuality stirred for Diane an experience of her sexuality that was new to her and also distressing. Diane is self-critical of never having allowed herself bodily pleasure. Alternatively, she now feels self-indulgent when sexually aroused. She shamefully acknowledges her pleasure in the fantasy of being penetrated. However, penetration, even if by a woman, necessitates her unbearable submission. She is in such conflict in experiencing her own vulnerability that relationships quickly become threatened by Diane's sadomasochistic contempt and readiness to be dismissive. She has struggled with her own and her parents' intolerance of her lesbianism, both within the religious doctrines and also within her cultural mores. Diane did not allow herself to become sexually active in her lesbianism until well in her twenties and she did this with much psychological conflict. She identified, through her analysis, that it was following her first lesbian relationship that her tendons and muscles in her legs tightened, serving to further debilitate her at the time when she was already debilitated by the foot difficulty she had. This additional problem actually put her on crutches and rendered her truly crippled, unable to walk.

Currently, Diane is working to fully accept her homosexuality and resolve the conflict-ridden eroticism she experiences with her female partner's penetrating strength and with her own passive receptive longings. Also, she is attempting to understand better her phallic sadistic strivings. Central to Diane's analysis is the problem of how pleasure can be realised while feeling like a denigrated disgusting hole. Diane describes her painful "submission" to her partner and her arousal in that pain. She was pained by her concern that it seemed "sadomasochistic". She loves her partner to "take her", to be strong and forceful, yet at the same time detests those masculine reminders. Along with the challenge of her relationship is her pervasive concern about regaining her full physical capacity.

Her consideration of her conflicts and limits has been distressingly challenging of her perfectionism. Her perfectionism for self and other extends to all areas of her life and is unrelenting. From early on in the analytic work, she repeatedly called on me to work at my best, questioned me if I was not speaking, and often doubted if I was adequately "on my game". Each time upon entering the consulting room, she examines me and checks me over for fatigue, distractedness, or any vulnerability that she believes could keep me from giving her my absolute best. I struggle with my own rage at having my competence and ethics constantly scrutinised. Diane is brutal in her assessments of me, always finding me deficient in my efforts. Often her exasperation with my not providing adequately for her threatens the treatment as she talks about wanting to find "better remedies". She gives me lashings for my substandard performance. She lives out an unconscious fantasy that threatens to destroy me and her, and our work together, showing the power of the unconscious sadomasochistic fantasy.

Listening to Diane's sense of dissatisfaction with me, with her work subordinates, with her family, friends, and dates, was excruciating. I will offer some process material between October 2006 and July 2007 as it proved to be a period of time when elements of sadomasochism came to the forefront of the analysis. Accompanying the sadomasochism are expressions of oral themes that are integrally interwoven with her sadism and masochism.

At the outset of this period of time, Diane expresses her pain and what appears as a merger with me, but also expresses concerns with harming me:

10/6/2006

Dream

PATIENT: I dreamt about you … I am sitting and talking about what pain I am in. I close my eyes and talk and when I open them you had moved to another chair because of your back pain. I ask about it and you say, "Didn't you see me"? I moved while you were talking. I say no and am sorry because my eyes are closed and you're in great pain and I get up to leave. I stand up and move next to you. I lift you up because you are in great pain and help move you back to the other chair and then I walk out. You are wearing Birkenstocks and M [*girlfriend*] wears Birkenstocks.

ANALYST: You are talking about your pain with your fear that it will break my back.

PATIENT: I cannot tell people about my pain.

ANALYST: You must not close your eyes.

PATIENT: I don't let people know … the old me is always positive, optimistic.

The patient does not allow herself to be aware of her wants, her desires, as her eyes are closed and she cannot see me. A mirror to her, I am rendered crippled in the dream, often the way I can feel in the countertransference with her. The sadomasochism in this analysis is excruciatingly painful for me. I struggle to bear both feeling empathically her chronic pain and also her rage at me for not being enough for her. Her wish to cripple me, to render me ineffectual, seems similar to the way she has crippled herself. As Diane experiences her toxicity, its effect on herself and others, she shifts to her conviction that she is lacking, insufficient, and ashamed, all of which she expresses in the following dream one month later.

11/6/2006

PATIENT: I dreamt of you outside, on a sunny day; you had not walked in yet. I had done something bad, like a little kid, and you asked me to bring someone to therapy and I brought Aunt Maureen, the nun; she walked into the circle and sat in my seat and my mom sat to the right of my seat and you would sit to left of me; Maureen was too close to your seat. I didn't have a seat. I felt ashamed ... you walked in; you wanted Aunt Maureen there because I did something bad. I was not focusing enough and not doing therapy well enough, not doing a good enough job. Mom was a huge force in the dream and you were too. Maureen was klutzy and was not doing the right thing. I don't know why she was sitting in your seat. I need to wake up for therapy. I felt ashamed, bad. Maureen is happy sitting in your seat. She was not going by the rules. She came to enjoy me, was there for me. I am happy to be there, like a little girl, present, eager, pure. I had no defence, no buffer ... and also I am in the shadow of my mother ... mom, Maureen, Betty, all three years apart. I WAS NOT enough in therapy. I had done something wrong and needed to bring in someone. I was not paying enough attention to the rules.

While Diane expressed her desire to be a little girl with me, she cannot yet fully own her little girl wishes. She believes she does not measure up and feels ashamed. She is bad as a defence against her wishes for closeness with me. In the transference she is not enough for me nor for herself. She shows her yearnings as expressed in not being enough. In the countertransference, I am put in the place of the disapproving mother and feel for Diane's struggle. Diane is self-driving and self-depriving, specifically around her wanting me in the way that the little girl wants her mother. The next session further develops her sense of herself as a fragile toddler as well as the grandiose toddler.

11/9/2006

PATIENT: I am not working my body hard enough. Some days I push to the end of the day ... When I don't push, I kick myself hard. I feel so guilty not going to the gym but I am just human ... This is a time when it is not acceptable to be human.

ANALYST: You have suffered because of your own and others' humanness.

PATIENT: I am living in too much humanness ... Humanness means human limits and errors. I walk around with the fragility of a toddler, unprotected.

ANALYST: I wonder if opening yourself to hunger, starvation, has to do with the feeling of fragility.

PATIENT: I don't know if this is connected, but I do know I want to kill Smith, Mary's father [*earlier partner*]. I wonder if I wanted to kill my dad.

ANALYST: You have any doubt about that?

PATIENT: Not that I wanted to castrate him like Smith. Dad had his last rites two times so he died a great Catholic. This is a deeply unacceptable thought. His penis is in my face. I want to cut it off. The only thing between you guys and me is the penis. You are just good at being men's men. It is likely that I wanted to kill him.

ANALYST: You hated him, that he never appreciated you.

PATIENT: My mother said he was proud of me. But I know he was forced into that. When I got a higher up job, I hit his world, like I did with tennis. He insisted on being my sponsor while other girls who were worse players than me had their own professional sponsors. I was not worthy of a professional coach. I am so fucking livid at him. I don't have access to any love.

ANALYST: For so long, you have had no access to your hate.

PATIENT: It is a relief to me that he is dead. Come to think of it, I had a great education.

ANALYST: Because of him?

PATIENT: No, because of me ... or maybe I had a great education because he fucked with my head and I wanted to leave everyone behind. I worked my butt off and wanted to get beyond that world that was killing me. It was time for him to go. Fuck you ... I want to blast him, but ...

ANALYST: Why not?

PATIENT: I am supposed to blame myself ... I would like to cast the blame to others and have it not be me. I would live in world of mediocrity, chaos ... if I stayed in that family.

ANALYST: Is that a risk now?

PATIENT: No. If I accept myself, I don't push myself. I then lose access. The flip side is maybe I would have less pain.

ANALYST: Maybe!

PATIENT: I think of my dad dying and my being misdiagnosed. How my muscular stiffness, psoriasis, tendon so tight, joints moving against each other, are connected with his dying.

ANALYST: How do you think?

PATIENT: I fought so hard against accepting myself. If I am accepting, I'd go down the drain.

ANALYST: You believe that—how does it work?

PATIENT: You go away and no one notices. You aren't substantial enough and you go down the drain.

ANALYST: You're dirt ...

PATIENT: No strength, no staying power, you don't count, you don't matter. It is the survival of the fittest.

ANALYST: The risk of many years of not counting and not mattering.

PATIENT: Right, because of the king. I was so afraid of him. He comes in the door, dinner is on the table, we lined up around the table. We got in our places. I was number six of seven. I'm the one who came three years after my parents had five children in six years. There was just not enough love to go around. Talking about food and eating ... love is food. Talking of our hunger, there was not enough food to eat. Irish cooking, bland, potatoes. I felt starvation for love.

Diane associates her pain with her hatred of her father. She must live beyond mediocrity; in mediocrity she does not exist. Perhaps it is that she believes she does not exist, can "go down the drain", in the minds of her mother and father. Here she disappears. Might body parts, like her imagined penis, also disappear down the drain? She hungers after mattering, being substantial enough to exist. Perhaps her rage turns against her own body in the form of physical dysfunction and autoimmune disease. In the countertransference, I cringe when I hear her ravenous hunger and her hatred, and feel that it is only a matter of time before I too become the object of her rage. I have come to ready myself for her criticisms of my insufficiencies. In the following session Diane expresses how she brings her ravenous hunger into her sexual intimacy.

12/7/2006

A further elaboration of her hunger ...

PATIENT: Sex is ninety-nine per cent tilted in the direction of oral sex for me. I think of a cow, like sucking on a nipple ... Susan [*then girlfriend*] sees me as malnourished. Mary [*earlier girlfriend*] saw me as starving. It is painful because I feel starved and need to be fed. I want her so bad, to be down on her so bad so much. I am so hungry, insatiable, ravenous for her.

ANALYST: When you are in that place of starvation there is a feeling of intensity and also excitement, exhilaration.

PATIENT: I am like a teenage boy; you got me there, you can't pull me back. Down there I come to life.

In her hunger she identifies with the male and finds her sexual arousal. Cunnilingus may involve a fetish for Diane. Could there be a denial of the "hole" of the vagina, and the search for a "something"? Nevertheless the identification is fraught with conflict. Something about the intensity of her longings feels like a potential threat to me in the countertransference. How can I possibly sate her? A few months later come Diane's expressions of her fury at masculinity and her compulsive drivenness.

2/14/2007

PATIENT: I am so busy, up at all hours. I am furious at Bob [*the man she supervises*]. He is a slacker. Goddamn it, he passes the buck with his incompetence. And now there is psoriasis all over my elbows and scalp this week. I have such rage. He needs to clean up his crap.

ANALYST: Something is stirred in you that has to do with his being a man?

PATIENT: Maybe it is my lens. I know from my past and my family life. I have broken the glass ceiling. It is a boys' club. I hate their behaviour because it violated me. It is the same shit, different day. He should take his own garbage out. Where will I put the anger of the past when I tell him to not scratch his penis.

ANALYST: Where will you put it?

PATIENT: I will just say this ... penis-scratching. I would love to let that image leave my head. Maybe this can change, now that dad died.

ANALYST: Change with me?

PATIENT: I do my best work when I am away from you.

ANALYST: You give me your garbage.

PATIENT: I am filling your space and energy with shit.

ANALYST: What Bob did to you.

PATIENT: I am doing what everyone else does, passing shit along. In my forum with you, either I am in space of agitation or in the heart of my anger where better work can happen.

ANALYST: Can we be in the heart of your anger.

PATIENT: When I get to the heart of it and throw a temper tantrum, you better be ready. I am not giving you a free ride. You have to be good partner. If I'm frenetic, I am weaker, and then the weaker I enable you to be. The stronger I am, the stronger you are. There is something big there.

ANALYST: Am I your match?

PATIENT: I'm looking to be better, and looking for my equal.

ANALYST: Perhaps your destiny is to find you don't have that equal.

PATIENT: If so, it'd be because people are lazy.

ANALYST: By nature. And I am lazy too.

PATIENT: By choice. I am not tough enough with myself. I let myself sleep too much. In order to be great, you have to work. But even Sea Biscuit slept long periods and ate a lot of food. Even that great horse needed rest and recovery.

ANALYST: Is that laziness?

PATIENT: Well-earned, but Bob is a slacker. He is dumping on others—and on me.

ANALYST: Intentionally?

PATIENT: I don't care if there is intention. The point is, you did it. I won't be compassionate. If you can't send me what I need, you are fired.

Diane's sadomasochism appears so closely associated with her ravenous hunger and oral deprivation. She hates others as she hates herself for her human limits. She strives to escape limits. Her pursuit is a grandiose pursuit, one intended to defy limits. She warns me that I must be her match, and in the countertransference I am convinced that she will find me lacking, deficient, as she finds most others and dreads finding herself. Limits are contemptible.

5/2/2007

Dream

PATIENT: I am at an anniversary party. Everyone I know is there. I am not in a deficient position. Phil walks in—I used to play tennis with him. When I dated him one summer, it was as if I was not there; he was rubbing himself, and pushing my head down. I instead used my hand to touch his penis. In the dream, he looked for my brothers. I am on skates, and am my old self. At a second party, there are huge displays of shelves with chocolate and candy. I can't figure out what I want. I don't want to get sick on sugar. I want to be selective. There is a handsome guy, but I was not confident, so nothing happened.

ANALYST: Did he show you interest?

PATIENT: He was a gentleman and waited for me. I tell the truth and am exposed—a huge botch and so I no longer can walk. And there is atrophy and joint pain. I was out of the closet with my shame. Now, I am so far beyond because of my success— that I leave everyone in shock. So if my Dad starts to pull any crap, I'll say what about my life is not good judgment!?

I need to read more about Roosevelt ... How does a man become president in a wheel chair? If he can do it, I can do it.

I see the chocolate, and can't figure out what I want, and I still don't grab a candy bar. I look at photographs of my parents' life. There is homogeneity that is dangerous and that could stuff me into a limited world. I skate back to the candy bar and am just about to pick something but I don't take the candy. There is such shame about being different that I will succeed by thirty because of my shame.

ANALYST: You accomplish great things and you did not take the candy many times.

PATIENT: And I did achieve it; I did all those things, at the same time, I did not indulge in candy, in desire. I was truly phobic of something catching me, stopping me if I indulged. I took some candy but am resentful that I did not take more. I had to be certain that I was gay before I could go after what I want.

It is in the defiance of limits, in the pursuit of grandiosity, that Diane can be sated, her hunger quelled. Diane's sadomasochism renders her unable to embrace the humanity of the self and the other, perhaps even the "sweetness" her analysis brings to her. Human limits mean for Diane ungratified urges that evoke her harsh condemnations and contempt. Her temptation is to destroy the other (before the self) and fall back into her isolation. I feel compassion for her deprivation under her self-imposed restrictiveness, and the aloneness she lives in because of her rejection of others.

Sadomasochism and the transference

PATIENT: Pat [*new partner*] loved my mother. My mother can chew my partners up. I have been thinking I want to reduce to three times a week. I want time for other healing, and I am not interested in the recycling that I am doing here. I need something else.

ANALYST: Are you concerned about chewing me up? [*I wonder if she feels concerned about the impact of both her criticisms of me, and her sadistic efforts at closeness.*]

PATIENT: No. I see that it will end with Pat. I should end it. When I look at her, I see the imperfections. The lines around her mouth, the way she scrunches her face, the lines. My friends are not enthusiastic about her, she is not a "power-house", she is "nice".

ANALYST: You search for imperfections—you fear being "adrift" if you don't find them—and in here, too, with your concern about recycling. Something is brewing in here with me.

PATIENT: I search for imperfections in my partner to stave off being had; the lines in her face [*referring to her partner's wrinkles*]. If I am not fully informed, then there can be a mistake. I stare in her face. I don't know if it is acceptable.

ANALYST: You search for the imperfections and stave off a deepening closeness.

PATIENT: I have Pat, and then I make her not right. She has to work at being a lover to me. She wants to attend to me, but she is involved with the pace of her own arousal, and loses me when she changes her pace.

ANALYST: You have an idea of the impact on me of a change of pace?

PATIENT: Something about ending here. I talked about it at the start, that I wanted it to be clear—to be an "aha" experience; to learn something new. That would be clear.

ANALYST: That I would be penetrating.

PATIENT: Yes. I want it to lead to something explosive, a bang, and it's not that way at all.

ANALYST: Like the climax of a penis, so clear.

PATIENT: Yes, it is so clear, and I like that and then they sleep.

ANALYST: And unclear with your vagina.

PATIENT: It could go on and on, and be not clear. Was it an orgasm or not. Not sure and I hate that.

ANALYST: And that's what it is like in here. You are not sure where it will lead and hate me because it is my imperfection and yours too.

PATIENT: I so hate that. I want the clarity, cannot stand the vagueness and unsurity.

ANALYST: You are talking about your femininity, your femaleness.

PATIENT: Am I? I think YOU are talking about my femininity.

For Diane, human limitation is contemptible and associated with versions of femininity and masculinity. She holds me in contempt for my femaleness and my maleness. For her, each proves limited and limiting. Diane is dismissive of my transference comments and "chews me up" with her contempt. She is tempted to reject me and the work we do together. She so fears her own vulnerability, and for that reason is always ready to dismiss and destroy.

In the analysis, Diane screams at me from her position of helplessness, despair, and rage at her life circumstance and at the slacking men that drain her. At times she berates me for what she sees as my slacking laziness. My countertransference informs me of the prevalence of sadomasochism in Diane's inner life. When I listen to her, I feel anxious and rageful because of the threat I experience to my analytic function. I clamour to find something to say to her, for a way to work with her and be grounded in my role as her analyst. I am tortured by her; often squirming, flushing, doubting my adequacy, feeling incompetent, struggling to save myself from feeling ripped apart. She tells me I am a slacker, that I am not penetrating her with knowledge. She accuses me of just "going along for the ride", and in the countertransference I feel like I am sucking off of her. I observe that I have the desire to want to speak to her with force, to pin her down, get her to submit to me, to my interpretations. While I accept her payments, I become identified countertransferentially with her rageful projections, and I question whether I am worthy as an analyst. I observe my worry that what I take from her could deprive her of what she needs to survive and see that my countertransference informs me that I am a participant in the sadomasochistic transference.

Where the structuralisation necessary for differentiation has been compromised, the sadomasochistic construction is a version of psychic structure allowing for some differentiation of the self and the other (Frosch, 1995). Fended off are the infantile longings. The longings to be loved, "... without the intervening step of a ... regression to an anal sadistic organization, [are] associated with the sense of annihilation" (Frosch, 1995, p. 444). The challenges for both patient and analyst are great when the psychoanalysis of sadomasochism calls forth rage at unmet needs and the threats of annihilation to self and other.

References

Chasseguet-Smirgel, J. (1991). Sado-masochism in the perversions: Some thoughts on the destruction of reality. *Journal of American Psychoanalytical Association*, 39: 399–415.

Frosch, A. (1995). The preconceptual organization of emotion. *Journal of American Psychoanalytical Association*, 43: 423–447.

CHAPTER FOUR

Discussion of the case of Diane

Alan Bass

From the welter of miseries that is Diane's treatment I choose an atypical moment. In the dream of 10/6/2006 Diane is talking to her analyst about her physical pain. In the dream the analyst then has severe back pain, and has moved to another chair. Diane says, "I stand up and move next to you. I lift you up because you're in great pain and help move you back to the other chair and then I walk out. You are wearing Birkenstocks and M [girlfriend] wears Birkenstocks." Diane, we know, has terrible foot and leg pains. Birkenstocks are therapeutic shoes. The analyst in great pain is wearing therapeutic shoes. (One wonders what kind of shoes Diane wears to take care of her injured feet and legs.) Most important, after projecting her pain into the analyst, Diane not only makes the analyst into her sensible shoe girlfriend, she cares for the analyst: "I lift you up because you're in great pain and help move you back to the other chair"—presumably the analyst's chair.

My purpose is to explain why I chose this moment as a guiding thread for a discussion of Ellman's paper. I hope to show that it says a great deal about the "life and death forces of sadomasochism". One immediately sees both sides in the transference: the "death" side of projection of Diane's own pain into the analyst, the "life" side of care for the analyst, who becomes her girlfriend. How to understand the interaction of the two? To answer this question I will meander through some of the case material, accompanied by my reactions. It is not often that we get such detailed reports, which are the best basis for thinking about the integration of theory and practice.

Ellman begins her account with Diane's bodily pain. Diane's "only interest" in treatment is being "freed of her pain", but the pain has gotten worse in her toe and ankle. Diane accuses the analyst of being incompetent in pursuing the question of early sexual abuse by her father. And how can the analyst be of any help when she has patients coming in and out of her office? Ellman revisits her own tortured feelings of inadequacy and of anger at Diane's lack of appreciation for her efforts. This beginning immediately made me think about Joyce McDougall.

Many years ago, when I read *Theaters of the Mind* I was quite impressed by McDougall's (1986) understanding of what she calls "psychosomatosis". McDougall takes elements of Freud, Klein, and Bion to explain this phenomenon. Extending Klein's idea that in fantasy the infant has access to the mother's insides, McDougall says that in a difficult dyad the baby discharges painful feelings through his/her own body *and*, in fantasy, through the mother's body, because the two bodies are not yet distinct. The attack on one's own body is also an attack on the mother's body. Mother and baby are joined in pain. The same dynamic will be repeated with the analyst. I wondered if this was the overarching structure of Diane's treatment. The first thing we hear about Diane is that her body is tortured, and that she tortures the analyst with her own torture.

A former patient of my own, who had sadomasochistic masturbation fantasies, shared many characteristics with Diane. My patient's mother was a physician, a Holocaust survivor, and probable borderline who tortured her children emotionally and stuffed them with medication. My patient compulsively tore at the skin on her fingers, even while on the couch, making me a passive witness of, or even participant in, her self-inflicted pain. I found McDougall's theory helpful in understanding this situation: my patient's attack on her own body was also an unconscious attack on the mother's body, or on my body. (For the moment I am leaving out the second generation Holocaust survivor aspects of the case. I will come back to this.) What I learned from McDougall is that in such treatments the analyst must accept being tortured. (McDougall herself relates her thinking to Bion on containment.) This is why I think that Ellman's feelings of being tortured by Diane should not be considered countertransference in the strict sense. Rather, the feeling of being tortured shows receptivity to the patient's communications, openness to the patient's sadistic claim on the analyst's "insides".

That was my first reaction to the opening of the report. Fast forwarding, I found related ideas in the literature. The Novicks (1987) published a comprehensive study of masochism, based on the treatments of children with beating fantasies and adults with masochistic issues. They cite "the unanimous report of the therapists of the children with fixed beating fantasies that the treatments were arduous, joyless, and ungratifying for a long time" (p. 355). Clearly the same holds for treatments like Diane's. While the Novicks explore masochistic dynamics on all developmental levels, they state that "the first layer of masochism must be sought in early infancy, in the child's adaptation to situation where safety resides only in a painful relationship with the mother" (p. 359).

Other theorists have come to the same conclusion. For example, in a famous paper contesting Freud's theory that masochism is sadism turned against oneself, Berliner (1947) said that masochism is the result of love for a sadistic object (p. 459). The dependent child "introjects the pain giving object because of an oral need for love" (p. 460). (We hear Diane speak many times of "being starved for love".) There is an appeal to Berliner's position: it eliminates the thorniness of Freud's drive-based theory of the turning of sadism upon oneself. McDougall is actually closer to Freud on this issue, adding the dynamics of sadism and projective identification found in Klein and Bion to explain how attack upon oneself *is* attack upon the other.

The Novicks also agree with Freud's position about a drive turned around upon oneself, and expand it. Sounding a bit like Berliner they state that "masochists are very active in their pursuit of pain and failure, in part to maintain the receptive relationship with an intrusive object" (p. 367). From their developmental perspective they state that the early association of mother and unpleasure "leads to the early adoption of an autoplastic [self directed], rather than alloplastic [other directed], mode of dealing with internal and external stimuli, which sets a pattern of discharge via the self which will affect all later developmental phases" (p. 362). In other words, the relatively unboundaried love for a painful mother stimulates discharge of pain through one's own body. The Novicks are particularly attentive to anal phase dynamics here: "The aggressive impulses of the anal phase are dealt with by the defense of turning the aggression against the self [Freud], which prevents destruction of the object and allows for discharge of aggression toward the internalized hated mother" (p. 369). In Freudian developmental terms, the Novicks basically come to the same conclusion as McDougall from her Freudian-Kleinian-Bionian perspective. I think that one sees all of this in Ellman's opening material, in the description of an analyst being tortured by a patient's self torture.

The next thing Ellman speaks of is Diane's distress at a girlfriend's demeaning remarks about Obama. Diane says: "She [the girlfriend] and I have been over that so many times", and then goes on to say that speaking to her mother about their own family problems is equally hopeless: "I continue to try to speak with my mother about the past ... but she is no longer willing to look back and discuss what has happened ..." Did Diane choose someone like her mother, with whom discussion of vital issues is hopeless? If so, there is more than one aspect to the problem. One wonders whether Diane also tortures herself by continuing to attempt something that she knows will not work. The Novicks think that in order for the masochist to break the preoedipal tie to mother, the patient "will have to become aware not only of his internal conflicts, but also of his mother's pathology" (p. 367). From a relational perspective, Ghent (1990) suggests that such apparently pain-seeking behavior is an attempt to "'take in' the inner truth, to perceive self and other as they really are ... The compulsion to repeat masochistically self destructive behavior may turn out to be another form of trying to 'take in' reality, in this case the unthinkable destructiveness of a significant other" (p. 127). The common denominator in these statements is that the masochism of repeated failed attempts to deal with an other's behaviour is grounded in denial of the true destructiveness of the object.

We know by Freud's own statement how much he struggled with recognising the role of destructiveness. "I remember my own defensive attitude when the idea of an instinct of destruction first emerged ... and how long it took before I became receptive to it" (1930, p. 120). Could Diane's struggle here be related to this issue, as both the Novicks and Ghent suggest? In other words, does Diane both understand and not understand the aggression originally directed against her, by both parents as it turns out? Is it the analyst's function to overcome the defence against recognising the parents' pathology (Novicks) or to acknowledge the distorted understanding of it (Ghent)? Either way, the analyst has to become receptive to the full extent of destructiveness. Whatever the merits of Freud's theory of innate human destructiveness (the death instinct), it enables us to think about this issue. To put it formulaically: self destructiveness is increased to the extent that the other's destructiveness is both felt and denied. I heard this simultaneous feeling and denial in my patient, who would repeatedly say, without a trace of irony: "The Nazis should have killed my mother." Of course my patient knew that she would not have been born if this had happened. The issue here, I believe, is that the patient did feel tortured by her mother, but could not really understand how entrenched the mother's pathology was. Nor could she really understand her mother's experience (survival of Auschwitz) of monstrous destructiveness.

For the destructive other to be able to enter into dialogue about the real effects of his or her actions, there has to be some depressive position integration, some recognition of one's own destructiveness. Klein teaches us that the depressive position is fraught with anxiety, an anxiety that blindly destructive people—whether abusive parents or perpetrators of genocide—cannot face. If so, trying to get them to see their destructiveness is impossible, but can become a compulsion. Ellman writes that Diane could "hear her mother's wish to protect herself from being riddled with regret ..." But does Diane really appreciate what this means, or is she endlessly compelled to attempt to get the other (mother, father, girlfriend, analyst) to admit a destructiveness that the other will never admit, no matter how much she suffers in the process?

The clinical problem here is profound. When the analyst uses the classical frame of non-self-disclosure, as Ellman does, and as do I, this can create an impasse. The analyst analyses without admitting anything, no matter how much inner turmoil he or she is in. A patient like Diane can concretely take this stance as repetition of the trauma of the parents who will not admit the cruelty and pain they have inflicted. Here I think that the analyst needs to interpret the patient's defences against understanding that the parents will never understand their destructiveness. Without such analysis, the patient can be involved in the kind of transference repetition Freud called "demonic" in *Beyond the Pleasure Principle* (1920): the endless repetition of a painful experience that exacerbates pain. For Freud this is a manifestation of the death instinct. It can seem that the masochistic patient will not permit the analyst to be on the side of life in such transference repetitions, and will concretely treat the analyst as the pain-inflicting parent.

We quickly learn about other painful aspects of Diane's past. She was raised in a family and a culture that valued boys over girls. She was the sixth of seven children. Her father seems to have been unconsciously exhibitionistic; one intuits that he could not imagine the impact of his crotch-scratching upon a child like Diane. Let us imagine Diane caught up in a kind of enraged penis envy, since she longed for the same kind of admiration from the parents that her oldest brother received. Maria Torok's account of penis envy is very enlightening here. Torok (1970) agrees with Freud that the girl reproaches the mother for having brought her into the world inadequately equipped. But she also thinks that in hopelessly envying men, the girl remains subservient to the mother, who in fantasy wishes to keep the girl in this tormented position. In Diane's case the longing for a mother who was overburdened with seven children, and the probable unconscious conviction that the mother wanted her to feel permanently inadequate, creates another transference dilemma: Diane hopelessly longs for exclusive attention from an analyst who has other patients, and who she unconsciously believes keeps her in an inadequate position. Hence, again, Diane can only take revenge by doing all she can to make the analyst feel inadequate.

All of this is exacerbated by Diane's own adolescent associations of sexuality with dirt and her mother's actual prohibitions against masturbation. The Novicks, as we saw above, pay special attention to the anal phase dynamics of masochism, following Freud. Torok, too, thinks that the girl's submission to the fantasy of the mother's command to hopelessly seek what she will never attain is a regression to the mother's control of the girl's inner body in the anal phase. Torok integrates anal phase dynamics with superego issues, which was also Freud's approach in "'A Child Is Being Beaten'" (1919). Later, in "Female Sexuality" (1931), Freud speculated that beating fantasies in women might be linked to maternal prohibition of masturbation—beating the clitoris. We do learn that Diane's mother forbade masturbation; Diane sometimes treats the analyst as someone who imposes "the rules". There seems to have been no path open to Diane to develop as a woman happy in her body. Everything about her is a source of pain to be overcome by inflicting more pain. The "rules" of analysis are only there to make her submit and suffer.

And so we arrive at Diane's athleticism. She excelled, often "outplaying boys". She drove herself to extremes of tennis practice, achieving great results, but with no one coaching her. The result was deterioration of the bones and muscles of her feet, to the extent that she could barely walk. I hear in this tragedy the superego command to become phallic by blindly inflicting more and more pain on herself. Such masochistic dynamics are not confined to women, as I learned with another patient, a man who was very much like Diane in this respect. This man's father was known for his arrogant brilliance. He was extremely successful, but unable to form ordinary ties to his wife and children. Like Diane's father, my patient's father was severely alcoholic; he was also adamant in his refusal to attend to his serious health problems. My patient, Mr. A, felt unable to compete with his father, but like Diane could not stop trying to get his father to deal with his health, alcoholism, and generally destructive effect on his family. Mr. A was athletically gifted, the only area in which he could do something that was beyond his father. Like Diane, he chose to train himself for a very demanding sport, and like Diane, inflicted more pain on himself when his body was injured. He had reasonable Olympic aspirations, but eventually could not compete with the men in his sport who had had supervised training. He came to treatment after his Olympic aspirations crashed, depressed, and entangled with a woman who treated him contemptuously, "borrowed" money from him, and saw another man on the side. And like Diane, my patient developed extremely painful leg symptoms—in his case lesions that were undiagnosable and untreatable. It took many years of treatment for him to understand the sadistic superego dictate that also plagued Diane: he could only excel by enacting a fantasy of becoming phallic by inflicting more and more pain on himself, leading to actual, severe injury.

But my patient did not have to face the issue of homosexuality. Diane's parents were contemptuous when she came out. Diane felt painfully alone, "cast out". Here one needs to consider the links between shame, masochism, and homophobia. There is nothing mysterious about the extreme shame that can accompany feeling sexually deviant in a culture that condemns homosexuality. However, we all too readily speak about "internalised homophobia" without going beyond shame and self-hatred. Homophobia is another form of entrenched destructiveness, which cannot be seen as such by those who practice it; hence gay bashings, and even murders (Matthew Shepherd). The familiar dynamics of the paranoid-schizoid position—projection onto the other of hated aspects of oneself—are patent in homophobia, as in any form of prejudice. But if one internalises homophobia, one internalises the destructiveness of the other. (This is akin to the problem of the unacknowledged destructiveness of the parent.) In Diane's case one sees how this could all too readily intersect with everything inside her that reacts to pain with more pain, as in her driven, fruitless attempts to make others admit their destructiveness, or in her approach to athletics. Her sexuality then can be nothing but masochistic. Ellman tells us that Diane is self-critical both for not allowing herself bodily pleasure and for feeling sexually aroused.

Which brings us to the crux of Diane's sexual conflicts. Diane shamefully acknowledges her pleasure in the fantasy of being penetrated. However, penetration, even if by a woman, necessitates her unbearable submission ... Diane describes her painful "submission" to her partner and her arousal in that pain. She was pained by her concern that it seemed "sadomasochistic". She loves her partner to "take her", to be strong and forceful, yet at the same time detests those masculine reminders.

There is a great deal to tease out here. Diane not only feels shame for being gay; she feels shame for enjoying penetration, because it reminds her of the "shame" of being a woman, for being the one who "submits". Further, Diane is ashamed that pain itself arouses her. This last factor is at the heart of Freud on masochism: pleasure in pain. Freud had many things to say about it, but let us start with his observation that for children all physical activity can be sexually arousing (1905, 1925). Pain can be particularly arousing, due to its intensity. Hence we all have the capacity to be aroused by pain. For Diane, however, it would be incomprehensible that her arousal by pain could be anything other than something affectively painful (shame), which is then to be treated with more pain.

This is where psychoanalytic tolerance for all forms of sexuality is crucial. Ellman says that a central issue in Diane's analysis is "the problem of how pleasure can be realised while feeling like a denigrated disgusting hole." The analyst has to be able to disentangle pleasure in pain from feeling "denigrated" and "disgusting". We do not know whether Ellman challenged Diane for her painful reaction to enjoying pain. However, if an analyst in this kind of situation thinks that the enjoyment of pain is in and of itself a problem, then there is the possibility of a countertransference impasse. The analyst could be in the position of the destructive parent and the destructive society. Ideally, treatment would include helping Diane to resolve her defensive shame about enjoyment of pain, and then see what happens. Diane, I guess, would find it completely counterintuitive that she could be a gay woman who sexually enjoys penetration and some degree of pain, and also be the kind of successful, authoritative person she is professionally. My related, simple guess is that Diane's sadistic contempt for others, her "readiness to be dismissive", is a version of the contempt for herself sexually. My second-generation Holocaust survivor patient had similar dynamics. She was deeply ashamed of her arousal by pain. She started treatment when her long road to professional success placed her in a position of authority which she wanted to quit, because of the combination of shame and arousal implicit in a job in which she would have to "give orders".

I believe that all these complex dynamics are active in Diane's case, but there is more. Let us look at another critical transferential issue, one in which Diane's sadism is more than contempt for herself. Ellman writes:

> Each time upon entering the consulting room, she examines me and checks me over for fatigue, distractedness or any vulnerability that she believes could keep me from giving her my absolute best. I struggle with my own rage at having my competence and ethics constantly scrutinised. Diane is brutal in her assessments of me, always finding me deficient in my efforts ... She gives me lashings for my substandard performance. She lives out an unconscious fantasy that threatens to destroy me and her, and our work together, showing the power of the unconscious sadomasochistic fantasy.

Above, I said that I think that Ellman's rage and feelings of being tortured are not countertransference *per se*, but rather the inevitable responses to the affective claims Diane makes on the analyst. However, I think that there is a possible countertransference problem, in the usual sense. Some aspects of Diane's masochism are due to her not understanding the destructiveness that has been directed against her. I speculate that she repeats this non-metabolised destructiveness with Ellman—a destructiveness that "threatens to destroy me and her, and our work together ..." What does one do in a situation that goes beyond feeling tortured and angry, a situation in which one encounters implacable negativity? One can feel persecuted in such a situation. (Kleinians such as Steiner and Rosenfeld have examined such situations in depth in their work on sadistic "gangs" of internal objects.) How does one resist despair, resignation, passivity, which I believe are built into this kind of clinical situation, and are more difficult to deal with?

This kind of destructiveness goes beyond sadomasochism in the sexual sense, because it is not linked to pleasure; it is more like blind hatred. It reminds me of Freud's controversial idea of primary masochism (1925). Freud thought that the self-destructiveness of the death drive is projected outward, becoming inevitable human aggression: we destroy each other in order not to destroy ourselves. This primary masochism can remain libidinally "bound" within the individual producing erotogenic, feminine, and moral masochism. But before this libidinal binding, there is blind self and other directed aggression.

What Freud might not have considered is that when boundaries between self and other are blurred, there is no distinction between destruction of oneself and destruction of the other, as in McDougall's theory. This seems to be a variation on Klein's paranoid-schizoid position, but I think there is more to it. Klein's formulations in her early phase would emphasise interpretation of aggression, and, in her late phase, interpretation of envy. I think that either would be counter-therapeutic here, making Diane feel more ashamed, exacerbating her vicious cycles of treating pain with pain. Freud's theory of primary masochism seems to say nothing at all about what to do clinically when "battling the life and death forces of sadomasochism". And McDougall seems to rely on a very traditional content based form of interpretation that spells out the patient's fantasies. As impressed as I am with her theorising, I am doubtful about the helpfulness of spelling out destructive fantasies. To get to a possibly effective clinical stance in such a difficult situation requires some theory. This theory will also justify my point of departure in a caring, non-destructive moment of Diane's dream.

In question are the complex relations between sadomasochism and the life and death drives. Let us take a quick glance at the development of Freud's thinking on this question. Freud was at first puzzled by masochism: how to explain a seeking of pain that appears to contradict the pleasure principle? One must always remember that the pleasure principle is really the pleasure-unpleasure principle: that is, pleasure as the avoidance of unpleasure, of pain. If the basic regulatory principle of the mind acts to avoid pain, what explains seeking pain, enjoyment of pain? Freud's first full answer to this question was in "Instincts and Their Vicissitudes" (1915): masochism is sadism turned against the self. In fact, the sadism that is turned against the self is not yet sexual sadism. Rather, Freud sees it as a manifestation of a drive to mastery, which can include cruel actions for their own sake, as in the example of a child who tears the legs off an insect without any thought of the insect's pain. Turning against the self is one of the basic "vicissitudes" of the drive. When original sadism or cruelty is turned against the self, the pain it causes can produce sexual excitation. This is masochism proper. Sexual sadism, in fact, derives from the masochism of non-sexual sadism turned against the self. The sexual sadist is someone who was originally masochistic, who enjoys being the object who does to the masochist what the masochist originally did to him or herself.

There are two important consequences here. The first is the old psychoanalytic idea that every sadist can become a masochist, and vice versa. This is absolutely necessary to Freud's theory of the component drives of infantile sexuality, which holds that such drives occur as active and passive pairs of opposites, such that each can turn into the other. (Freud gives a similar account of voyeurism and exhibitionism.) The second consequence has been pointed out by Laplanche (1980). Even if Freud derives sexual masochism from non-sexual sadism, from the point of view of sexuality masochism is always primary in his theory. Laplanche goes further, positing an essentially masochistic nature of sexuality itself. In this conception, masochism is an irreducible issue. From Laplanche's point of view, Diane teaches us something about sexuality itself.

The next step in Freud on masochism is "'A Child Is Being Beaten'". Here, Freud for the first time provides a complex set of psychodynamics to explain a "perversion"—beating fantasies—rather than simply seeing it as a fixation to a component drive of infantile sexuality. Without going into all the details, Freud finds in beating fantasies Oedipal wishes, regression to anality, and simultaneous gratification and punishment (the beating fantasy as a regressive, anal expression of the sexual wish for the father and punishment for that wish). Laplanche (1980) again finds in this paper evidence that for Freud masochism is always sexually primary. He says that Freud's three stage derivation of the beating fantasy—my father is beating the child who I hate, my father is beating me, a child is being beaten—replicates the schema of "Instincts and Their Vicissitudes": gratification of non-sexual sadism (sibling rivalry), turning of that sadism against the self (sexual masochism), identification with both beater and beaten in masturbatory fantasy. This suggests a question about Diane: is it possible that one aspect of her self-torture is simultaneous gratification and punishment for Oedipal wishes? She is both aroused by and ashamed of her wishes to be penetrated. Sexual wishes for men do come up in her material. (This in no way eliminates crucial pre-oedipal dynamics.)

All of this is complicated by the introduction of the life and death drives in *Beyond the Pleasure Principle*. Freud's idea is that there is in the organism a silent force that tends toward the elimination of all tension, toward death, as a consequence of the emergence of organic from inorganic life. However debatable this theory might be, it does open psychoanalysis to some of the darkest and most difficult issues. This is where Freud begins to think about innate human aggression, because the self-destructive force of the death drive is deflected outward, directed against another. Freud now sees sadism as a fusion of the death drive and libido: pleasure in the other's destruction, pleasure in cruelty for its own sake. This gives a different picture of the child tearing legs off an insect. Such a child might not care about inflicting pain upon another, but may be enjoying his/her own cruelty.

The death drive's antagonist is the life drive, Eros. But what is Eros? It is not simply sexuality. Freud is specific: Eros is the conjoint force of sexuality and self-preservation. This is a reversal of the original theory, derived from the study of the neuroses, in which self preservation and sexuality were in conflict. As a simultaneous expression of sexuality and self preservation, Freud says, Eros "introduces fresh vital tensions" (1920, p. 55) into the organism. Thus, the death drive, the drive to eliminate tension, attempts to suppress the force of Eros. When Freud subsequently sees primary masochism as that remainder of the death drive libidinally bound within the psyche (1925), he is clearly implying that erotogenic, feminine, and moral masochism are also a kind of lethal pleasure in self-destruction. How can one not think of Diane? But is Diane completely dominated by primary masochism, or even by the blind destructiveness that precedes it? Would despair and resignation on the analyst's part actually be justified? Has death won out over life?

To answer we need to understand more about Eros. Loewald (1980), more than anyone else, has seen what is novel in the life drive. Previously for Freud, all drive gratification was a question of tension reduction. (This is why Freud can say in *Beyond the Pleasure Principle* that the death drive, as the drive to eliminate tension, serves the pleasure principle.) Now, Loewald says, Freud has introduced a basic psychic force that tends toward tension increase, not decrease. This is the force that is responsible for structure formation, for the holding together of a more complex, more "energy filled" psychic organisation in dynamic interaction with the environment. It is the motor of psychic change.

Loewald, however, does not look at a basic paradox clearly described by Freud. Precisely because there is also a self-destructive force of tension reduction in the psyche, Eros is a "mischief maker", a disturbance of the trend toward tension reduction. This is why in my own work (Bass, 2000) I speak of the "trauma of Eros": integrated sexuality and self-preservation do raise tension levels, and in some situations this raised tension is experienced as trauma, as too much tension. In such situations, sexuality and self-preservation are split, so that sexuality is more on the side of death, self destruction. (Laplanche (1997) also speaks of a "sexuality of life and a sexuality of death".) But then Eros, the force that keeps the psyche in dynamic interaction with the environment, is stalemated. Is this a negative therapeutic reaction that the analyst must resign him or herself to?

I think not, and this is where I come back to my point of departure in Diane's dream. What happens in this fragment? First Diane projects her pain into the analyst—for reasons already discussed. But then Diane cares for the analyst. She takes the analyst from the "chair of pain" back to her own chair, the chair in which she treats Diane. In caring for the analyst who contains her pain, in taking the analyst back to her chair, Diane is unconsciously caring for herself. And then the analyst is wearing the Birkenstocks that her girlfriend wears—that is, the analyst is her girlfriend who is careful about her feet. Sexuality and self-preservation are reintegrated in these dream images via the analyst.

Here I would enter into collegial discussion with Ellman. She stresses that Diane cripples her in the dream, a reflection of how crippled she so often feels in this treatment. Any analyst would understand Ellman's reactions here. But this is where theory counts. Theory gives us tools to see things, to think in unaccustomed ways. The theory of the life drive as tension-raising, as potentially traumatic integration, says that what might be most threatening to Diane is recognition of the analyst's help and care, and with it the possible emergence from her own vicious cycles of pain met with more pain. Or I should really say, emergence from meeting pain with pain, to meeting pain with a different pain. In other words, Diane does indeed take cruel, self-perpetuating pleasure in destroying herself and the analyst. To counter this, she would also have to deal with the pain, the increased tension, of life—the "trauma of Eros". Just as our original theory allowed us to hear derivatives of sexuality in unusual places, the theory I am advocating helps us to hear derivatives of the life drive in unusual places—here in a brief moment from the dream of a sadomasochistic patient. This would produce a different interpretive stance. I am not advocating support: "You are kind to me in the dream, and you make me into your girlfriend who is also kind to her feet." Rather, I would approach the issue from the defensive side: "I think it might be very upsetting to you to think about taking care of me—and yourself, because I contain your pain—and maybe even more upsetting to think of making me into your girlfriend—who takes care of her feet."

My guess is that Diane would reject such an intervention out of hand. But that would be fine, especially if one hypothesises that her rejection is motivated by intense anxiety. The same topic comes up again later, when Diane seems unable to extend to herself the need for rest and food of a great race horse (Sea Biscuit); I speculate here that Diane also does not want to acknowledge her need for the analyst's care. Diane claims that she concretely needs physical pain relief from the analyst; she seeks out many alternative treatments. Here I am reminded of a supervised case, a woman who, like Diane, tortured herself and her analyst with the analyst's inadequacy. This patient sought out almost every kind of alternative treatment imaginable, including having all the fillings in her teeth changed, and yet never left her analysis. I think one sees an extreme splitting defence here, splitting against the unconscious knowledge that analytic care is precisely what is needed and desired, and yet extreme anxiety at the possibility of internalisation of analytic care.

Ellman raises an analogous issue in her concluding remark. Citing Frosch, she speaks of compromised differentiation between self and other, and says that "the psychoanalysis of sadomasochism calls forth rage at unmet needs and the threat of annihilation of self and other." I am suggesting a related version of these dynamics: there is not only rage at unmet needs (what could be clearer in Diane's case?), but also intense anxiety about the analytic meeting of these needs, via the integration of sexuality and self-preservation. The "annihilation" of self and other, or the entrapment of self and other in vicious cycles of destructiveness, is due to another form of splitting: the defensive splitting of self-preservation and sexuality, the defence against life itself in its tension-raising aspect, with consequent enhancement of the anti-life force of undifferentiated self and other directed destructiveness. I believe there is clinical evidence for this position in Diane's dream.

There is one more difficult issue here. The first part of this paper dealt with sadomasochism from the point of view of psychic content (Freud, Klein, McDougall, the Novicks, Berliner, Ghent, Steiner, Rosenfeld—a list that I know is partial at best; I have not mentioned Bach's crucial work on sadomasochism and self and object constancy because I assume he will do so elsewhere in this volume). All of this, and much more, is completely necessary, and gives a clear indication of how complex the dynamics of sadomasochism really are. However, when speaking of sadomasochism in terms of the life and death drives, which appear to be more abstract metapsychological formulations, I am also alleging that they provide a way to think about how sadomasochism functions in relation to the analytic process itself. Diane, like so many patients who need to keep self preservation and sexuality split, that is, who defend against the analytic process as a manifestation of Eros, uses the content of transference fantasies as a defensive barrier between herself and the analyst. (This, again, is why I think that simply articulating the patient's fantasies does not help.) Elsewhere I have cited Betty Joseph on this question. Joseph writes:

> ... conflict is constantly introduced, as Freud showed, by the life instinct. It manifests itself in a need to love and be dependent ... of [which] the analyst is the *prime and most disturbing current representative. Each time these carriers of the life instinct disturb the patient's peace, a situation akin to trauma arises* ... (1989, p. 32; my emphasis)

By maintaining the analytic environment and the analytic process, for some patients, like Diane, the content of sadomasochistic dynamics will be played out as a global defence against internalisation of that process. As difficult as such situations are, this is also the antidote to resignation and despair. Although we can feel daunted at the prospect of helping the neurotic emerge from inhibition, guilt, and anxiety, or the narcissist from grandiosity and devaluation, we think that his or her very pathology defends against those possibilities, possibilities that are "there" in the patient, but lost to defence. So, too, the pathology of patients who seem to be caught in a sadomasochistic, life-and-death struggle with the analyst, indicates a defensive structure with both content and process aspects. The content aspects are the more familiar psychodynamic factors, the drives, object relations, fantasies, anxieties, defences, that create sadomasochism. The process aspects are the less familiar anxiety-filled response to the analyst as disturber of the peace, such that any integration of sexuality and self-preservation becomes a threat. This is why we need to be attentive to any derivatives of such integration, as in Diane's dream, and even her passing mention of Sea Biscuit. They are the possibility of successful treatment.

References

Bach, S. (1994). *The Language of Perversion and the Language of Love*. Northvale, NJ: Jason Aronson.

Bass, A. (2000). *Difference and Disavowal: The Trauma of Eros*. Stanford: Stanford University Press.

Berliner, B. (1947). On some psychodynamics of masochism. *Psychoanalytic Quarterly*, 16: 459–471.

Freud, S. (1905). *Three Essays on the Theory of Sexuality. S. E., 7*. London: Hogarth.

Freud, S. (1915). Instincts and their vicissitudes. *S. E., 14*. London: Hogarth.

Freud, S. (1919). "A child is being beaten." *S. E., 17*. London: Hogarth.

Freud, S. (1920). *Beyond the Pleasure Principle. S. E., 18*. London: Hogarth.

Freud, S. (1925). The economic problem of masochism. *S. E., 19*. London: Hogarth.

Freud, S. (1930). *Civilization and Its Discontents. S. E., 21*. London: Hogarth.

Freud, S. (1931). Female sexuality. *S. E., 21*. London: Hogarth.

Frosch, A. (1995). The preconceptual organization of emotion. *Journal of American Psychoanalytic Association*, 43: 423–447.

Ghent, E. (1990). Masochism, submission, surrender—masochism as a perversion of surrender. *Contemporary Psychoanalysis*, 26: 108–136.

Joseph, B. (1989). *Psychic Equilibrium and Psychic Change*. London: Routledge.

Klein, M. (1986). *The Selected Melanie Klein* (Ed., J. Mitchell). New York: Free Press.

Laplanche, J. (1980). *Life and Death in Psychoanalysis* (Trans., J. Mehlmann). Baltimore: Johns Hopkins University Press.

Laplanche, J. (1997). Aims of the psychoanalytic process. *Journal of European Psychoanalysis*, 5: 69–79.

Loewald, H. (1980). *Papers on Psychoanalysis*. New Haven: Yale University Press.

McDougall, J. (1986). *Theaters of the Mind*. London: Free Association Books.

Novick, K. K. & Novick, J. (1987). The essence of masochism. *Psychoanalytic Study of the Child*, 42: 353–384.

Rosenfeld, H. (1971). A clinical approach to the psychoanalytic theory of the life and death instincts. *International Journal of Psychoanalysis*, 52: 169–178.

Steiner, J. (1993). *Psychic Retreats*. London: Routledge.

Torok, M. (1970). The significance of penis envy in women. In: J. Chasseguet-Smirgel (Ed.), *Female Sexuality*. Ann Arbor: University of Michigan Press.

CHAPTER FIVE

Discussion of the case of Diane

Jack Novick and Kerry Kelly Novick

Our first response to Dr. Ellman's vivid and moving account of her work with "Diane" and her honest portrayal of her own reactions is to acknowledge that she is not alone. In our years of working with sadomasochism, we have found, as have others from Freud on (Freud, 1909, 1940; Meyers, 1988) that the analyses were long and arduous because of the self-destructive nature of the pathology, its roots at every level of development, the multiple functions it serves, and the intense countertransference reactions it evokes. In 1909 Freud wrote to Jung: "In my practice, I am chiefly concerned with the problem of repressed sadism in my patients; I regard it as the most frequent cause of failure of therapy ... In general, sadism is becoming more and more important to me" (cited in Bergmann and Hartman, 1976, p. 33). Freud remained intrigued by the complexity of sadomasochism and each major shift in psychoanalytic theory stemmed directly from his clinical experience with masochistic phenomena. However, by the end of his career even Freud had to note that "... we are especially inadequate" in dealing with masochistic patients (1940 [1938], p. 180).

Analysts are still challenged and fascinated by the complexity and counter-intuitiveness of sadomasochism. The overarching regulatory principle is the pleasure principle, so how and why do people do things that are obviously self-destructive and painful? Freud's last solution was contained in his conceptualisation of Eros as opposed to the death instinct, two forces that operate beyond interpretation, a discouraged model he came to in the face of seemingly intractable pathology (1940 [1938]).

We have been grappling with understanding sadomasochism since the late 1960s and our detailed formulations are contained in a long series of papers and books (1972, 1987, 1991, 1996a, 1996b, 1997, 1998, 1999, 2000, 2001, 2002, 2003, 2004, 2005, 2006, 2007, 2010, 2012). Here we will briefly summarise the central points in the latest iteration of our evolving model. It is a privilege to have someone else's case material to test and expand our ideas.

From our clinical work on sadomasochistic power relationships and the defensive omnipotent beliefs and fantasies that organise them we have built on Freud's dual-track developmental model (1915) to postulate two systems of self-regulation and conflict resolution that address the universal need to defend against helplessness and potential traumatisation (Novick, J. & Novick, K. K., 2001). One system, the open system, is attuned to reality and characterised by joy, competence, and creativity. The other, the closed system, avoids reality and is characterised by power dynamics, omnipotence, and stasis.

In closed-system functioning, relationships have a perverse, sadomasochistic pattern; the psyche is organised according to magical, omnipotent beliefs; hostile, painful feelings and aggressive, self-destructive behaviour cycles repeatedly with no real change or growth. Omnipotent beliefs are invoked as the main defensive self-protection against trauma. Externalisation, denial, and avoidance are used to support those beliefs. The aim is to control the other, rather than change the self. Reality-based pleasure is experienced as a threat to omnipotent beliefs, since the closed system depends on feeling victimised. Ego capacities and executive personality functions are co-opted in the service of maintaining omnipotent defences and beliefs. Rules of any sort, from the laws of physics to the conventions of society and the patterns of games, are undermined and denied.

Pain is central to the closed system, as a means for attachment, defence, and gratification. Diane's experience and expressions of psychic and physical pain are central to her self-representation. A patient may present herself as a suffering victim, but in our model the passively experienced pain from trauma becomes transformed and actively sought as a marker of attachment, as a defence against omnipotent rage, and as a sadistic thrill in rendering the other a victim. A closed-system response becomes an active construction that appears to solve the problem but actually prevents change and growth. There has always been controversy over how to define perversion. Patients who live out an unchanging cycle, rarely improving or constantly sliding back into old patterns, who stay in treatment for a long time without an end in sight, offer a challenge to our understanding and our techniques. This static and sterile repetition defines perversion, in our view, as a deviation from the path of progressive development.

The aim is the same in both systems of self-regulation, that is, protection against helplessness. In the closed system the basis for defence is omnipotent belief in the power and necessity to be a perpetrator or victim in order to survive. In the open system the maximum use of one's genuine mental and physical capacities to be realistically effective and competent is the method of mastering inner and outer forces. Two important technical ideas derive from the concept of the open system. One is the analyst's "objective love" for the patient (Novick, J. & Novick, K. K., 2000; Winnicott, 1949), in contrast to sadomasochistic victimisation and enthrallment.

The second is the sequence of therapeutic alliance tasks throughout the unfolding phases of treatment. The therapeutic alliance operationalises the open system; mastery of therapeutic alliance tasks builds on and enhances open-system functioning (Novick, K. K. & Novick, J., 1998). Children, adolescents, and adults finish good enough treatment with the potential for adaptive transformations in response to the vicissitudes of life. From the alliance task of being with comes confidence in the capacity to be alone with oneself, to value oneself and to cooperate in a trusting, mutually enhancing relationship with others. The new level and range of ego functions used to work together in alliance with the analyst can be used for living and for self-analysis whenever necessary. The explicit inclusion of self-analysis as a goal arises in the context of pre-termination phase focus on issues around independent therapeutic work; thus self-analysis may be seen as one of the tools for living that will be available to the patient after finishing. Each therapeutic alliance task accomplished and internalised equips the patient in specific ways (Novick, J. & Novick, K. K., 2007 [1996]).

The closed and open systems do not differentiate people, that is, they are not diagnostic categories. Rather, the constructs describe potential choices of adaptation available within each individual at *any* challenging point throughout development and allow for a metapsychological or multidimensional description of the components of the individual's relation to himself and others. This has profound implications for technique, as it allows for addressing the whole of the patient's personality throughout the treatment (Novick, J. & Novick, K. K., 2003). Rather than characterising treatment as a progression along a path from pathology to health, or from closed-system to open-system functioning, we see simultaneous potential for both systems operating throughout in both patient and analyst. With a two-system model, "Restoration of the capacity to choose between closed, self-destructive and open, competent, and creative systems of self-regulation is the overarching goal of all therapies" (Novick, J. & Novick, K. K., 2006, p. 137).

Dr. Ellman starts her account of her work with "Diane" with a description of her "tortured feelings of failing her, having nothing to offer her—not being good enough", and her anger at the patient not appreciating her efforts. She gives us a tangible sense of Diane's sadism, her closed-system stasis, from the start of the treatment. We began describing in 1987 how a patient's persistent search for pain or humiliation will be figured in the therapeutic relationship (Novick, K. K. & Novick, J.).

The counter-reactions and countertransferences of the therapist may provide the first clue of underlying omnipotent beliefs and sadomasochistic fantasies in the patient. The epigenetic layering of sadomasochism and its multiple functions emerge within the therapeutic relationship and must be dealt with in that context.

We have suggested that pain-seeking behaviour and attachment to pain are derived first from disturbances in the pleasure-pain economy in early mother-child interactions (Novick, J. & Novick, K. K., 1987, [1996] 2007). Derivatives from this level can appear in the form of an externalising transference, where the analyst may experience pain, helplessness, lack of attention or focus. Awareness that this may represent a recreation of an early disturbance can help the analyst first bear and contain responses to being rendered ineffective, stay open to the patient, and then eventually reconstruct the early addiction to pain. Through this work, the therapist will not only interpret the aggressive components in the interaction, but can begin to identify the use of pain to maintain a tie to the other person.

Patients like Diane have been variously described as "borderline", severely neurotic, or other diagnostic labels that attempt to capture the extreme difficulty in engaging with and facilitating change. At the end of the nineteenth century a psychiatrist (Hughes, 1884) described such patients as living in a "borderland". Rather than relying on a nosological approach that could create a static "us and them", the two systems model borrows the spatial metaphor of "borderland", a place any one of us may go when challenged by the trauma of helplessness. The closed-system sadomasochistic/omnipotent mode of self-regulation with its "vicious circles" (Wurmser, 2007) and magical omnipotent defences operates in the borderland.

During the beginning phase of treatment when the analyst makes maximum use of empathy, the analyst can find herself totally caught in the never-changing pain, helplessness, omnipotent rage, sadistic attack, omnipotent guilt, victimisation, and helplessness that leads to further entitled omnipotent rage. Dr. Ellman's presentation vividly depicts Diane's repetitive cycles of omnipotent expectations of self and others, the vicious attack on the other for failing and then the attack on herself for not being good enough.

In the manifest content of the first dream described by Dr. Ellman (10/6/06) we see the patient constructing the never-ending sadomasochistic circle where the pain shifts from herself to her analyst. She apologises for not noticing her analyst's pain; then the patient becomes the powerful healer who carries her denigrated, crippled analyst to her chair—"... and then I walk out." In the borderland of the closed system, separation is the worst crime. In our 1972 study of beating fantasies in children we found that the beating fantasy, what Freud called "the essence of masochism" (1919, p. 189), appeared after normal developmental moments of increased physical separation from mother. Wurmser (ibid.) suggests that at such moments patients feel "separation guilt" where every experience of separateness is experienced as murder. So when Diane says calmly, "and then I walked out", she is, in her closed-system world, committing a most heinous crime, deserving of severe punishment. This then leads to a further vicious cycle, what Wurmser calls the "symbiotic circle" (ibid., p. 39).

Dr. Ellman's clinical presentation of these repetitive sadomasochistic cycles highlights the main technical issue in such work. She notes that Diane "repetitively called on [me] to work at my best, question me if I was not speaking, and often doubted if I was adequately 'on my game'. Each time upon entering the consulting room, she examines me and checks me over for fatigue, distractedness, or any vulnerability that she believes could keep me from giving her my absolute best. I struggle with my own rage at having my competence and ethics constantly scrutinised. Diane is brutal in her assessments of me, always finding me deficient in my efforts. Often her exasperation with my not providing adequately for her threatens the treatment as she talks about wanting to find 'better remedies'. She gives me lashings for my substandard performance. She lives out an unconscious fantasy that threatens to destroy me and her, and our work together, showing the power of the unconscious sadomasochistic fantasy."

The aim of the closed system is to deny the reality of time and oppose change; such a world, as described by Hegel and Marx (cited in Rathbone, 2001), consists only and entirely of dominance and submission. The empathy of the analyst leaves her in danger of being swept up in the tsunami of the patient's closed system. Patients do not come to treatment to have the closed, omnipotent system removed. Just as Diane did, they come because the omnipotent system is not working as well as they think it should. They attribute omnipotence to the therapist and then demand instant results to fix it.

If we engage our empathy too fully with a patient's pain, victimisation, and justified rage we will soon become part of the closed system they operate with. As in the case described, we soon feel like failures, victims of attack, helpless and filled with rage. We may become even more masochistic, accepting the patient's externalisations and feeling like the denigrated, unappreciated, yet guilty, partner in the sadomasochistic partnership. Dr. Ellman bravely shares feelings we all have had. She talks of " ... years of working with Diane, my tortured feelings of failing her, having nothing to offer her—not being good enough and my anger at her not appreciating my efforts." Often in such situations the partners shift and the analyst can become the sadistic one, subtly pushing patients to do what they often threaten to do, that is, leave the analyst.

What can analysis offer in these seemingly endless cycles of closed-system functioning? This is where a two-system model can be helpful. At the beginning of treatment the two systems model exists mainly in the mind of the analyst. We do not see omnipotence as a normal phase of childhood as described by Ferenczi (1913) and posited by many others. Rather, we see omnipotence as a defence mobilised against helplessness (trauma) experienced and expected when reality (the parents) fails to meet a child's basic needs and fails to protect a child from being overwhelmed by negative affects. It is then actively maintained and layers of meaning and adaptation are added throughout development. To the patient the alternative to the closed, omnipotent system of self-regulation is helplessness, that is, trauma. The closed system is *not* a deficit to be made up or a pathology to be eradicated but has been a highly effective and cherished means of self-regulation which includes a powerful magical omnipotent defence against retraumatisation.

Just as we do not conceptualise normal development as movement from universal omnipotence to reality, we do not think of the passage through treatment as a journey from closed- to open-system functioning. Infants have an innate capacity to perceive and effectively engage with reality. This is the root of competence and the open system. It coexists with the potential for creating omnipotent defences from birth to death, just as we all have the potential to reach for closed-system ways of being and relating whenever we are threatened with helplessness. What analysis can and does change is the intensity and automatic recourse to closed-system modes of self-regulation. This is an economic shift.

The goal of analysis is not to do away with the closed system, but rather to help the patient realise and experience the value of an open-system mode of adaptation and self-regulation as a viable alternative. From the very beginning the analyst has to enter into the borderland with the patient, but also always keep one foot in the world of reality, in the open system.

We noted earlier that the successive tasks of the therapeutic alliance, highlighted in each phase of treatment, represent an open-system alternative for both patient and analyst. Here we will use some of the material from Dr. Ellman's case to comment briefly on how an open-system concept of the therapeutic alliance can help the analyst stay grounded in reality from the very beginning of treatment, expand the available techniques, and hopefully move the process forward so the patient feels more free to choose the life force of "progressive development" (Freud, A. 1965).

Evaluation

The evaluation phase has hitherto been somewhat neglected, often dispensed with, and rarely thought about as the crucial foundation for a successful treatment (Novick, K. K. & Novick, J., 2005). In our model the evaluation is not only to diagnose the patient, but mainly to develop a working relationship. This starts the process of turning a patient into a partner who can work together with the therapist. During the evaluation, patient and analyst begin a series of transformations: of self-help to joint work; chaos to order and meaning; fantasies to realistic goals; external complaints and circumstantial explanations to internal meanings, motivations, and conflicts; helplessness to competence; despair to hopefulness. The analyst can learn a great deal about the patient and the prospects for the treatment from the initial responses to these tasks. Making a start lays the foundation for a relationship of collaboration and mutuality between therapist and patient.

Diane's presenting urgency created enormous pressure on the analyst immediately. With the support of a model that emphasises the substantive work of evaluation, an analyst can withstand the omnipotent demandingness couched as distress. The pitfall is being pulled into the patient's sadomasochistic search for an omnipotent solution. Analysis provides the time and space for a mutual exploration of the patient's whole person, their history, and the complexity of their current functioning. The two-systems model encompasses that complexity in examining the strengths as well as the closed-system adaptations the patient has made.

We can look at Diane's material in relation to the transformative tasks. For instance, when Diane says that she read that psychoanalysis could help her access her unconscious rage, we might hear that as a promising effort to transform self-help into joint effort with an analyst. Her understanding that her feelings relate to early life experiences maps a pathway to her history, to reconstruction and working through. The analyst needs to find evidence during the evaluation of open-system capacities or potential in order to have the conviction that the patient will eventually be able to access and develop these potentials of the personality.

But Diane presents her ideas on the basis of a cathartic model of cure that she has devised, which would depend on the omnipotence of the analyst and be a quick solution, in itself an omnipotent belief. Diane makes explicit something we have found in almost all patients; they come in with a plan, conscious or unconscious. Our model suggests a period of evaluation to explore more fully Diane's ideas about how treatment works. If we fail to explore their fantasies and expectations of treatment, the patients' plans will prevail, often leading to a premature termination. Here is an entry into a core issue. Through this we would make explicit the essential partnership involved in an analysis, how the relationship between patient and analyst becomes the arena for understanding patterns and history in the patient's interactions with others. The recommendation for analysis has to spring from an experience of working together and a process of mutual assessment, where both analyst and patient feel there is some hope of change and growth toward shared goals, and some sense of mutual respect. The description of Diane's achievements does not include any sense of pleasure beyond occasional sadistic triumph. This is a crucial piece of information to feed back to the patient, since the pursuit of authentic and dependable good feelings can become a shared goal of treatment.

In reading about Diane we are struck by her great strengths, her intellectual power, her tenacity and persistence, her capacity for hard work and courage in the face of neglect, discouragement, and pain. This perception would be a pillar of the ongoing analytic work, creating a framework for the analyst's reality-testing, a bridge out of the borderland, and one side of a conflict between closed- and open-system functioning that will eventually be fostered by the work of analysis.

Holding on to the knowledge of Diane's strengths allows us to hear the unfolding history in additional ways. Her major emphasis is on the iniquities of her father and the unfairness of men. With an open-system emphasis, we would also hear the reality that she is the sixth of seven children, with a three-year gap between her and the next oldest. Given that her mother previously had children every year for five years, we might infer one or two miscarriages before Diane's birth. Whether that is so or not, this might signal a depression and mourning on top of overburdened and overstretched parenting. Diane's story emphasises basking in her mother's preference, which may reflect a strong investment in this child, but we would wonder about the basis in daily experience for that feeling. We might inquire about the three-year gap and what the family stories are about her birth and infancy. This could stretch the limits of her closed-system self-image as simply a victimised female child.

Her childhood and adult competence and effectiveness imply that she was always a capable person, in sharp contrast to an overburdened, inattentive, perhaps depressed mother. This is a typical configuration, where a child, actually incapable of meeting an adult's needs, is thrust into that position, and then comes to omnipotently value the role of striving to accomplish the impossible. The centrality of Diane's perfectionism in her mental economy indicates that her frantic need to be the absolute best (and to demand the same of others) rests on an impossible mission to repair her mother. The idea that she tried to meet such expectations can be floated during the evaluation, as a hypothesis for both to test. It may give the patient a feeling of being understood for the first time. This can be a more realistic basis for a therapeutic alliance than empathy with pain, which is part of Diane's closed-system effort toward perfection. Such a different suggestion might also intrigue the patient and engage her intellect in the quest for understanding. A glimmer of a positive response to such a dialogue would give the analyst hope that this treatment has a future.

Another effect of such exchanges in the early meetings is to demonstrate to the patient that the analyst is a competent, intelligent person with something substantive to offer. This is real, in contrast to the transference role the patient will surely cast the analyst in. This open-system reality contrast allows the transference to be an experience accessible to interpretation, rather than a closed-system enactment and delusion that engulfs both people.

In our paper on love in the therapeutic alliance, we noted "The result of the transformations of the evaluation phase is a shift from separately held beliefs to the beginning of shared, reality-based respect and conviction about this particular partnership. This joint confidence will be repeatedly assailed throughout treatment—hence its importance for the maintenance of the therapist's conviction in the face of inevitable undermining from the transference of the patient's pathology during treatment. Thus the evaluation can provide the building blocks—in the form of respect, hope, and a sense of potential partnership—for the therapist's 'objective love' for the patient, to use Winnicott's term" (Novick, J. & Novick, K. K., 2000, p. 197).

Beginning

In the beginning phase the patient's therapeutic alliance task is to *be with* the therapist; the analyst strives to *feel with* the patient. The therapist intervenes actively when obstacles to being together arise from within the patient, from the environment, or from the therapist. These tasks of being with and feeling with will persist throughout treatment, but predominate at the beginning. The model for this attunement is the early mother-child relationship. Fluctuations in attunement may draw on and relate to issues of mother-child attachment during infancy and toddlerhood. The nature of that attachment will be played out in the therapeutic relationship.

From the start Diane creates a transference relationship of doubt, mistrust, denigration, and assumption that the analyst is incompetent and not really there for her. Dr. Ellman experiences this as central to the case. The analytic content about the incompetence of the analyst confirms aspects of the history indicated in the evaluation related to Diane's position as sixth of seven children with a depressed and overwhelmed mother, who was too exhausted and depleted to meet Diane's needs. In our model sadomasochism springs first from a painful mother-infant interaction, vividly borne out in Diane's transference. Disruptions and deviations in being with are our first indicators of resistance to engaging in the therapeutic process and direct our attention to describing the conditions under which the patient can feel safe with the therapist.

What appears throughout the case report is that Diane's sadomasochism is her way of attaching and staying with her analyst at the deepest level. As Dr. Ellman notes, "for Diane, any sign of separateness of the other is not tolerable." Sadomasochism is a highly effective method of staying connected and denying separateness.

The analyst's therapeutic alliance task at the beginning is to *feel with* the patient. But what should the analyst be connecting to? What feelings are useful to empathise with? And what are the sources of the analyst's feelings—not everything comes from the patient. Rage at a patient may be a counter-reaction to being rendered helpless by the patient's sadistic attack and not necessarily an internalisation of the patient's rage. We think here about the advantages and limitations of empathy.

Empathy demands an act of imagination to put oneself in another's shoes and therefore assumes separateness. We see this as an open-system mental function, in contrast to a closed-system pressure coming from the patient to deny boundaries and separateness, to be as one. Part of what helps the analyst keep one foot outside the borderland is to maintain open-system empathy, to feel with the patient in the present and the past, but maintain the reality of the present.

We notice the occurrence of "developmental images" in our own minds, generic patterns of interaction that illuminate and suggest possibilities for exploration and reconstruction with the patient. For instance, developmental images that occur to us in relation to Diane include one of a spirited, capable toddler, into everything, whose curiosity was ignored or frustrated, and whose bodily pleasures were curtailed or forbidden as dirty. The developmental image allows us to make a general, educational statement about the legitimacy and normality of such toddler needs, before engaging with what the patient has done with her particular experience. This is a useful precursor to interpretation with Diane, for instance, of her transference to her partner of frustration at her partner's unavailability for intimacy.

Such a line of interpretation, however valid, still resides in the territory of Diane's victimhood and pain, in the sadomasochistic format of relating that she mandates. There are several different, but linked, transitions that come into play at this point in a treatment when we apply our model to understanding the material. The therapeutic alliance task for both patient and analyst in the middle phase of treatment is the maximum use of ego capacities to work together. Conflicts and resistances around this task highlight the contrast between open- and closed-system functioning.

Middle

For the analyst, even delineating this task conceptually engages with the separateness of the patient, which the patient combats continually in a sadomasochistic interaction. When we see the sadomasochism as a defence against the terror of separateness, the uncertainty of the pleasures of collaboration, and the avoidance of being the agent of one's own life in order to maintain the license of justified rage and sadism, we can open up several lines of inquiry and work. There is also a developmental transition from passive victimisation in infancy to an active toddler and childhood construction of an organising set of omnipotent beliefs and a beating fantasy.

This seems crucial to Diane's case. Her beating fantasy was probably enacted in her athletic pursuits. She ignored actual physical pain from overuse and the signal of pain became the symbol of her omnipotent triumph over her father and brother and all men. Too much empathy with this pain can miss the point that, for the sadomasochist, "pain is the affect which triggers the defense of omnipotence, pain is the magical means by which all wishes are gratified and pain justifies the omnipotent hostility and revenge contained in the sadomasochistic fantasy" (Novick, J. & Novick, K. K., 2007 [1996], p. 64).

Dr. Ellman describes: "Most glaring in Diane's clinical presentation was the massive physical disability of her lower limbs that had developed within the years preceding her entry to therapy, rendering her unable to participate in the athletic lifestyle she had previously embraced; in fact, she was barely able to walk. With many possible medical diagnoses, no treatment was definitive. Diane believed that she had inadvertently made demanding choices that were, by nature, 'being the best she can be' that resulted in her current disabled state." We think that Diane's belief can be turned to good account by helping her see that she is at the centre of her pathology. Her omnipotent belief in perfection, and conviction that she could attain it, emerged out of painful interactions in infancy and came to serve through subsequent phases as a defence against the feeling of helplessness and inadequacy. Pain became the motivator, indicator, reinforcer and proof of her perfectionist quest.

The open-system alternative would be to listen to her body signals as an ingredient in self-regulation. Throughout her development Diane denied the actuality and meaning of her bodily signals, as when she equated excited vaginal wetness with incontinence. Diane does not report any kind of ordinary pleasure, past or current. Trying was never gratifying. She could not allow herself to enjoy and get reinforcement from mastery and realistic satisfaction from her achievements. Even her current sexual activities are described in terms only of arousing, painful submission to her partner.

The analyst's therapeutic leverage in addressing these issues can be the open-system conviction that pleasure in general can be found in respectful mutuality in all relationships. We imagine that a highly intelligent patient like Diane might be intrigued to explore such alternative possibilities.

In the rich dream material Dr. Ellman provides, we can see the crux of Diane's pathology as it is played out in the therapeutic relationship in the middle phase, when the task is to work together. Diane tries to stay in the manifest content of the dreams, where she is always the victim in pain, or the denigrated, naughty child. Her analyst tries to pull her into the work, telling her to "not to close [her] eyes". Diane dreams a month later about falling short in her therapeutic efforts—in her dream she "did something bad. I was not focusing enough and not doing therapy well enough, not doing a good job … I WAS NOT enough in therapy." We think Diane was right in her dream. She was not being perfection-istic; rather she was aware that she was not using her full ego capacities in the work. This is a clear sign that Diane was now experiencing a middle-phase conflict between closed-system habits and new open-system possibilities.

In the middle phase, the conflict between open- and closed-system modes of functioning that has been externalised into the outside world and played out in the sadomasochistic transference can become increasingly experienced internally. Diane's third dream expresses the intense conflict between her actual open-system humanness and her closed-system pressure toward perfection. She also expresses clearly what to her still represents her only alternative to closed-system omnipotence, when she says, "humanness means human limits and errors. I walk around with the fragility of a toddler, unprotected." She fears that the only alternative to her omnipotent sadomasochism is the helplessness she felt in childhood.

Her treatment is giving her the experience of a different alternative, in realistic open-system humanness. The battle is joined in this middle phase of Diane's analysis. She will never give up her sadomasochistic solutions. She may, however, with the further work to come in her treatment, be able to generate and experience the pleasure and dependability of open-system alternatives for safety, gratification, and self-regulation. Then she eventually might set aside her closed-system solutions. Like Mr. M, who started his analysis beating himself with his fists on the couch, she may be able to say, as he did near the end of his eleven-year analysis, "It's my life— I have only one life and I have to choose. It's hard to admit that I was wrong, hard to admit that my pain buys me nothing but aspirin. But then I never knew that I had a choice, that I could choose to live a real life, with real pleasure" (Novick, J. & Novick, K. K., 2007 [1996] p. 309).

References

Ferenczi, S. (1913). Stages in the development of the sense of reality. In: *First Contributions to Psychoanalysis* (pp. 213–239). New York: Brunner/Mazel, 1980.

Freud, A. (1965). *Normality and Pathology in Childhood. Writings* 6: 3–273. New York: International Universities Press.

Freud, S. (1909). Letter to Jung. In: M. S. Bergmann & F. R. Hartman (Eds.), *The Evolution of Psychoanalytic Technique*. New York: Basic Books, 1976.

Freud, S. (1915). Instincts and their vicissitudes. *S. E., 14*: 117–140. London: Hogarth.

Freud, S. (1919). "A child is being beaten". *S. E., 17*: 175–204. London: Hogarth.

Freud, S. (1940 [1938]). An Outline of Psychoanalysis. *S. E., 23*: 141–207. London: Hogarth.

Hughes, C. H. (1884). Borderline psychiatric records: Prodromal symptoms of psychical impairment. *Alienist and Neurologist*, 5: 85–91.

Meyers, H. (1988). A consideration of treatment techniques in relation to the functions of masochism. In: R. A. Glick & D. I. Meyers (Eds.), *Masochism: Current Psychoanalytic Perspectives* (pp. 175–189). Hillsdale, NJ: Analytic Press.

Novick, J. & Novick, K. K. (1972). Beating fantasies in children. *International Journal of Psycho-analysis*, 53: 237–242.

Novick, J. & Novick, K. K. (1991). Some comments on masochism and the delusion of omnipotence from a developmental perspective. *Journal of American Psychoanalytic Association*, 39: 307–331.

Novick, J. & Novick, K. K. (1996a). A developmental perspective on omnipotence. *Journal of Clinical Psychoanalysis*, 5: 124–173.

Novick, J. & Novick, K. K. (1996b). *Fearful Symmetry: The Development and Treatment of Sadomasochism*. Northvale, NJ: Jason Aronson.

Novick, J. & Novick, K. K. (1997). Omnipotence, pathology and resistance. In: C. Ellman (Ed.), *Omnipotent Fantasies and the Vulnerable Self* (pp. 39–78). Northvale, NJ: Jason Aronson.

Novick, J. & Novick, K. K. (2000). Love in the therapeutic alliance. *Journal of American Psychoanalytic Association*, 48: 189–218.

Novick, J. & Novick, K. K. (2001). Two systems of self-regulation. *Journal of Psychiatric Social Work*, 8: 95–122.

Novick, J. & Novick, K. K. (2003). Two systems of self-regulation and the differential application of psychoanalytic technique. *American Journal of Psychoanalysis*, 63: 1–19.

Novick, J. & Novick, K. K. (2004). The superego and the two-system model. *Psychoanalytic Inquiry*, 24: 232–256.

Novick, J. & Novick, K. K. (2006). *Good Goodbyes: Knowing How to End in Psychoanalysis and Psychotherapy*. Maryland: Jason Aronson/Rowman and Littlefield.

Novick, J. & Novick, K. K. (2007). *Fearful Symmetry: The Development and Treatment of Sadomasochism*. Maryland: Jason Aronson/Rowman and Littlefield.

Novick, K. K. & Novick, J. (1987). The essence of masochism. *Psychoanalytic Study of the Child*, 42: 353–383. New Haven: Yale University Press.

Novick, K. K. & Novick, J. (1998). An application of the concept of the therapeutic alliance to sadomasochistic pathology. *Journal of American Psychoanalytic Association*, 46: 813–846.

Novick, K. K. & Novick, J. (1999). Creativity and compliance: An introduction to Anna Freud's "The relation of beating fantasies to day dream." In: D. Bassin (Ed.), *Female Sexuality: Contemporary Engagements* (pp. 63–70). Northvale, NJ: Jason Aronson, 1999.

Novick, K. K. & Novick, J. (2002). Une théorie développementale du sadomasochisme. *Revue Française de Psychanalyse*, 66: 1133–1156.

Novick, K. K. & Novick, J. (2005). *Working With Parents Makes Therapy Work.* Lanham, MD: Aronson.

Novick, K. K. & Novick, J. (2010). *Emotional Muscle: Strong Parents, Strong Children*. Indiana: XLibris.

Novick, K. K. & Novick, J. (2011). Building emotional muscle in children and parents. *Psa. Study Child*, 65: 131–151.

Rathbone, J. (2001). *Anatomy of Masochism*. New York: Kluver Academic/ Plenum Publishers.

Winnicott, D. W. (1949). Hate in the countertransference. In: D. Goldmand (Ed.), *In One's Bones: The Clinical Genius of Winnicott* (pp. 15–24). Northvale, NJ: Jason Aronson.

Wurmser, L. (2007). *Torment Me, But Don't Abandon Me: Psychoanalysis of the Severe Neurosis in a New Key*. Maryland: Jason Aronson/Rowman and Littlefield.

CHAPTER SIX

Diane *vs.* reality: unconscious fantasies at impasse? discussion of the case of Diane

Marianne Robinson

I am pleased to have this opportunity to discuss Paula Ellman's compelling case of sadomasochism as described in her paper.

The initial reading of this paper was a powerful psychosomatic event for me. I experienced a relentless squeezing out of any potential psychic space for mindful thinking until it seemed there was nowhere to go. I dozed off twice and then realised that I felt hopelessly entrapped. I imagined that being Diane's psychoanalyst would be similar to the experience of the brave student in Tian An Min Square facing an oncoming tank during the 17 September 1989 student uprising against the current oppressive regime. The determination to meet such destructiveness, whether concrete or psychic, while also being in contact with one's human vulnerability, is a daunting task. However, only in that state can one come to understand what it is like for Diane to be in the path of the desperate power of a "regime" whose continued survival is paramount, regardless of cost. For the Chinese student then, as for the student of psychoanalysis now (however experienced and skilled), only faith (Bion, 1970) that transformation is possible would make it bearable to go on—faith that something will emerge that will impact the relentless, destructive repetition. Enduring the knowledge that Dr. Ellman will live or die as Diane's psychoanalyst is made possible by the faith that, whichever the outcome, she will have the ability to survive and investigate and digest what happened.

Before discussing the clinical material I want to, in broad brush strokes, outline the theoretical concepts I found myself using during the reading in order to gain some understanding of Diane's internal world and describe how I see her core struggle.

As I free associate to the clinical sessions provided I find myself focusing on the unconscious fantasies inferred from Diane's dreams and associations and their influence on Diane's internal and external relationships.

In Kleinian theory unconscious fantasies underlie every mental process and accompany all mental activity (Bion, 1962; Hinshelwood, 1989; Isaacs, 1948; Klein, 1923; Segal, 1991). Unconscious fantasies are the mental representation of those somatic events in the body that comprise the instincts, and are physical sensations interpreted as relationships with objects that cause those sensations. Fantasy is the mental expression of both libidinal and aggressive impulses and can also be defence mechanisms against those impulses. Much of the therapeutic activity of psychoanalysis can be described as an attempt to convert unconscious fantasy into conscious thought.

Freud (1911) introduced the concept of unconscious fantasy and fantasising, which *he* thought of as a phylogenetically inherited capacity of the human mind. Klein adopted his idea of unconscious fantasy but broadened it considerably because her work with children gave her extensive experience with the wide-ranging content of children's fantasies. She and her successors have emphasised that fantasies interact reciprocally with experience (Segal, 1991) to form the developing intellectual and emotional characteristics of the individual; fantasies are considered to be a basic capacity underlying and shaping thought, dreams, symptoms, and patterns of defence.

I believe the clinical material shows how Diane unconsciously registers the emergence of important aspects of her object relations. At the same time, the extent to which this threatens her sadomasochistic psychic retreat (Steiner, 1987) or psychic equilibrium (Joseph, 1992) is seen in the way the material shows that the destruction of her analyst's usefulness matches the extent of her perceived threat at that moment in the relationship.

I would summarise Diane's dilemma as follows. Unconsciously she wishes for a "cure" that involves a seamless relationship with a mother/analyst who reads her mind and who tends to her every need before Diane herself becomes aware that there is an outside object on whom she depends. She wants to be one with her object—a wish represented orally in her unconscious as an act of gobbling up her object ("*if I am accepted* [taken in], *I go down the drain*"). This leads to variously expressed fears of being annihilated, going down the drain being one of those expressions.

On the other hand, and with equal force, Diane strives for a "cure" that would free her from any reminders of her human vulnerabilities by moving in the opposite direction and rejecting awareness of any nurture from an outside object in order to preserve her conviction of invulnerability. Toward that end she uses the defences (Klein, 1935) *of* splitting, projection, idealisation/denigration in an effort to triumph over psychic reality as well as over the object that put her in touch with that reality.

Also, and on a more concrete elemental level, Diane desperately tries to make her body armour stronger by muscular activity (Bick, 1968). In the process she deadens the senses that register her experience in order to keep out the unwelcome reality, and she therefore lives a constricted existence of mutilated perceptual capacities with a vicious vigilance against anything resembling a connection to aliveness. Such aliveness would bring awareness of dependency, neediness, and inability to achieve complete control over her internal and external world, all of which Diane has avoided with her sadomasochism. Bion (1957) describes the dilemma when splitting and projection become overactive, resulting in unbearable confusional states:

> The mental and other activities by which the dominant impulse, be it of life or death instincts, strives to express itself, are at once subjected to mutilation by the temporarily subordinated impulse. Harassed by the mutilations and striving to escape the confusional states, the patient returns to the restricted relationship. Oscillation between the attempt to broaden the contact and the attempt to restrict continues throughout the analysis. (p. 266)

I believe that sadomasochism belongs on a spectrum of intensity of hatred of psychic reality which is expressed in various levels of destructiveness. The amount of cruelty in a sadomasochistic relationship is related to the intensity of erotised hatred of reality which in turn is related to the capacity to tolerate frustration. Bion (1967) emphasises this and describes it as a differential ability to hold discrepancies between expectations and reality. The individual level of frustration tolerance may be present even before birth. I am referring here to Freud's (1911) famous statement:

> There is much more continuity between intra-uterine life and earliest infancy than the impressive caesura of the act of *birth* would have us believe. What happens is the child's biological situation as a foetus is replaced for it by a psychical object-relation to its mother (p. 138)

and to the subsequent body of work on prenatal aspects in postnatal life as they manifest in the clinical situation. The same individual level of frustration tolerance may also, or instead, later be an outcome of traumatic environmental conditions.

I want to emphasise that my "free associations" about Diane's destructiveness come from my conviction that *it is her* split-off traumatic overload that powers what in her object relations emerges as cruelty and destructiveness. To keep *myself* in touch with that experience I often think of a frightened wounded animal whose internal state is pain and terror but in relation to whom anyone who approaches meets tearing claws and biting teeth.

Association to the clinical material

In her 10/6/06 session Diane brings a dream in which she is having therapy sitting up ("*I am sitting and talking*"). It is not clear from the material if she uses the couch in her analysis. If she does, taking the sitting position in the dream would seem to convey an unwillingness to recognise her role as a patient. Instead she relates to her analyst and the analysis as if to an equal, in the process denying her dependency on a nurturing relationship.

In the dream Diane is "*talking about what pain I am in. I close my eyes and talk*". She is not using her long-distance sense of sight which would convey acceptance of separateness but seems to be in an unmentalised (Mitrani, 1995), not-yet-emerged state of mind. The use of words for symbolic communication is also related to recognition of separateness, the state rejected by her closed eyes. I believe that Diane is not in emotional touch with what she is saying and that the debilitating effect of her "words" on her analyst makes it clear that she is using speech as action (Bion, 1970). Her use of words is not symbolic but is instead connected to an unconscious fantasy that her words concretely hold her "bad" painful thoughts and feelings and carry them away from herself and into her analyst. Talking is therefore unconsciously equated with performing a harmful action, not communicating painful experience. As a result, Diane feels that her analyst is containing the "badness" that she has evacuated in an act of splitting. This puts emotional distance between them (*"you had moved to another chair because of your back pain"*). When Diane realises (*"when I open them"* [*her eyes*]) she notices that something has happened which her analyst experienced but that she herself was blind to (*"you say, 'didn't you see me?' I moved while you were talking"*). This is a very disturbing discovery to the part of Diane that needs to feel in control and insists on knowing everything in order to maintain a fantasy of being protected from surprising experiences from within and without.

When Diane realises the damage she has done to her object she is upset (*"I say ... [I] am sorry because my eyes are closed"*). Her feeling of being sorry suggests a beginning realisation that her analyst has value and she has concern for her well-being. This is a depressive anxiety (Klein, 1935) showing movement toward whole object function and separateness.

However, Diane's subsequent action in the dream seems to show that she is not yet able to deal with the pain of that depressive anxiety because she now wants to make it all better and completely restore the analyst to the place she occupied before the assault (*"I stand up and move next to you. I lift you up because you are in great pain and help move you back to the other chair"*). This is omnipotent repair (Klein, 1935) with Diane in the role of the caretaker of her analyst who is in need. Reparation would involve dealing with her concern by mourning the damage she fears her needs have inflicted on to her object and recognising both her own and her object's pain with a symbolic gesture of gratitude. Instead Diane splits and the roles are reversed in an interplay, the dynamics of which form an ongoing theme in the sessions presented. Having thus omnipotently restored her object Diane splits (*"and then I walk out"*), unconsciously believing it possible to leave her "bad" painful parts in her analyst.

While exiting, Diane notices that her analyst is wearing Birkenstocks just like her girlfriend does. I believe this shows that in her state of projection, boundaries blur between Diane and her objects and confusion sets in about who is who and which of them contains what. When Diane is in pain her objects become undifferentiated receptacles of her projection. She now relates to her analyst as to her girlfriend which adds to her sense of being trapped in a world where there is no escape. This is the inevitable imprisoning effect of splitting and projection because they distort the object and leave her entrapped in the projections of her own internal world. She fantasies that she avoids her psychic pain but the price is imprisoning confusion.

The description of how Diane "repairs" her wounded analyst may also clarify why she feels herself to be a perennial caretaker of others. Her modus operandi is to project her pain into her object and then minister to it there. It is possible that she unconsciously finds needy people who are only too happy to cooperate in that arrangement for a time.

Later in that session Diane says, "*I cannot tell people about my pain*". In so far as she does not use words to talk about her pain, that statement is accurate. She does however very eloquently communicate her suffering on pre-verbal and non-verbal levels in ways that are powerfully received by others who tune in to those wavelengths. However, this creates in Diane the unconscious knowledge that rules have been broken and that "relationship crimes" have been committed *because projection on this level is unconsciously registered as a destructive assault on the object*. This gives rise to unconscious guilt, as discussed earlier. In that way she unconsciously continues to replenish evidence for her conscious conviction that she is toxic. Diane feels helpless, useless, and impotent when she has not already successfully controlled her experience of internal or external events. When she looks at the world through the lens of that sense of helplessness she sees an ineffectual analyst in a useless, unhelpful object world.

Projective identification (Klein, 1946) is unconsciously perceived as a concrete action that includes two components: one is the projection into the object of an unbearable experience, the other is the subsequent treatment of that object to induce the projected state of mind. Diane treats her analyst with the cruel disdain she feels for her own vulnerability. In the projective process she moves from being the suffering, weak, out-of-control victim of her own sadism to becoming the sadistic attacker of her object who now is felt to contain the despised weaknesses.

Within that concrete state of mind, Diane now actually feels herself to be in the presence of a helpless damaged and useless analyst who is unable to give her what she feels entitled to receive. Expressing her conviction in accusing and attacking words (*"You cannot help me ... You were not on my case adequately"*) encourages the analyst to conform to the projective identification. And in the state of reverie (Bion, 1970) the analyst, like a sensitive tuning fork, experiences Diane's feelings while it also stirs up her own discomfort with inevitable human imperfection and shortcomings.

In the 11/6/2006 session Diane brings another dream where shifting of seats is again a feature, as I will discuss below. Also the analytic field (Baranger, 1993) is expanded to include her mother and Aunt Maureen and the internal parts they represent.

It seems Diane is increasingly aware of her destructiveness (*"I had done something bad"*). This may have a two-fold meaning. On the one hand, the "bad" she has done consists of attacking her object with her projective identification. On the other hand, when the part of her that hates reality senses any psychic movement and growth toward separation as a result of the analysis (*"I dreamt of you outside"*) she feels she has done something wrong, "bad". In that way. Diane and her analyst are working at cross purposes. Diane unconsciously wishes for a "cure" without change, a wish that is powered by an unconscious fantasy that there is a way to avoid going through the pain of becoming separate (a process also referred to as emergence or psychic birth) while her analyst, by extending the relationship that stimulates emergence, hopes to share and make bearable Diane's pains of emergence.

In the dream Diane also realises that the relationship with her analyst does not end when she (Diane) has been "bad" (*"you asked me to bring someone to therapy"*). With that she becomes aware that her analyst can contain and think about what Diane projects into her, and that capacity enables her to continue their relationship. In that way her analyst is different from Diane herself who walked out (split) after being "bad" in the first dream. Diane now has a glimmer of an analyst with an open mind, more benevolent than her own, who is encouraging her to risk more of herself by bringing more into the analytic relationship.

Following that thought, it seems Diane is split and Aunt Maureen seems to represent Diane's own idealised pure and innocent part. She had expected to sit between the two mother figures (*"Mom was a huge force in the dream and you were too"*), showing her fantasy of having all the goodness to herself. She is dismayed that her idealised omnipotent part gets the closeness to the analyst (*"Maureen was too close to your seat"*) and in fact happily takes her place (*"Maureen is happy sitting in your seat"*).

I believe this expresses envy of an idealised part of herself. Instead of the eagerly hoped-for exclusive nourishment from two mother figures (breasts) the vulnerable part of Diane (experienced as bad) feels that another part of her is getting the nourishment she lacks and she feels left out and left behind in a very inadequate and painful state. This provokes her anger and envy of the nourished Aunt Maureen part who was supposed to feed Diane. Every interpretation given is evidence that her analyst is a thinking containing object whose reverie enables her to transform Diane's productions into thoughts that she can give back to Diane in tolerable amounts. Since this is a function Diane herself cannot perform, it stimulates her envy both of her analyst and of the capacity inside herself to have such a relationship. The latter is elaborated as self-envy by López-Corvo (1991).

The fact that *"Maureen is happy sitting in your seat"* may be connected to Diane's sadistic manoeuvre of becoming the superior caretaker by changing places with her analyst with the unconscious fantasy that she (Diane) has all the nourishment and can feed her own needy part, now felt to be located in her analyst. However she now feels herself increasingly in the *"shadow of my mother"*, the analyst who with her nurturing presence refutes the fantasy that Diane possess the nurturing function.

Diane's relationship to pain is interesting in two ways. On the one hand, whenever she is in pain she feels that something must have gone wrong and there must have been rules she was not adequate enough to pay attention to. On the other hand, because of her analytic relationship, Diane has a beginning realisation that there are rules and consequences in the unconscious that she disobeys by evacuating, splitting, projecting, and acting out in her efforts to modify, evade, or destroy reality. Her comment, *"I need to wake up for therapy"* seems to convey her realisation that a different state of mind is needed in order to engage in an analytic partnership and grow. Her struggle now seems to centre on the dilemma between the pursuit of suffering her growing pains or continuation of the pursuit of suffering the pains of her destructive defences.

In her session on 11/9/2006 Diane shows the impact of the analytic work. She seems to be in touch with her increased vulnerability and neediness (*"I walk around with the fragility of a toddler, unprotected"*). As a consequence her defensive efforts are increasing but she realises that it does not help (*"This is a time when it is not acceptable to be human"*).

I believe that Diane's comment, *"I am not working my body hard enough"*, refers to her second skin formation (Bick, 1968), enlisted to form a hard protective action with the unconscious fantasy that this will actually replace the maternal holding and containing she now destroys and that she may not have experienced early on. This manoeuvre is based on an unconscious fantasy that the action of her concrete muscular bracing actually protects her from reality breaking into her experience and awareness. In that state of mind, internal sensations, including thoughts and fantasies, are perceived as coming from outside. In her attempt to perfect the protection of her second skin she engages in ruthless uncompromising activity that has little empathy for her vulnerable "human" aspects. She performs actions to increase her imperviousness to the experience of vulnerability (*"some days I push to the end of the day [in the gym]"*). In the process she pushes out of her mind the awareness of vulnerability and need for a containing object. She acts when she should feel.

Diane experiences her humanness as a defeat, not as the potential wellspring for growth in her analytic partnership (*"I am living in too much humanness"*). Her associations seem to show that she feels pummeled by a reality that, until now, has been denied and that she has previously dealt with through the familiar manoeuvre of becoming the superior caretaker in relation to her object who is seen as the inferior, needy one, in the process forcing into her object the experience of how murdered and castrated she feels. The moment of new awareness of her vulnerability quickly turns into a feeling of lacking invulnerability with the fantasy that others (including her analyst) have what she lacks. (*"I do know I want to kill Smith, Mary's father ([Diane's] earlier partner). I wonder if I wanted to kill my dad … Not that I wanted to castrate him like Smith. Dad had his last rights two times so he died a great Catholic. This is a deeply unaccep*table *thought. His penis is in my face. I want to cut it off."*) In this session what Diane lacks is called "a penis" (father's) and life (Mr. Smith's). The full explosive exchange conveys Diane's emerging realisation that her analyst is potent (represented as having a penis) which is in Diane's face (awareness) right there in the session. (*"I want to cut it off. The only thing between you guys and me is the penis. You are just good at being men's men."*)

When Diane feels fragile her father comes to mind (possibly in the form of his seemingly triumphant scratching of his penis) and she wants to banish the image from her mind (*"Fuck you (father) … I want to blast him, but …"*).

As additional historic information unfolds in that session it seems to have been Diane's sad reality to have had a possessive father who wanted her achievements to reinforce his inflated importance, in the process diminishing the appreciation of Diane's talent. This sadomasochistic part of the father/daughter relationship seems to have been stirred up in the analyst's countertransference ("I observed that I have the desire to want to speak to her with force, to pin her down, and get her to submit to me and value me") showing how Diane's internal world unfolds in the analytic relationship.

In her determination not to succumb to a dependent relationship and accept what father had to give, Diane used her talents and accomplishments to become superior (*"I hit his world like I did with tennis"*). This gives insight into Diane's grievance (Steiner, 1996), the hating aspects of which are now emerging in the analysis, crowding out any access to loving internal parts (*"I don't have access to any love"*). Her efforts to compensate for deprivation have been motivated by hate and she can therefore feel neither proud of her achievements nor grateful for what she has received. The unfortunate outcome is that any pride her father may have had for her is felt as having been extracted by the force of her hatred and therefore cannot be warmly received and appreciated.

It seems that on some level Diane feels her crippling symptoms are deserved paternal punishment for her murderous hatred (*"I was not worthy of a professional coach"*). She connects her bodily pain with her father's death by referring to her increased symptoms at the time of his death (*"How my muscular stiffness, psoriasis, tendon so tight, joints moving against each other, are connected with his dying"*).

Sadly, in her family Diane was not able to find the opportunity to differentiate between the perceived "mediocrity" of being human with its potential for growth, separateness, and interdependence and the "mediocrity" of a mediocre family whose members may have been unable to nurture or even recognise her talents and potential.

In the face of the opportunity for a continued partnership that her analyst offers, Diane fears that if she opens the door to being human she would be annihilated (*"if I am accepting, I'd go down the drain"*). Her psychic paralysis is evident and the complexity of her dilemma can be seen to stem from the different levels of her struggle. As the sixth of seven children, born after her parents had five children in six years, her reality may have been that, unless she held on by sheer force, no one would be there for her. This would lead to a conviction that the object would only be there as a result of her own singular efforts. The other level of her struggle is in the area of separateness. "Letting go" is felt as a death of the old way of being without the yet-to-be-established introjected holding analytic relationship. Until that happens, if it can, Diane lives in a ruthless world (*"you don't count, you don't matter. It is the survival of the fittest"*) the tragedy of which Diane is now coming in touch with. Confronted with such ruthlessness the analyst's efforts to stay potent and boundaried become a struggle ("I cringe when I hear her ravenous hunger and her hatred, and feel that it is only a matter of time before I too become the object of her rage. I have come to ready myself for her criticisms of my insufficiencies"). The analyst puts words to the temptation to harden up and develop her own second skin (Bick, 1968).

The session on 12/7/2006, although short, seems to further elaborate Diane's experience of her hunger. It has become enlisted in the service of her sexuality. In the "down there" position of pleasuring her girlfriend she is filling the hole in her object, not being "up there" by her analyst's nourishing breast filling the hole of her own lack.

Now the analyst also gets blamed for her patient's hatred of needs (*"you got me there, you can't pull me back"*), showing her paranoid blame of her object for having put the awareness of a potentially healthy hunger into Diane. With that statement Diane conveys her entitlement to satisfaction, thereby dismissing any need to feel grateful. Unfortunately in the process she also destroys the value of what she is given, thus increasing her hunger and greed (Bion, 1970).

In her session on 2/14/2007 Diane again uses manic defences in her disdain for her "slacker" supervisee. She is triumphantly dismissive of her analyst/slacker, (*"I do my best work away from you"*) apparently with the unconscious fantasy that she can grow and feed herself without having to recognise the analytic partnership which she realises she is destroying inside herself (*"I am filling your space and energy with shit"*). Diane is here stating a conscious realisation of how she is treating her analyst but she may not be aware of the unconscious guilt that accumulates as a result.

In addition Diane seems to indulge in the fantasy that she makes her analyst a good strong partner solely by the force of her own efforts. The reality is in fact the reverse; she herself is stronger as a result of her analyst's hard work and containment. Her fear that the analyst might not be able to bear the force of her emotional presence (a situation she experienced with her parents) turns into entitlement—"*When I get to the heart of it and throw a temper tantrum, you better be ready. I am not giving you a free ride. You have to be a good partner. I won't be compassionate*". Holding on to that fantasy enables Diane to feel that she is superior to her analyst. Diane wants to be perfect, that is, without equal.

There is, however, also the reference to Sea Biscuit, a great horse who "*ate a lot of food*". This seems to allow space for her needs and at that moment Diane's grandiosity is tempered by realistic ambition ("*even that great horse needed rest and recovery*"). After this Diane realises that being more in touch with her reality will confront her with what to do with her anger from the past ("*where will I put the anger of the past*"). Her hatred and entitled anger has powered much of Diane's achievements and filled her identity. She will feel empty without it and has to await a sense of adequacy that facing and bearing reality gives over time.

In the final session of this paper on 5/2/07, after seven turbulent months, Diane brings a dream which further widens the analytic field ("*everyone I know is there*"). She acknowledges her former tennis partner's potency/penis ("*instead I used my hand to touch his penis*") and projects her wish to suck on it ("*he was rubbing himself, and pushing my head down*"). Now, instead of being tempted by her greed for all the erotised sweets, she wants to be selective of what she takes in. It seems Diane is able to differentiate what is nourishing to her growth and what is not. In that process she meets a handsome/potent part of herself and in that state of mind she is able to meet her own vulnerability. She is humbled ("*I was not confident ... I tell the truth*") in a hopeful whole-object moment encompassing both her able and humble/truthful parts.

The next sequence is a meaningful emotional confrontation with all the missed opportunities as a result of her destructiveness ("*I tell the truth and am exposed—a huge botch and so I no longer can walk. And there is atrophy and joint pain*"). If she proceeds, Diane will face the need to mourn missed opportunities and the destructive effects of her sadomasochism, some of which cannot be repaired.

In this last session both core parts of Diane's splitting appear in a mixture of, on the one hand, awareness of her frailty with recognition of damage done by her destructiveness, and the old superior sadomasochistic attitude on the other. "*I am so far beyond because of my success— I leave everyone in shock ...*" are statements of sadistic, manic, superiority while *"What about my life is not good judgment?!"* reveals a desperate doubt about her judgment.

It is an important moment where recognising the real achievement, although initially obtained by motivation of hatred, can be gratefully received and appreciated by the vulnerable part rather than attacked by the envious left behind part.

Diane's subsequent statement, *"I was truly phobic of something catching me, stopping me if I indulged"*, relates closely to the state of mind described in Bion's (1970) quote from Samuel Taylor Coleridge's poem:

> Like one that on a lonesome road
> Doth walk in fear and dread;
> And having once turned round walks on,
> And turns no more his head;
> Because he knows a frightful fiend
> Doth close behind him tread.
>
> —*"The Rime of the Ancient Mariner"*, Samuel Taylor Coleridge

Bion makes the point that the "frightful fiend" represents indifferently the quest for truth or the active defences against it, depending on the state of mind. He goes on to comment that it may seem improbable that dread should be associated with analytic progress towards a more realistic outlook.

When coming to the end of the clinical material, while not knowing how Diane's treatment proceeded, I found something in the session that gives direction to my conjecture that Diane is plateauing and needing time to consolidate before a possible next phase of turmoil. In her dream Diane describes that she is *"on skates and am my old self"*. From that I infer that she is moving fast and has reconstituted her old ways of avoiding reality. She says *"I skate back to the candy bar and am just about to pick something but I don't take the candy"*. I believe that the seven sessions in Dr. Paula Ellman's paper describe an intense and turbulent period of Diane's analysis which shows psychic movement from severe sadomasochistic internal and external relationships toward space and capacity to endure the pain and recognition of psychic reality with potential for incremental amendment of her sadomasochistic entrenchment. Whether, and to what extent, Diane will allow herself to become conscious of that movement is uncertain. I find myself wondering how many cycles of progression/regression accompanied by identifiable change Diane will endure and how much of her analytic relationship she will be able to introject.

References

Baranger, M. (1993). The mind of the analyst: From listening to interpretation. *International Journal of Psychoanalysis*, 74: 15–24.

Bick, E (1968). The experience of the skin in early object relations. *International Journal of Psychoanalysis*, 49: 484–486.

Bion, W. R. (1957). Differentiation of the psychotic from the non-psychotic personalities. *International Journal of Psychoanalysis*, 38: 266–275.

Bion, W. R. (1962). *Learning from Experience*. London: Tavistock.

Bion, W. R. (1967). *Second Thoughts*. London: Heinemann.

Bion, W. R. (1970). *Attention and Interpretation: A Scientific Approach to Insight in PsychoAnalysis and Groups*. London: Karnac, 1984.

Freud, S. (1911). Formulations on the two principles of mental functioning. *S. E., 12*. London: Hogarth.

Hinshelwood, R. D. (1989). *A Dictionary of Kleinian Thought*. London: Free Association Books. London.

Isaacs, S. (1948). The nature and function of phantasy. *International Journal of Psychoanalysis*, 29: 73–97.

Joseph, B. (1992). Psychic change: Some perspectives. *International Journal of Psychoanalysis*, 73: 237–243.

Klein, M. (1923). The development of a child. *International Journal of Psychoanalysis*, 4: 419–474.

Klein, M. (1935). A contribution to the psychogenesis of manic-depressive states. *International Journal of Psychoanalysis*, 16: 145–174.

Klein, M. (1946). Notes on some schizoid mechanisms. *International Journal of Psychoanalysis*, 27: 99–110.

López-Corvo, R. (1999). Self-envy and intrapsychic interpretation. *Psychoanalytic Quarterly*, 68: 209–219.

Mitrani, J. L. (1995). Toward an understanding of unmentalized experience. *Psychoanalytic Quarterly*, 64: 68–112.

Segal, H. (1991). *Dream, Phantasy and Art*. London: Routledge.

Steiner, J. (1987). The interplay between pathological organizations and the paranoid-schizoid and depressive positions. *International Journal of Psychoanalysis*, 68: 69–80.

Steiner, J. (1996). Revenge And resentment in the "Oedipus situation". *International Journal of Psychoanalysis*, 77: 433–443.

PART II

CASE PRESENTED
BY NANCY R. GOODMAN AND
DISCUSSIONS

CHAPTER SEVEN

Sailing with Mr. B through waters of "hurting love"

Nancy R. Goodman

"Oh no, not again" was a constant and loud refrain ringing in my inner psychoanalytic ear as I listened to Mr. B and to the counter feelings in my own psyche. Over his six-year analysis, he taught me about the way he had evolved, and now used, internal scenes of what I came to think of as "hurting love". They took place again and again, marking their import in his psychic organisation. At times he was the one being hurt and at times he was bringing hurt to others. Fear of annihilation/castration ruled his psyche and the terror about this was avoided and managed with the clarity of an expected sadomasochistic object relationship. The repetition compulsion was alive in regard to constant replaying of someone attacking the other resulting in a sense of psychic death or a state of overwhelming stimulation. Mr. B's special way of getting rid of someone was to find fault and to "x" them out. Both of us suffered often with the sense that a place of disappointment and detachment would appear again and again. His annihilating capacity staved off his own terror about being annihilated. In his inner life a danger signal aroused the desire to get rid of the other as soon as possible.

After a year of two times a week therapy he started a four times a week analysis and began to often enact deadness with me as he

95

fell asleep or was what he called "floating" on the couch. For Mr. B issues of autonomy and separateness and dangers of body intrusion coalesced around a regressive use of anal stage organisation in which dominance and submission, and control and omnipotence, were at play. Countertransferentially I became familiar with all facets of these methods of being with someone. We were often involved in fluctuating configurations of "who was going to hurt whom" as "hurting love" was played out on our analytic stage. I came to appreciate the way in which a representation of relationship centred on someone causing pain for the other can function. Similar to the way someone uses a fetish to keep terror away, Mr. B at times used the "hurting love" scene between us to disavow the catastrophe signaled by separateness. I am grateful for Mr. B's honesty and capacity to discover and his generosity in granting me permission to write about "sailing with Mr. B".

The case of Mr. B: in the beginning

Mr. B walked into my office, sat down across from me, and began to speak about recent feelings of sadness, despair, and fears of being invisible to others. Even before hearing verbal accounts of the recent break-up of a relationship and the history of old break-ups, I could feel that sadness was in the room. He recognised that somehow he was creating his problems and felt desperate enough to seek therapy. He was fifty-seven years old and had recently retired from an engineering company. He organised his life with a full schedule of exercise, social commitments including card games, and volunteer work in professional organisations. He was sure that his married sons and daughters did not need him and would gladly ignore his existence. His depression reminded him of the way he had felt after the break-up of his marriage ten years previously. I was deeply concerned about his despair and sense of emptiness. I wanted to help and took on the sending in of treatment forms to his insurance company on a monthly basis. He later said that I had taken him on even though the forms were "a pain in the ass". This was the beginning of our alliance, that I would be the one receiving the pain in the ass—a central image in many derivative forms in his hurting love scenes.

Mr. B told me of early childhood experiences he thought I would want to know. As an infant and toddler, he was kept in his highchair until he had eaten what his mother wanted him to eat. His aunt informed him of this and as if to ensure that I could vividly know the truth of this experience, he described how now he often fell asleep with his head lying on the table after "my lonely dinner". As a toddler he received an enema every three days if he was not producing a bowel movement. Numbers were now very important to Mr. B. He wanted to optimise time and money by spending very little of each commodity. He described the many ways he would save money, for example, driving home to get a coupon if he had forgotten it knowing full well that the gasoline costs might be greater than the value of the coupon. He had to go through almost ritualistic machinations to manage a feeling of being taken advantage of or a sense that his resources were wasted and misused. Dread about helplessness and the idea of possible misuse by others was often in his mind.

Another story took place on his eighth birthday and became the prototype for a need to always win negotiations and to never compromise. He had been clear that he wanted a particular baseball glove with a signature from a favoured player. His father presented him with a different one and when he protested, his father told him "take it or leave it". There was no negotiating. He left it and preferred to have no glove than to have one he felt he was forced to accept. When I spoke to him about including this in my write-up, he said: "It was the feeling that I did not matter that was so awful. Why wouldn't he care to know why it mattered to me?"

You will hear the symbolic significance of these stories in descriptions of the analytic work, especially in the fantasies and enactments taking place between Mr. B and me. From the beginning of treatment, the question of who would control whom or who would force whom into submission was often an active dynamic. His highly cathected representation of a sadomasochistic object relationship would catch each of us in imagined and enacted active and passive positions. Sometimes I wanted to absolutely force life into him. Other times, I wanted to merge into his sleepiness to deny my anxiety of not understanding and to just find a way to join with him. He produced an agonising deadness in me. It took time for us together to face the remnants in his mind of the experiences and internal fantasies about having been so often a thing-baby. A solid belief in destruction and helplessness produced by the narcissistic needs of another was a monument marking a place of "ground zero" in his psychic organisation. Later in the analysis, I was amazed to learn about the empathy and attunement which also existed in Mr. B's mind. When grandchildren entered his life, I heard about interactions with babies and toddlers which showed caring and sensitive intimacy.

He told me stories about being with the babies which brought forth representations of tender, attentive, and consistent attunement. These descriptions were valuable in our work as he then realised so fully the unmet wishes he had and the pain of making them conscious.

Finding a relationship: search and destroy or be destroyed

After about a year of bringing his helpless despair to the sessions and gaining a sense that there was something in his psyche to be understood, Mr. B was ready to resume going out on dates with women. Mr. B was searching for a relationship like a detective looking for clues for a "who done it" or "who might do it" crime series. He had a list of requirements of particular traits which were necessary in a potential partner. He had a subjective barometer for measuring the truth of his observations; if he were excited, it meant that his scanning had found no fault. Excitement referred to sexual desire and to a general internal experience of being alive. However, if just one of the traits on his list was absent, he was willing to accept his loneliness and isolation and return to perusing Match.com. He maintained a vague hope that he would eventually locate the right woman. He spoke of a fantasy of half merger with a woman: "We are in beautiful water and our legs are completely wrapped around each other." As I saw it, this wrapping around could be a safely felt union that was wished for because of the pleasure anticipated and because of the safety it offers from contemplating difference which can arouse desire and fear.

Mr. B describes his rejecting in the following way: "It is like I sail into a harbour. The water is beautiful and all of the houses on the hills of the coast are colourful and perfect. If one rooftop is awry or one façade unpainted, I will not stay. I will sail away and look for another harbour which is perfect."

He also let me know that analytic sailing with me at this time would not happen. There was no reason to wonder about the harbour, the visual scanning, and the absolute rejection. The metaphoric meaning was thrown overboard so he could sail alone. I was left alone with hypotheses about his idealising, searching for the phallic woman, terrors about difference. This moment captured the tension in our sado/masochistic coupling in which someone is forced into submission. He withheld a treasure of associations from me and like the mother giving enemas, I wanted to make him give me more of what was inside of him.

The word match in Match.com expressed well his psychic searching for the perfect fit between his internal idealised harbour of perfection and the actual find. He had two ways to feel alive: holding onto the ideal because it could be dreamt of without fear of annihilation or demeaning the found object, beating it into annihilation because it did not match. As I continued to reflect on his wishes and disappointed responses, he too began to wonder about his pattern of reactions which he called "my knee jerk reactions" and the need for this within him.

Weapons of mass destruction: character assassination

Mr. B dated about thirty women and delighted in bringing me stories of women who got no further than a walk or one dinner. "Her waist was not thin, her hair was too short, she was not enthusiastic about the meal, she did not smile at me, she does not read the editorial page, she has some arthritis, she has that menopausal weight gain around her middle." There was always something not to be found and the mantra of complaint was: "she did not excite me". Each date was a search and destroy mission and I, another postmenopausal woman, could not get him excited about a date. I listened to details of each miserable encounter and felt dizzied by his constant lack of excitement and attacking of the image of each woman. He disagreed with me that he was being aggressive telling me: "I just do not feel excited with that one." Over and over, he displayed a scene to me of what was not to be found and what was not getting excited and I was the stunned voyeur to it. Various unconscious scenes occurred to me; for example, never finding a needed mother and a negative primal scene without excitement and without intercourse. I was made to feel the helplessness of endlessly watching these scenes and their deadness. Eventually we were able to talk about the delight he got in holding onto his harsh devaluing and making me feel that my words could not in any way bring life to his inner world. His lack of enthusiasm was the invitation for the sado-masochistic relationship with me. I wanted to penetrate his inability to be excited and his inability was a penetration of my psyche meant to numb me and place me under his control—a wish for timeless sleeping togetherness. I invited reflection: "you are giving me a picture of how you feel excitement—it has to come from someone else" and he responded with disdain: "I know when I am excited and why should I feel it on my own?"

Indicative of his belief in either helpless overstimulation or self-maintained under-stimulation, he described a previous relationship in which he was the erotic plaything for a woman who would show up and sneak into his home. This was another "toomuchness" to try to control by rejecting every woman. In exasperation I say to him in a session, "Well all of these women you are rejecting can be sexual, they all have vaginas and you keep assassinating them before anything can happen." He thought my comment was outrageous and delighted in telling me so. I was also aware that I enacted bringing sexual difference into the session in a sudden and shocking way. He seemed to like the recognition of his power when I referred to his rejections of all these women as character assassinations. Devaluing was his favoured method of attack and his victim was helpless. He devalued my reflecting on what he might be up to in his concrete enactments of someone "shooting down" the other. He could tell that I was the one frustrated. He began to use a tone of voice which was teasing about my inability to change him. I found myself wondering if something like "preplay" was developing, or maybe, foreplay. I was enjoying his teasing.

He had a dream about a Barbie Doll as some kind of a "sexual tool". His curiosity came alive as he stated, "It is such a funny thing an actual Barbie Doll attached to my hip." He needed it to ignite a feeling strong enough to overcome his reluctance. He realised that the Barbie Doll in his dream was a sexualised image of an unreal woman that made him not want to fully know a real woman but made him feel very sexy. I began to see his "hurting love" object representation as another kind of object attached to him. Like the Barbie Doll, it was attached to his psyche, lending potency and preventing terror. As he gained a capacity to acknowledge how his rejecting thoughts and behaviours concerning the women he went out with were contemptuous and cruel, his collapse of excitement began to be countered.

Finding the sado/masochistic representation in the analytic room

At this time, a way of attacking me was to claim me unworthy of attack. When I wondered to him how this process of search and destroy related to the analytic sessions and to me, he stated that he did not think about me as a real person but as a doctor with knowledge similar to an instrument which he needed in order to get better. "Basically," he said, "I feel detached here and look at this as a business transaction." He also often retreated to a type of self-hypnotic state in which he spoke slowly and softly and fell asleep, and told me he was removed and floating. This too, he claimed as having nothing to do with the session or with me. His moods, his activity of inaction in the sessions, his dreams, his fears were unconnected, of course, to the analysis and the analyst. He told me: "You are like a gasoline station attendant who puts gas in the car. You do not have a relationship with your gasoline attendant, you just pay the bill. That is the way it is." At other times he told me I was the Wooden Indian in front of a cigar store. These pictures of me in his mind were creative constructions of his psyche. They were full of multiple meanings about connections, disconnections, openings, and entrances. He wanted to see them as concrete expressions without metaphoric meaning and would close down, enacting closed space. I wanted metaphoric exploration; he wanted "not that". We were different. We were into the feeling of a sadomasochistic world. He mostly needed me to be quiet and tolerate his deadness and the sadism in both of us. I had joined a Bion study group and was thinking a lot about containment and metabolising of affect. I was still and quiet.

Countertransference: living with pain

During this time, strong affective experience entered my countertransference involving suffering and oscillations between analyst as masochist and analyst as sadist. He brought his agony to me in sessions where he stated he was floating, detached, and appeared to be asleep. I sat in my chair enduring awful nothingness. I spoke to him about what was occurring to me as I sat with him—what I thought he was feeling or what he was perhaps wishing that I would feel. I found anchoring in the "screen scenes" of his babyhood and childhood and wondered if he was conveying to me how the baby induced sleepiness in himself when in the highchair prison or floated away during the enemas. Had he not been held in mind by a mother who had fear and dread of her baby's separateness of experience and need? I was imagining what might be happening within him when he was so detached and yet with me in the room on the analytic couch.

I often felt I was "right on" with what I was saying to him and he let me know the next day that he did not remember anything I had said to him. He asked why in the world I thought he would remember and I felt confused by his questioning. I really wanted to yell at him to wake up and listen and as a result I became more and more quiet. Sometimes I felt pressure in my left eye, becoming aware that I was holding my hand over my eye. He had terrible migraines and now with him I had the pain. My psyche resonated with his attraction to character assassination. At this time I could have convinced anyone that Mr. B was, at core, unanalyseable. I realised how annihilating and destructive I wanted to be to keep myself from feeling like a failure. I kept telling myself that holding and metabolising these feelings were primary. My mantra was "just wait and tolerate the nothing". I began to imagine that contact between us would bring about a conflagration of degrading each other. His mind was doing something to my mind and I wanted to figure out how to get him to know this.

He persisted in telling me I was the "gas station attendant". Sometimes I argued: "I'm a gas station attendant? Why are you so determined to see me as the enema mother who sticks things in you?" I was complaining and ashamed of my whining. What kind of analyst am I becoming, I wondered. He would tell me that he did not mean to hurt me but needed to tell the truth. My psyche was infused with thoughts about the enemas. I wondered if any other analysts lived with constant images of enemas in their minds. Then I thought about the infant held in the highchair and thought that that was even more unthinkable.

Mr. B began to tell me that in order for him to hear what I was saying I would probably have to hit him over the head. I often thought about wanting to hit him over the head. Once in a while I hit on some words or affect that brought on a response from him of sneezing. He always took this as an indication that he was feeling something, but he did not know what. He liked it when he sneezed with a lover; it meant he felt alive. We both looked forward to his sneezes, it meant something was happening. He did not sneeze often. Occasionally I wondered out loud if he was inviting me to penetrate him like an enema which would produce an overwhelming outpouring type of orgasm. He told me he liked orgasms which lasted a long time. I felt more alive when he was speaking to me, even derogating me, but silence still dominated. Sometimes he said he saw geometric figures when drifting. "Almost something I can reach out and grab." Maybe the outline of a relationship, I thought and hoped. To have a relationship there has to be some recognition of separateness and the shock of difference was to soon be the focus of our sessions.

The shock of difference

In the fifth year of the analysis the shock of difference entered the analysis, first in the displacement and then directly in the transference. Mr. B began to have more than one date with two women and quickly settled on one woman. He could not believe that he was tolerating her short hair and felt excited about her and about feeling excited. After three months of being involved and seeing each other almost every day, he announced that his goal for treatment had been reached and he would now stop analysis the next day. He said this at the end of a session as he was sitting up to leave. My interpretation was an astonished "What in the world are you talking about?" I went on, "We need to think more about this tomorrow".

At the next session he told me he was amazed at my reaction. He thought I would just say "okay". I had sounded shocked when he told me his idea about stopping. He could hear that I was not expecting this and could not understand my surprise. Why would I think he needed to talk more? I said that I had been having the idea that we would now be able to understand more deeply how he lived in a relationship. Something very particular occurred here in his recognition of me as someone who had real feeling reactions about him and the analytic work. I could almost sense him trying to figure out what to do with his de-animated pictures of me now that he knew I reacted to his announcement of ending treatment. We were separate people who could have different feelings and different thoughts and he could shock me. We worked with acknowledging how differently we saw things and agreed to disagree and continue three times a week.

While Mr. B was interested in discovering the difference between us, the work was in the displacement with intensified scrutiny of differences with his girlfriend. He wanted me to know about each and every twist, turn, and strain in his relationship. He would report the tensions of the last twenty-four hours, relishing each detail. It made me think of something going through his digestive canal and I was to hear each gurgle of the process. "She does not read the paper; I read it every day. She wants to go on vacation and just let things happen; I want to plan out everything. She does not eat dinner at the same time each day; I want a schedule. She does not like the spices I like on steaks we barbecue. We both like a lot of sex."

Importantly, he was able to wonder about his terrible anxiety at noting their differences. He tells me he needs to protect himself against some kind of danger and wonders what it is. "It is like holding my hands out and saying, oh no there cannot be a difference, I have to 'x' it out." At this time, he had a series of dreams full of anxiety and I felt hope that he was symbolising his experience in a new way and that he was less anxious about being open to his own mind and open to me. In one dream he is alone and lost in water and on ice. He states: "Death can easily occur, there is no help." In another, he reaches out over a slab of ice and the SS is on the other side ready to torture. He wakes up in a state of fear from a dream in which he is being tortured, being burned on his fingers, and he does not feel anything and is glad to be numb. As awful as these images are, I felt a relief that he was dreaming and wanting to tell me his dreams. He notices gaps everywhere—between the kitchen cabinet and the stove, between tiles on the roof where water has been leaking, and constantly between himself and his girlfriend. He and I associate to "gaps" for months. In the following vignette, Mr. B is describing differences between his girlfriend and him in the way they think about the vacation they will be taking to France. He feels that frustration is building up.

ANALYST: Something about seeing the gap between you brings about pressure.

MR. B: It brings about more than that. Like something is in my face that I have no control over.

ANALYST: Could you tell me more about the gap?

MR. B: It is nothing there, no one is there. It is blackness, nothing … coming face to face with emptiness, blankness, in fact she looks blank and I cannot stand it … I don't know why it is something that fills me with dread. I don't want to see it. Yes, dread. [He is silent for minutes.]

ANALYST: Is there something difficult about telling me about your dread, you have become quiet.

MR. B: I started drifting—just a little. I can almost reach for something [holds arm out with hand reaching] but there is nothing there.

ANALYST: When you drift you create the nothing that makes you feel dread, that may be one way to feel in control of what is frightening.

MR. B: I don't even know what would make me feel so anxious.

ANALYST: We have spoken often about your reactions to being face to face with gaps and how intolerable it is. The thought of separate people ignites the certainty that someone will be tortured and the gap is the girls genital, that made the little boy frightened.

MR. B: [Laughing with gusto] I cannot believe that you say those Freudian things [more laughter], I guess you are earning your pay, I know you are Freudian. It is laughable.

ANALYST: Maybe tomorrow we can understand more about why you are assassinating me and my knowledge now.

Mr. B is enjoying being dismissive of me and derisive of my ideas. I find this lively and not deadening. He is being direct with me and we are both in the room. Over the next weeks he complains that I am not a friend and am not making him warm soups. He is hungry.

Crises with his girlfriend intensify for a while as I again sit in the background feeling masochistically strangled to not mention the transference right now and to ponder rather obsessively about my own analytic beliefs—does there have to be transference work? I tell him: "When you are angry it seems to be like a drop of something toxic in a bowl of water that contaminates the whole thing. There is no room for any other way of feeling." He begins to feel that he can tolerate the imperfections he so often sees, he finds that he feels a kind of loving for his girlfriend when she does something imperfect that she then realises hurts him. He keeps wondering how he can be so excited with a woman who is not perfect. He wants to delight me with his new found capacity to tolerate ambivalence and to quiet his wishes to assassinate. He states emphatically that it is time to terminate in three months and expects me to not respect his decision. I feel it is very important to accept his wish to separate and tell him we can together assess if we need to do more work over the three months.

Pain and collapse

Two weeks before we are to terminate, Mr. B misses Monday and Tuesday because of illness, and reports in the session on Wednesday that he has been having the worse migraine of his life.

MR. B: Four days of agony. I took my pills and even they did not help. I finally got my Doc to order a narcotic. The pain was all over my head, not just on the left side where it usually is. I stayed in bed the whole time. I had awful dreams, awful nightmares. I was lost in tunnels. I was alone. The tunnels were built into the ground and very dirty. I could look up and see that overhead there were sort of panels which held up part of the ceiling of the tunnels, they were made of shiny metal. But, there did not seem to be enough of them and the whole thing could collapse and cave in and I would suffocate. I was really scared and did not know what direction to go in and there were these offshoots where I had not been and I had to take them to get out but I did not know what directions to go in and I needed time to figure it out before everything collapsed.

ANALYST: I can hear how imminent the danger was.

MR. B: What kind of tunnels are these? They were almost collapsing and there was only this sort of flimsy structure preventing everything from just falling in, it was not like there was an actual ceiling, just places here and there where the metal held things up. I get frightened just telling you.

ANALYST: You are letting me know how frightened you are at a time we are planning to stop.

MR. B: That is right, maybe I need to talk some more.

ANALYST: You were in these tunnels and all alone and have been ambivalent about wanting anything from me. I hear your wishing to be on more solid ground and to discover more about how to make the tunnels safer and stronger before you do leave. Is it so frightening to need me at this time?

MR. B: It would feel better to take time to figure it out.

ANALYST: I have been active in trying to respond to your distress in telling you what I think right away, I wonder how you have experienced that?

MR. B: My head feels better, no pain. I want to keep meeting for awhile.

Listening to Mr. B's nightmare and fear, I felt an urgency to shore things up and not allow a collapse. We did not take time to hear associations to the tunnels which sounded so much like a fantasy of the inside of the anal canal where he felt frantic in wanting more from me. The wishes and fears collecting around this imagery would develop in the next phase of our work.

Prelude to the storm and the storm

The sadomasochism in the sessions appeared to be becoming more sublimated in forms of his teasing me and a liveliness between us. He was letting me know that he knew me, how I thought, how I often spoke, what I responded to. I was letting him know how I knew him, I remembered his dreams, I remembered his ways of responding to me. We now had history together. A session during this time indicates the knowledge he was putting together; it also shows how he was using isolation and withholding of affect as a way to continue bringing "hurting love" to me and to deflate me.

MR. B: Just the thought that someone I am close to would be used by someone triggers off the feeling that I have to do something, I get invested in their interest as if my own—it may have to do with attachment and emotional involvement. Just the thought triggers this in me

ANALYST: I recall when you were dating, one thing that was not right and you had to "x" it out or drift away, it may seem like passivity but you are actively doing something.

MR. B: As I listen, these are psychological devices, what would be most available to me as a small child, as an adult I do it in action, could distance, just black it out like erasing it, as an adult try to solve it and that makes me confident, maybe different over development how change dependency and helplessness, the tools change over time. I head off things, optimise, all my manoeuvres. Most of my life expanding my tools for warding off helplessness.

ANALYST: You use the word black out, that is something a child could do, any other thoughts about "black out"?

MR. B: Destroy something, get rid of it, erasing it—I cannot let my feeling about the person get in the way of my having to do something. It is necessary to get rid of the helplessness I feel, the attachment is an impediment, this sounds right, but it sounds so academic, I do not feel it although I can imagine it happening cognitively, it doesn't stir up anything.

ANALYST: You sound lonely for feeling something.

MR. B: I can be ruthless and just paint over things with black in order to take care of myself.

ANALYST: "Painting over with black"—perhaps you are now showing me how you can blacken out feelings for me in order to leave me feeling helpless. You can conquer any ideas I have about you feeling and then I am the one helpless and defeated.

MR. B: I can blacken you out.

Mr. B was integrating thoughts about himself and his childhood and acknowledging the wish to use "blacking out". In another session, he reports having a sensation of aliveness and connection: "I had a strange feeling in the waiting room of wanting to reach out and touch someone's coat on the coat rack which I suddenly thought was maybe yours. It would be so nice to just stroke it. Maybe this is something about wishing to feel your skin. Maybe I will feel sad when I leave … and it will be soon."

There were many more dreams symbolising fears and wishes, including a dream of a woman who greeted him at the entrance to a museum. She seemed familiar and took him through the museum. He liked this woman but did not know who she was. The work was interesting to me and felt more collaborative—then his announcement: "I am done, I have no more curiosity and no more interest." He came to sessions and said absolutely nothing. He lay down on the couch; after about five minutes I asked what his quiet might be about? "I have nothing to say", he said. After seven minutes I told him that I wondered what he might be trying to have me feel with his having nothing to say. He said, "I am done." I said, "I wonder if we could be curious about your being done in this way?" He said, "I am not curious and you cannot make me curious." Silence. The next sessions were all about his leaving, his being done, and about a growing desperate feeling in me—a pressure to say the right thing, a need to come up with something powerful. The sessions were extremely tense—(the enema in the room, the tunnels— the cloaca which would collapse under the force of pressure). Someone would be excitedly evacuated.

I say to him: "I think we are in a crisis. There is no way we can speak to each other." He says: "I absolutely agree and feel like just giving in and waiting until you say I can go; or, I will just walk out. This feels like a war." I tell him that I absolutely agree and that he does not have to be curious just because I am; but, I am curious. I ask: "What is so important about being in a battle, is it a way to not experience saying goodbye"? He says: "Aha, I hear another six years coming on, six years to get in and six years to get out." We both laugh out loud.

When he returns to silence in sessions, I wonder to him why it is so important to so often keep the relationship with the analysis and with me as a place of no feeling.

ANALYST: You are getting across to me vividly what it means to be treated as a not and you must feel the same way. Someone is about to be dehumanised and forced into submission.

MR. B: You mean I would be like my mother?

ANALYST: I think you have an unconscious belief that if two people are separate and different there will be an annihilation, there is only a question of who will do it to whom.

MR. B: Maybe ... I still do not feel anything toward you and have nothing to say.

ANALYST: Your nothing to say attacks me as your analyst and the analysis, you are collapsing any space to think and for us to speak. What is so risky, now?

MR. B: Is this some kind of technique you have been taught to ask about how I feel about you? Is this what you are instructed to ask in your books? Do I have to do it your way or I have failed?

These questions really make me think and I let him know that. I eventually tell him that in fact it is a way I think about how to learn about his mind by attending to ideas and feeling that develop about our relationship and he was probably very attuned to that being important to me. He also seems to be thinking that if I bring this up it is about doing it by the book and not about real interest on my part. He remarked that he knew I liked dreams also and did not know if he was interested in dreams. "Your interest might also be because you are supposed to pay attention to dreams" he says to me. I state that I could understand, that it made sense to me that he would expect me to be another mother who would use knowledge from books to torture him and make him feel his authentic experience did not matter, what mattered was what the doctor ordered. As we spoke in this session, it felt like we were listening to each other in a different way. We soon agree to pick a termination date two months later.

I appreciate Mr. B's creativity and ability to bring about states of mind and compromise formations which did keep him alive as he went on his searches from harbour to harbour. He needed to try to control everything in his path and annihilate anything that was not as he wanted. Much discovery of the depths of his mind, and of mine, took place as he was telling me he was floating or sleepy and we were both learning to listen to his deep unconscious. While the "oh no, not again" was available in his mind when needed, we managed together to sail through often tortured waters finding courage and enlivenment and more space for a "yes" in his mind as well.

CHAPTER EIGHT

Discussion of the case of Mr. B

James S. Grotstein

General comments

I found myself irresistibly drawn into the narrative by the beckoning text of the author. We are immediately introduced to a tumultuous "love-hate affair" between two involved but wary "lovers", except for the fact that this is not a love-hurting affair in the ordinary understanding of that idea because it is a *"psychoanalytic affair"*, not a real life one. It is a psychoanalytic story by mutual agreement and arrangement between the analysand and the analyst and by virtue of the fact that the analytic frame is being rigorously observed. Once the frame and all that it suggests in terms of self-restraint of impulsive actions are in place, the analysand as well as the analyst become able to suspend their respective "realistic" impulses (suspend reality in order safely to experience their own respective freely associative phantasies). It is a pre-arranged dramatic, seemingly improvisational, and yet paradoxically pre-scripted, dramatic play taking place in a world that is *un*conscious to the participants. The situation is more an intersubjective "group dream" (co-constructed by analyst and analysand) *and* their two individual dreams.

When I say a "love-hate (hurting) affair", I am not necessarily alluding to an erotised transference ↔ countertransference ↔ intersubjective

111

situation, but I am not excluding it. I am attempting to illuminate an aspect of the interrelationship between the analytic couple that para-doxically belongs to the transference ↔ countertransference ↔ inter-subjective situation and yet at the same time lies beyond it. Put another way, the quality of the *psychic* experience of "analytic sex", for the analysand but also including the analyst, is quite different than that of physical sex in real life. "Psychoanalytic sex" is the inverse of body-participating sex. Because of the mandatory barrier against physical action, the analysand, despite, and yet because of, enforced frustration, is able to become aware of the fuller measure and deeper font of his/her capacity for passionate desire. The experience of frustration on the part of the analysand, however, may stimulate such frustration that (s)he may begin to perceive the analyst as a cruel and sadistic tempter or temptress and begin to develop powerful emotions of envy along with hate and resentment and may wish to punish the analyst for his/her unwarranted, even cruel, seductive intimidations. What I am getting at is that "analytic sex" is the reciprocal of real sex. They are separate domains with differing aims. Actual sexual relations aim at the achieve-ment of the ecstasy of mind-body union (communion) both within the self and between the participating couple. "Psychoanalytic sex", by contrast, aims primarily at the exploration, discovery, and acceptance of the fuller measure and meaning of one's sexual capacity as well as illuminating one's unconscious infantile sexual history.

One of the ironies of the emotional involvement of the analytic couple is that they are each constrained to allow themselves to feel their emo-tions toward one another but only the analysand is compelled to reveal them in this foreordained imbalanced situation, while the analyst must make private note of his or her own passions, experience them, then distance him/her self from them, and finally interpret from them, but *not* reveal them directly to the analysand. Further, the psychical inti-macy that transpires between the analysand and the analyst can be so intense that the former has understandable difficulty in realising that the latter may have similar experiences with his or her other patients and thus may be demeaned as a "prostitute", as they may have once thought about their mothers in regard to her love being able to encom-pass other siblings as well as father.

"Hurting love", in other words, can all too easily emerge as a con-sequence of inevitable analytic intimacy, and it is understandable that the analyst would be held responsible for its inevitable frustrating pain.

The analysand, in this case, Mr. B, probably felt tricked, tantalised, and deceived by the emotions he was compelled to experience in his analytic regression, including dependency, neediness, passionate desire, and envy of his analyst. In so doing, he was moving epigenetically from the position of the passive, shamefully inadequate helpless victim to the active role in which he in turn sought to tempt and frustrate his analyst. In other words, he employed the manic defenses (Klein, 1935, 1940) in which he, in unconscious phantasy, reversed the dependency hierarchy with his analyst and experiencing triumph over, demeaning contempt for, and control of her and her emotional life.

Now, where do sadism and masochism fit in to "painful love"? Were Mr. B's masochism and sadism defensive alternative responses to his perception of his strict frame-minding and regressive transference-inducing analyst? Or did his "inherent armory", that is, his instinctual-drives, inaugurate his transference behaviour—or both? My tentative answer at this juncture is that we cannot really know, that is, we cannot really reconstruct his origins with certainty. We can only know our experience of the current transference ↔ countertransference evidence in the here and now.

Let us pursue sadism a step further however. One of the chief components of sadism has long been thought of as the enjoyment of being cruel to an object, the desire to and pleasure in inflicting pain and suffering in the object. Another component of sadism is the subject's pleasure in controlling the object, a tendency which is included in the Kleinian concept of the manic defence. I believe that sadism may constitute a part-instinctual drive subserving what Bowlby (1969, and personal communication) calls the "prey-predator instinct", as in stalking and hunting prey, an atavistic residue of our animal (creature) prehistory and geared to be an evolutionary adaptive instrument for our survival.

Another line of associations now suggests itself in regard to Mr. B's analysis and again in the transference ↔ countertransference context. Winnicott (1969) speaks of the concept of the "subjective object" (p. 91), the infant's phantasied perception of the object which (s)he interposes (projects) into the potential space between him/herself and the object, thereby distorting her/his image of the real object. One can readily see that this idea graphically illustrates the phenomenon of the parallax of transference. Winnicott goes on, however, to say something even more interesting. He states that the infant seeks to destroy the (subjective) object yet hopes that the real object survives. It must be realised that the infant, like the analysand, is in a state of transference and consequently cannot distinguish between the self-constructed image of the object and the real object itself.

Yet there is a deeper layer to "hurting-love", a layer which is all too obvious and yet paradoxically mysterious. We all realise that there can be no love without the occurrence of hate. Put another way, hate through wanting to hurt the object, helps to define love, as Winnicott (1945) remind us, but why is this so? The infliction by and the corresponding experience of pain inflicted on an object with whom one is intimately involved seem to be the emotional certification, a veritable "branding" by the act of inflicting and of suffering pain in regard to the other. We are reminded of this by the labour pains mothers have timelessly suffered for the birth of their beloved infants. This pain constitutes the sacred bonding link between the two and is the hidden order of the depressive position. The crucifixion of Christ designates the sacred act whereby the God-appointed scapegoat or Pascal Lamb willingly suffers for those who cannot tolerate their pain. The Eucharist designates the ritualisation of inflicting suffering upon the sacred scapegoat by which act a sacred covenant (in regard to the relationship to the sacrificial object) emerges, and obligatory guilt becomes etched into one's very being (soul). This sacrificial act introduces the birth of the superego.

Winnicott (1945) grasped the essence of this irony that "hateful love" poses in the following:

> It seems to me that there is in it [the baby's injuring his fingers or mouth by too vigorously sucking his thumb or hand] the element that something must suffer if the object is to have pleasure: the object of primitive love suffers by being loved, apart from being hated. (p. 155)

> (I am grateful to Thomas Ogden for referring me to this citation.)

First conclusion: Destructive aggression against the infantile transference (subjective) object by the infant and analytic interpretation in addition to the analysand's attacks against the transference object have the same motive: to rid oneself of the part-object interferences which keep one from experiencing the truly intimate reality of the object ("Now through a glass darkly/Then face to face ..."). May this aggression on the part of the analysand not be a hidden motive for achieving closeness for real?

Second conclusion: May the real relationship between the analysand and the analyst be the secret template underlying transference ↔ countertransference and constitute its hidden order—ever to be sought after but never achieved? To achieve it, including self-disclosure by the analyst, is sacrilegious to the analytic endeavor. Put another way, the analysand forever seeks to destroy the transference object (illusion, phantasy, suspension of disbelief) to achieve possession ("knowing") of the real object and yet must always be kept from doing so. The analyst, on the other hand, is always seeking the analysand's transference so as to eradicate it so that (s)he can become more evolved (real) and be able to experience the realness of the analyst.

Third conclusion: The infliction and experience of suffering unites the two participant objects by a "branding pain" and an obligatory guilt that galvanises the intimacy of a relationship between the two and certifies its sanctity. I believe theology and anthropology (particularly Shamanism) need to be invoked for further enlightenment on this seemingly obvious yet truly mysterious sacred phenomenon we are dealing with.

Fourth conclusion: It is important to distinguish between "sex" and "erotism", the former being a natural consequence and achievement of normal libidinal development, and the second being a purloining or misuse of sexual impulses for defensive reasons and/or perverse motives (Lichtenberg, 2007). Mr. M., like so many analytic patients, disguises his shameful dependency needs for what pretend to be sexual needs in order to level the playing field. Dependency connotes a hierarchic relationship in which the infant or the infantile portion of the personality feels inferior to or less than the object of their dependency, the original experience being the breast. Erotic sex, on the other hand, connotes a prematurely achieved later stage of development in which the erotised partner and the self are considered to be equal in their erotised enthrallment.

Specific comments

The patient seemed to have better adjusted to the analysis than he had let on. He moved easily from a twice-weekly psychotherapy to a four times a week psychoanalysis. One of his first responses after making the change was to "enact deadness", according to the author, and also to fall asleep. My own "reverie-at-one-remove" was to think of him as having experienced a deep regression into a womb-like state. I think I might have understood this as his desire both to become unborn and also to become *re*born with the analyst-as-mother. I felt confirmed in this speculation a short while later when he told his analyst that he felt "invisible to others". I took this remark to suggest the operation of projective identification, an unconscious phantasy by which he seeks to become unborn and therefore invisible by disappearing inside the analyst-mother's body.

The author comments on how sad and alone he felt. He was divorced and retired and seemed unable to handle the spaces of unshared time. He believed his children didn't need him, a comment that suggested to me that he was being unconsciously reminded of. how needy he was becoming—and needed to deny by using projective identification. We learn from his history that his mother had apparently created a power struggle with him over his eating. His resultant frustration must certainly have made his needy dependency feelings shameful or even humiliating to bear. His feeding trauma became re-enacted in the transference ↔ countertransference as "painful love" because of *painful need*. The trauma resulting from his many childhood experiences seemed to have activated and confirmed his negativity in regard to his neediness, and it must have heightened his envy of his needed objects. It may also have pushed him from feelings of being shamefully powerless as a helpless infant to that of being a precociously erotic infant or child, as I alluded to earlier, who, with his discovery of his new erotic capability, could now equalise the distribution of power with the object and no longer be the shamefully powerless and vulnerable infant.

The analytic "passion play"

We also learn that his mother gave him enemas every three days. This act too must have been traumatic—in several ways: childhood molestation (rape) and theft of his own valuable internal objects (highly valuable faeces), but utmostly he must have felt that his budding capacity for autonomy underwent foreclosure. He must also have felt the same when his father wouldn't negotiate with him about the choice of a baseball mitt on his eighth birthday. We see these events as model scenes which become repeated in his later life—in relationships with women and in the transference. After poignantly describing her experiences of a sadomasochistic tug-of-war in the transference and in the countertransference, the author reveals the drama that was unconsciously ordained to take place, a scene within an analytic "passion play", an intersubjective co-construction within the analytic field (Baranger, M. & Baranger, W., 1961–1962; Bion, 1976; Grotstein, 1981, 2000, 2008, 2009a, 2009b, 2009c; Ogden, 1994; Stolorow, 1988). "His highly cathected representation of a sadomasochistic object relationship would catch each of us in imagined and enacted active and passive positions. Sometimes I wanted to absolutely force life into him [as if she were his anxious mother]. Other times, I wanted to merge into his sleepiness to deny my anxiety of not understanding and to just find a way to join with him [mutual projective identification to create the imagined pre-natal state of bliss]. He produced an agonizing deadness within me."

Freud (1915) stated that psychoanalysis cannot effectively treat a *psychoneurosis*, only a *transference* neurosis. Today we would say a "transference" and a "countertransference neurosis" (a "double" one-person model) or an "intersubjective" (two-person model as an irreducible "group") "analytic field". I have postulated that psychoanalysis constitutes a passion play, a drama in which the analysand and analyst are unconsciously assigned roles in order to play out troubling themes emerging from within the former (Grotstein, 1981, 2000, 2009a, 2009b, 2009c); McDougall (1986, 1989) and Lothane, (2001) have also explored the theatrical perspective of clinical psychoanalysis. Ogden (1994) postulates a specific "subjugating third analytic subject" which, like a preternatural theatrical director, unconsciously subjects the analysand and analyst to "enact" (Shapiro, 2004) a pre-arranged script (which is experienced by the analytic players as improvisational) that dramatises important themes that need to be emotionally experienced both by the analyst as well as by the analysand. This dramatic catharsis is, in my opinion, exactly what transpired between the author and her analysand.

Other issues in the case

There were many possible reasons why the patient experienced difficulties in finding a mate. I should like to offer a few which suggested themselves to me: (A) One was *claustrophobic anxiety*. By that I mean that as soon as he found himself becoming emotionally close to any of his potential mates and to his analyst, he would begin to feel more needy, then would unconsciously project his undesirable, shameful neediness into them, and then felt suffocated and controlled by *their* neediness and putative undesirability; (B) A second factor was his *aversion to differences* between them and him. Here, I thought of the concept of contingency and non-contingency, as they are thought of in infant development research. In brief, contingency refers to the early infant's need for his mother and her responses to be in "lock-step" symmetry with his/her needy states so as to be able to achieve a sense of self-continuity (Brooks & Lewis, 1976, in Lichtenberg, 1989, p. 91). I believe that the author's patient succeeded in achieving a deep analytic regression and was unconsciously pinpointing the need to repeat and restore his archaic development of self-and object-constancy.

(C) and (D) A third and fourth factor that caught my eye were, in my rational conjecture, his *envy* of women and his use of the manic defence to overcome and reverse the emotional power struggle set in train by his envy. In the manic defence the patient reverses the field by assuming the analyst's power and authority, projects his impotent vulnerability into the analyst, and displays triumph over and contempt and control of her. The author states:

> I was made to feel the helplessness of endlessly watching these scenes and their deadness. Eventually we were able to talk about the delight he got in holding onto his harsh devaluing and making me feel that my words could not in any way bring life to his inner world. His lack of enthusiasm was the invitation for the sadomasochistic relationship with me.

The patient reported a dream about a Barbie Doll as some form of a sexual tool that was attached to him. (D) I thought that the Barbie Doll represented the recovery of an archaic unconscious infantile act or phantasy in which he fled the persecutory breast and precociously sought his soothing from his penis in *masturbation*.

Part three: "hurting love" as the major theme of the analysis

The author suggests that the Barbie Doll also represented a "hurting love object". I think that "hurting love" constitutes the Ariadne's thread of the whole analysis. His archaic relationships with his mother and his father were reported by him as having been painful. Whether he was the helpless victim of their parental ineptitude, neglect, or abuse, and/or whether his inherent personality constituted an ongoing mismatch, the patient, though not necessarily guilty for what had happened in his infancy and childhood, is nevertheless psychically responsible for what became activated in his internal world as a consequence of his parents' impingements and/or neglect of him. He is unconsciously mandated to repeat these ancient mishaps and their effects in him in the analysis as a passion play in which he recreates, re-enacts, and re-dreams his "painful loving"—for the analyst now to feel the pain that he has felt lifelong. That the analyst must feel his pain is absolutely necessary, states Bion (1978, and personal communication). The analyst must feel the patient's pain so as to achieve the cure of the pain—as an exorcistic transfer of "demons" (bad objects) from the patient to the analyst. The analyst must then feel the patient's transferred pain *instead of the patient* and must also *vicariously* feel the guilt and regret that the original parents did not or could not reveal or express. The act is one of vicarious atonement. This healing act is shamanistic. I term it the "Pieta transference ↔ countertransference" (Grotstein, 2008a, p. 21).

Conclusion

In the course of an infancy and childhood background characterised by faulty attachment with injury to his developing self-esteem, this patient seems to have tightly joined sadism and its twin, masochism, to his capacity to love. What he is beginning to learn in his analysis is that true love must always be associated with pain—the pain that inevitably comes with *caring*—but it must become "divorced" from its unnecessary but persistently persuasive dark side, sadism and masochism.

References

Baranger, M. & Baranger, W. (1961–62). La situation analitico como campo dinamico. In: *Problemas del Campo Analitico*. Buenas Aires: *Revista Uruguayo de Psicoanálisis*, 4: 3–554.
Bion, W. R. (1976 [2005]). *The Tavistock Seminars* (Ed., Francesca Bion). London: Karnac.

Bion, W. R. (1978 [2005]). *The Tavistock Seminars* (Ed., Francesca Bion). London: Karnac.

Bowlby, J. (1969). *Attachment and Loss. Vol. I: Attachment*. New York: Basic Books.

Brooks, J. & Lewis, M. (1976). Visual self-recognition in infancy: Contingency and the self-other distinction. In: J. Lichtenberg, *Psychoanalysis and Motivation* (p. 93). *Hillsdale, NJ: Analytic Press*, 1989.

Freud, S. (1915 [1941]b). Observations on transference-love (Further recommendations on the technique of psycho-analysis, III). In: *Remembering, Repeating, and Working-Through* (pp. 157–171). London: Hogarth Press.

Grotstein, J. (1981). Who is the dreamer who dreams the dream and who is the dreamer who understands it? (Revised). In: J. S. Grotstein (Ed.), *Do I Dare Disturb the Universe? A Memorial to Wilfred R. Bion* (pp. 357–416). Beverly Hills: Caesura Press.

Grotstein, J. (2000). *Who is the Dreamer Who Dreams the Dream?: A Study of Psychic Presences*. Hillsdale, NJ: The Analytic Press.

Grotstein, J. (2008). *A Beam of Intense Darkness: Wilfred Bion's Legacy to Psychoanalysis*. London: Karnac.

Grotstein, J. (2009a). *"But at the Same Time and on Another Level ...": Psychoanalytic Theory and Technique in the Kleinian/Bionian Mode. Volume 1:* London: Karnac.

Grotstein, J. (2009b). *"But at the Same Time and on Another Level ...": Clinical Application in the Kleinian/Bionian Mode. Volume 2*. London: Karnac.

Grotstein, J. (2009c). "The play's the thing wherein I'll catch the conscience of the king!" Psychoanalysis as a passion play. In: A. Ferro & R. Basile (Eds.), *The Analytic Field: A Clinical Concept* (pp. 189–212). London: Karnac.

Klein, M. (1935). A contribution to the psychogenesis of manic-depressive states. In: *Contributions to Psycho-Analysis, 1921–1945* (pp. 282–310). London: Hogarth Press, 1950.

Klein, M. (1940). Mourning and its relation to manic-depressive states. In: *Contributions to Psycho-Analysis, 1921–1945* (pp. 311–338). London: Hogarth Press, 1950.

Lichtenberg, J. (1989). *Psychoanalysis and Motivation*. Hillsdale, NJ: Analytic Press.

Lichtenberg, J. (2007). *Sensuality and Sexuality across the Divide of Shame*: London: Routledge.

Lothane, Z. (2001). Freud's alleged repudiation of the seduction theory revisited. *Psychoanalytic Review*, 88: 673–723.

McDougall, J. (1986). *Theatres of the Mind*. Stanmore: Free Association Books.

McDougall, J. (1989). *Theatres of the Body*. Stanmore: Free Association Books.

Ogden, T. (1994). *Subjects of Analysis*. Northvale, NJ: Jason Aronson.

Shapiro, T. (2004). Use your words! *Journal of the American Psychoanalytic Association*, 52: 331–353.

Stolorow, R. (1988). Intersubjectivity, psychoanalytic knowing, and reality. *Contemporary Psychoanalysis*, 24: 331–338.

Winnicott, D. W. (1945). Primitive emotional development. In: *Through Paediatrics to Psycho-Analysis* (pp. 145–156). New York: Basic Books, 1958.

Winnicott, D. W. (1969). The use of an object. *International Journal of Psycho-Analysis*, 50: 711–716.

CHAPTER NINE

Discussion of the case of Mr. B

Margaret Ann Hanly

In "Sailing with Mr. B", the author presents a vivid and convincing narrative of a six-year psychoanalysis with a difficult patient engaged in a sadomasochistic transference. Mr. B was fifty-seven when he came for analysis because of a depression with feelings of "despair and a sense of emptiness", a depression like one he had suffered after the break-up of his marriage ten years previously. He organised his life with a full schedule of exercise, social commitments, and volunteer work in professional organisations. He had no sense that he could really relate to others, "sure that his married sons and daughters did not need him and would gladly ignore his existence … He had to go through almost ritualistic machinations to manage a feeling of being taken advantage of or a sense that his resources were wasted and misused." He would drive home "to get a coupon if he had forgotten it knowing full well that the gasoline costs might be greater than the value of the coupon."

Dr. Goodman builds a complex formulation into the clinical narrative, and she provides clear indications of the nature of the transformations in the patient's psychic functioning and life which take place through the analytic process. Between the formulation and description of change, the analyst shows how she saw the past coming into the present and tells us what she did and said to further the process and to create change. In this discussion I will try to make more explicit what is sometimes implicit in her working formulations and descriptions of change in Mr. B.

Formulation of sadomasochistic dynamics in a traumatised patient

Goodman's working formulation about the patient's sadomasochistic functioning emerges in the course of her reflection on the associations, the transference, countertransference, and enactments. She explicitly formulates the patient's "regressive use of anal stage organisation in which dominance and submission, and control and omnipotence were at play". Central to understanding her patient was the analyst's discovery of a serious "annihilation anxiety" in the patient, which he kept out of consciousness through sadomasochistic relationships and through the projection into the analyst of states of helplessness and rage. "Mr. B's special way of getting rid of someone was to find fault and to 'x' them out".

Annihilation anxiety tallies with much that Goodman formulates about the cumulative trauma suffered by her patient and the effects on his intrapsychic dynamics and his struggles in relationships. Hurvich (2003) describes concepts closely related to annihilation anxiety, which include: "traumatic anxiety (Freud, 1926); ... psychotic anxiety (Klein, 1935); instinctual anxiety (A. Freud, 1936); schizoid anxiety (Fairbairn, 1940); ... unthinkable anxiety (Winnicott, 1960; ... disintegration anxiety (Kohut, 1977); ... too muchness (Shengold, 1989)" (p. 580). According to Hurvich, these terms have been used to describe "fears of being over-whelmed, of ego disintegration ... of the disorganising effects of impinge-ment, of a breakdown of self- and object representations ... the terror of twoness ... overstimulation, and the absence of internal space" (p. 580). The terror of twoness in Mr. B seems to have been linked to a terror of mutual hurting or domination, to the point of annihilation of self or other. This terror seems to have resulted in his attacks, withdrawals, or wishes for merger or for revenge, including his attempts to humiliate or to "cas-trate" his partners who were experienced as sadistic, and his attempts to create guilt and shame in others. Goodman came to view these sadistic tendencies as an enacted revenge for childhood humiliations and pain-ful intrusions and constraints. Chasseguet-Smirgel (1991a) articulates the link between trauma and these perverse fantasies:

My views come close to those of Stoller ... for whom perversion
is an erotized form of hate. The object is to act out a fantasy of
revenge which transforms an infantile trauma into an adult
triumph. (p. 401)

Three screen memories in particular were found to be useful in understanding the link between the cumulative trauma in childhood and
Mr. B's powerful revenge impulses. His mother had forced him to sit
alone in his highchair when he was an infant "until he ate everything".
She gave him enemas every three days when he had difficulty with his
bowel movements. His father also seems to have been arbitrary and
rigid, refusing his son a longed-for baseball glove signed by a loved
player, and giving him one that had no meaning. Later Mr. B could say:
"Why wouldn't he care to know why it mattered to me?"

These patterns of ruthless demands and denial of meaning resulted
in an intense dread of helplessness in Mr. B, an unconscious desire
for revenge, and a defensive oscillating between identifying with the
aggressor and with the victim: "from the beginning of treatment, the
question of who would control whom or who would force whom into
submission was an active dynamic." For instance, in an early session,
the analyst found herself offering to fill in and send out the patient's
insurance forms, an act which she later reflected on as meaning to the
patient a first "submission" in what became recurring sadomasochistic
dynamics in the analytic relationship. Coen (1998) describes the analyst's role playing within the sadomasochistic dynamics, that is pro-
gressively understood and spoken.

My patients ... felt relieved to be contained, held, and challenged in their sadomasochistic object relating; in it they did not
have to feel separate and alone with their intolerable feelings and
needs ... Dread of intimacy (disappointment, subjugation, merger/
disorganization) activated perverse and narcissistic defenses
against need. (pp. 1172–1173)

Coen's description of perverse defences fits well with several aspects of
Goodman's analysis. Mr. B tries to make her feel distant and objectified:
"I feel detached here and look at this as a business transaction." The
deadening of experience and the provoking of deadened states in the
analyst comprised Mr. B's most entrenched defence against emotional
vulnerability. Much later in the analysis, there emerged more positive

capacities, which had been split off in the service of defence. The analyst was amazed to hear about a playful empathy and attunement with his grandchildren which also existed in Mr. B's mind, "interactions with babies and toddlers which showed caring and sensitive intimacy".

Reflecting on the countertransference and helping the patient to own aggressive impulses was the first step in analysing the revenge wishes and the traumatically intrusive experiences leading to them. But at first Mr. B rejected all interpretations concerning his aggressive impulses towards the women he dated and towards the analyst. During the second year of the analysis, Mr. B dated thirty women, and it became clear that he was looking for a woman who would be so perfect that he would not have any impulse to reject or humiliate her. However, eventually the analyst and patient were "able to talk about the delight he took in his harsh devaluations of women", and in his insinuations that the analyst's words could never enliven his inner world. For a long period he forced a "sadomasochistic coupling" on the analysis: as Mr. B "withheld a treasure of associations", the analyst caught sight of her wish to force him to "give more", "like the mother giving enemas". The acknowledgement in herself of these countertransferential impulses to intrude aggressively, together with reflection on what this indicated about the patient's past experiences, was an important factor in effecting change.

> Patients whose transferences take the form of sadomasochistic fantasy enactments may, by their insistent invitation to attack, induce similar conflicts in the therapist. Sometimes in subtle ways, sometimes overtly, the therapist may be placed in a position requiring submission or some aggressive behavior. (Grossman, 1991, p. 42)

Throughout the paper, Nancy Goodman builds up a reconstruction, an implicit formulation that the patient suffered cumulatively from traumatic experiences, that the mother's cruelties (Berliner, 1958) and intrusions, resulted in a lack of internal space and had a disorganising effect which negatively affected the patient's capacity for symbolisation and triangulation. "Once in a while I hit on some words or affect that brought on a response from him of sneezing. He always took this as an indication that he was feeling something, but he did not know what." He could not link his bodily sensations with affects or words. How was the analyst to facilitate Mr. B's capacity for symbolisation, that is, "the linking of experiences from distinct spheres of the mind, where one represents the other" (Freedman & Russell, 2003, p. 39)? When the analysis threatened the patient with a re-experience of previously traumatic situations, a process of desymbolisation would start. Mr. B would become concrete, would foreclose affect, or disavow experience. Thus, the analyst reflects: "he told me I was the wooden Indian in front of a cigar store". These pictures of the analyst "were full of multiple meanings" in the analyst's mind. However, the patient wanted to see the pictures of her "as concrete expressions without metaphoric meaning and would close down, enacting a closed space". The analyst describes defensive disavowal in Mr. B in that one of his ways of attacking her "was to claim me unworthy of attack". The first step in the complex process of facilitating symbolisation in such a patient was for the analyst to bear the projections of deadness and to conceptualise the desymbolisation as it occurred.

Several analysts have explored the idea that an important therapeutic action takes place through the analysis of a destructive primal scene fantasy which leads to the opening up of a capacity for linking and thus symbolisation. As Dr. Goodman reflected on her own experiences in the countertransference over a period of years, the concept of a destructive primal scene robbed of true intercourse and of procreativity (Britton, 1989; Chasseguet-Smirgel, 1991b) became important to her reconstruction of his unconscious fantasies of the couple in the patient's mind. She was aware that the patient oscillated between helpless overstimulation and self-maintained under-stimulation, forging in the analyst a role of passive voyeur/pervert: "Over and over, he displayed a scene to me of what was not to be found and of not getting excited and I was the stunned voyeur. Various unconscious scenes occurred to me; for example, … a negative primal scene without excitement and without intercourse. I was made to feel the helplessness of endlessly watching these scenes and their deadness". This deadening of mind about sexual intercourse seemed at the heart of the desymbolising forces of disavowal and affect foreclosure.

As Mr. B came more to life in the analysis, a perverse transference (Rosenfeld, 1978) showed up in two specific fantasies. The first was a fetishistic image of a phallic woman, a Barbie doll, attached to his hip, which allowed his erection to continue; the fantasy "could ignite a feeling strong enough to overcome his reluctance". The second was a cluster of revenge fantasies about the analyst which seemed directly linked to the analyst's idea that as a baby and little child he felt he was a "thing" for his mother. Thus he says to his analyst "that he does not think about her as a real person but as a doctor with knowledge similar to an instrument". He sees the analysis as a "business transaction", and concludes: "You are like a gasoline station attendant who puts gas in the car".

The fantasy of sadistic anal intrusion (the gas hose) seemed linked to the overstimulating passive experience caused by the mother's injection of the enema "instruments" into his rectum; the passive intrusion experience/fantasy is transformed into the active wishful fantasy of the analyst viewed as gas station attendant, in a projective identification.

The next part of the discussion will focus on the termination phase, which gathered and intensified Goodman's ways of facilitating change for the patient.

The termination phase and the transformational process

Interpretation of sexual fantasies and sadistic impulses, as well as the analysis of enactments and containment of projective identifications, helped to facilitate the therapeutic action. In the case of Mr. B, Goodman's clinical descriptions indicate that she valued spontaneous interpretation followed by a careful listening to the patient's response in order to elaborate split-off experience and re-start a truncated process of fantasy elaboration. She indicates that the impact of trauma on psychosexual development was a fundamental idea in her thinking about Mr. B.

Many months before the actual end of the analysis, Mr. B began his first serious relationship and, in a sudden enactment, abruptly announced that he would leave the analysis the next day. The startled analyst intervened spontaneously, "What in the world are you talking about? ... we need to think more about this tomorrow". Mr. B returned the next day, and stayed in the analysis. A very difficult and very fruitful termination phase ensued.

In the termination phase of the analysis, the return of previously split-off traumatic experience was intense and harrowing (Freud, 1938). Infantile and childhood proto-experiences and fantasies that had never been elaborated, remembered, or worked through, returned in anxiety-ridden experiences, and were felt in the analysis in "deferred actions" (Faimberg, 2005). But the patient was no longer alone with intolerable feelings and needs.

... psychological development organizes the formation of fantasy structures to regulate the responses to pain and the attendant aggression. The affectionate and sexual relationships with other people are the matrix for this process. (Grossman, 1991, p. 39)

An essential development in the analysis functioned in just the way Grossman's complex theorising describes: the analyst named and facilitated "fantasy structures" to regulate Mr. B's earlier responses to pain, and his sexual relationships were the matrix for this process, as was a transference "foreplay". The analyst brought into consciousness Mr. B's sadistic response to the dangerous female vagina. Here is Goodman's account:

"Indicative of his belief in either helpless overstimulation or self-maintained under-stimulation, he described a previous relationship in which he was the erotic plaything for a woman who would show up and sneak into his home. In exasperation I say to him in a session, 'well all of these women you are rejecting can be sexual, they all have vaginas and you keep assassinating them before anything can happen.' He thought my comment was outrageous and delighted in telling me so. I was also aware that I enacted action of bringing sexual difference into the session in a sudden and shocking way. He seemed to like the recognition of his power ... He began to use a tone of voice which was teasing about my inability to change him. I found myself wondering if something like "preplay" was developing, or maybe, foreplay. I was enjoying his teasing.

The fantasy structure which had regulated Mr. B's responses to pain involved a fear of "sexual difference", now analysed by Goodman through reference to implicit castration anxiety: "they all have vaginas and you keep assassinating them before anything can happen." Within this condensed portrayal of a segment of analysis, Goodman's spontaneous interpretation seems to have emerged partially from unconscious to unconscious communications. A teasing and being teased (Brenman, 1952) dynamic next entered the transference/countertransference with a more explicit sexual aspect: a "foreplay" was elaborated in the transference and important functional change was initiated.

During this phase of the analysis, Mr. B not only humiliated the analyst as powerless to help him, but also tried to erase her, to "x her out".

Through the analysis of this transference, the intention to annihilate a woman, which underlay the sadism to women, became conscious and changes took place.

> As he gained a capacity to acknowledge that his rejecting thoughts and behaviours concerning the women he dated were contemptuous and cruel, the collapse of his [sic] excitement began to be countered.

Goodman notes an important functional gain, as Mr. B began to sustain a sexual and emotional aliveness with a woman.

Given that Mr. B had formed a defensive internal fantasy of assassinating potential sexual partners, we can more fully understand why he attempted to end the analysis by annihilation, announcing he would stop the next day. The analyst responded: "What in the world are you talking about? ... we need to think more about this tomorrow". Mr. B had, pre-consciously, dared to test how he existed for the analyst, and the analyst answered with complete spontaneity, indicating he was very alive in her mind, and in her therapeutic space.

After Mr. B decided to continue the analysis, a decision grounded in the now alive analytic relationship, he gained a new ability to "tolerate ambivalence". Mr. B decided, for the second time, that he was ready to leave the analysis, and gave himself three months to prepare. A crucial interpretation during this termination phase helped the patient to elaborate the impact on his psychosexual development of the traumatic experiences of his childhood. The analyst interpreted that "someone will be tortured and the gap is the girl's genital, that made the little boy frightened". Leading up to this interpretation, the analyst describes a period in the analysis in which the patient reported more dreams, now symbolic rather than evacuative, and associations, indicating Mr. B's growing capacity for linking experiences from distinct spheres of the mind (sadistic desires and cruel punishments). Grinberg (1987) describes the changes that take place in a patient's psychic functioning showing up in the difference between early dreams in the analysis which have an evacuative function and later dreams which show a greater capacity for symbolizstion.

> Freud (1900) referred indirectly to the function of discharge in dreaming when he stated: "Dreaming has taken on the task of

bringing back under control of the preconscious the excitation in the Ucs. which has been left free; in so doing, it discharges the Ucs. excitation, serves it as a safety valve ... (p. 579)". Segal (1981) also pointed out that "dreams may be used for purposes of evacuation ... A patient can use dreams for getting rid of, rather than working through, unwanted parts of the self and objects, and he can use them in analysis for projective identification (p. 99)". (Grinberg, 1987, pp. 162–163)

The links between Mr. B's *fear* about his *wish* to annihilate, his self-punishment, and his states of aloneness and deadness became represented in the dreams and associations of this period. In one dream Mr. B is alone and lost in water and on ice. He states: "death can easily occur, there is no help." In another dream, he reaches out over a slab of ice and the German SS are on the other side ready to torture him. He wakes up in a state of fear from a dream in which he is being tortured, being burned on his fingers, and he does not feel anything and is glad to be numb. For the first time, he puts his defensive disavowal of affect into words, "glad to be numb", now conscious of and owning the state he had evacuated and projected into the analyst earlier in the analytic process.

After analysing Mr. B's dreams and dread of gaps for months ("coming face to face with emptiness, blankness; in fact she looks blank and I cannot stand it"), the analyst makes the interpretation linking the patient's fear of female genitals, his conflicted sexual desire, his castration anxiety, and his torture fantasies.

> "We have spoken often about your reactions to being face to face with gaps and how intolerable it is. The thought of separate people ignites the certainty that someone will be tortured and the gap is the girl's genitals, that made the little boy frightened". *Mr. B:.* [*Laughing with gusto*] "*I cannot believe that you say those Freudian things* [*more laughter*], *I guess you are earning your pay.*"

Mr. B showed signs that he had a new ability to take in the analyst's interpretation of his castration anxiety and unconscious castration fantasies (Freud, 1915), expressing some relief in his laughter, but also trying to dismiss the analyst as she brought the fantasy into consciousness.

With these anxiety/punishment dreams and associations Mr. B showed a new capacity for symbolisation as the analyst helped him to understand the impact on his sexuality of his traumatic experiences. The analyst's idea that the patient's sadomasochistic provocative words and behaviours had defended against annihilation anxiety was confirmed. As Mr. B's annihilation anxiety became more conscious and more threatening, his sadomasochistic defensive activities reemerged strongly in the transference in the last months of the analysis.

Two weeks before planned termination, Mr. B experienced four days of agony with a migraine. He dreamt of tunnels that would collapse and suffocate him. The analyst noted that his associations to the tunnels … sounded "much like a fantasy of the inside of the anal canal where he felt frantic". Again the analyst was able to interpret more about the impingement of the powerful childhood experiences on the anal developmental issues of control, sadism, helpless sexual submission, and vengeful rage at maltreatment at the hands of the other.

Mr. B again delayed ending the analysis, and the next months were marked by his renewed withholding of affect, and by continuing a "hurting love" toward the analyst, geared to "deflate" her. But although he was repeating earlier strategies (as happens typically in termination), Mr. B could now put into words what had only existed in action. Mr. B understood that for most of his life he had been engaged in "expanding his tools for warding off helplessness". Finally he was able to bring his destructive impulses into the here and now with the analyst. Picking up on Mr. B's associations about a blackout, the analyst asks him for his thoughts on "black out", and he thinks, "get rid of, erase". The analyst directly analyses Mr. B's destructive wish and projection of helplessness in the transference fantasy: "perhaps you are now showing me how you can blacken out feelings for me in order to leave me feeling helpless. You can conquer any ideas I have about you, feeling that then I am the one helpless and defeated." Mr. B can make a direct emotional contact with his destructive impulse: "I can blacken you out". To recognise his desire to annihilate her, the analyst had used her countertransference to reverberate with the patient, and he now could associate to the symbolic language, "blacken out", and work with the analyst.

> … "reverberation time" is also the building block of a psychoanalysis, leading to "unfreezing" psychic time and enabling the reconnection of "here and now" with "there and then" in a flexible way

which promotes open possibilities, and ... this takes place via the analyst's reverie, or time of reverberation. (Birksted-Breen, 2009, p. 35)

The termination phase of this analysis signified evacuation and rejection to the patient, and so was experienced as a traumatic situation. But due to the gains made earlier in the analysis, through the interpretation of sexual fantasies and annihilation fears, the patient's experience of affects and impulses of a more tender nature oscillated with his impulses to evacuate and erase. He told the analyst that he had wanted to touch her coat in the waiting room; he thought of wishing to feel her skin. The analyst helped Mr. B to put previously enacted anal fantasies and ambivalence into words. She understood that he wanted to love and to be loved, to desire and to be desired, but that he was also experiencing the end of analysis as an excited child "being evacuated". Dr. Goodman was able to interpret that "someone" felt about to be dehumanised and forced into submission again.

The wider-ranging emotional communication and the lessening of the intensity of the projections were important indicators of change in the patient's psychic functioning. In the middle phase of the analysis, the analyst had felt penetrated by his inner states: "He had terrible migraines and now with him I had the pain. My psyche resonated with his attraction to character assassination" In the termination phase, while there was a repetition of the deadening, annihilating, withholding impulses, the analyst could "return" meanings to the patient. Each enactment allowed some aspect of the early trauma and proto-fantasies to become a reverie in the analyst's mind, which facilitated a set of interpretations linking the patient's defensive and sadistic responses to trauma with current experience in the analysis.

The patient had challenged the analyst, trying to push her away: "Is this some kind of technique you have been taught to ask about how I feel about you? Is this what you are instructed to ask in your books? Do I have to do it your way or I have failed?". The analyst in this last phase, makes a direct transference interpretation of the projection of the torturing mother onto her, saying that she could understand "that it made sense ... that he would expect me to be another mother who would use knowledge from books to torture him and make him feel his authentic experience did not matter, what mattered was what the doctor ordered". And the analyst reports the important observation that the patient was now hearing her interpretation: "it felt like we were listening to each other in a different way". Important transformations could be seen in his ability to sustain a love relationship, despite his fears, which had been his reason for entering analysis.

Conclusions about therapeutic action in the analysis of Mr. B

Mr. B's presenting complaints included fears of being "invisible", and worries about his "relationships breaking up". Between these two conscious ideas lay a whole world of split-off and repressed experiences, repeated but not known. Dr. Goodman's presentation of the case makes clear that the mother's failure to contain affects and hostile impulses in the patient's childhood led to his excessive and unsuccessful use of projection as a means of attempted communication. The parental "object" was experienced as unable or unwilling to contain and transform the infant's unmentalised states (Bion, 1959, 1962) and was experienced as attacking the child's self in a destructive manner (Rosenfeld, 1983) as if willfully misunderstanding the infant/child's projections: "He produced an agonising deadness in me. It took time for us to together face the remnants in his mind of the experiences and internal fantasies about having been so often a thing-baby".

In Mr. B's unconscious scenarios and impulses, being in a relationship meant submitting to cruelty or perpetrating a sadistic revenge. In the ending phase of the analysis, the analyst brought Mr. B, ineluctably, into a partially interpreted and partially enacted sadomasochistic relationship with herself. Therapeutic action was achieved through bringing the patient's split-off experiences into the analytic setting, through the analyst's self-analysis of the patient's projective identifications, and through putting into words the patient's transference fantasies through analysis of countertransference fantasies. Mr. B now became conscious that he was afraid of being tortured and annihilated, and aware of his impulses to torture or to annihilate the analyst, but also conscious of "tender feelings".

Goodman's paper concludes with a modest but condensed articulation of the changes the analysis facilitated in Mr. B.

> Much discovery of the depths of his mind, and of mine, took place
> as he was telling me he was floating or sleepy and we were both
> learning to listen to his deep unconscious. While the "oh no, not

again" was available in his mind when needed, we managed together to sail through often tortured waters finding courage and enlivenment and more space for a "yes" in his mind as well.

Here is a portrait of an analytic couple working together to find the "deep unconscious", to uncover defensive dissociative states (floating or sleepy) and to come to a mutual acceptance ("both listening") of the defensive negations ("oh no, not again") which signified the painful and mind numbing experiences ("tortured waters") which lead to their creation. And a "yes" to the risks of love emerged.

I have explored several technical approaches which resulted in therapeutic action in the analysis, approaches which significantly increased Mr. B's capacity for symbolisation, a new tolerance for discordant affects rather than disavowal, a capacity to imagine a more loving primal scene, and thus a capacity for being in relationship (Britton, 1989; Freedman & Russell, 2003). Changes in Mr. B's psychic functioning were facilitated by periods of close attention to countertransference fantasies and feelings, followed by powerful integrative interpretations some of which arose spontaneously out of the long and somewhat painful countertransference experience and observation. The analyst experienced, understood, and put into words, the impact of the early trauma on the infantile unconscious sexual fantasies. Through the many patient-generated enactments, the analyst's ability to digest, reverberate with, and return affects and fantasies provoked in her (Bion, 1959; Birkstead-Breen, 2009), the analytic work gradually led to the owning of childhood experience, including suffering, by the patient. This produced reduction of his narcissistic and sadomasochistic defences. In the therapeutic ending of the analysis, Mr. B came to know emotionally that he was not "invisible" to his analyst, and that sexual and loving relationships could hold together.

References

Berliner, B. (1958). The role of object relations in moral masochism. *Psychoanalytic Quarterly*. 27: 38–56.

Bion, W. R. (1959). Attacks on linking. *International Journal of Psycho-Analysis*, 40: 308–315.

Bion, W. R. (1962). The psycho-analytic study of thinking. *International Journal of Psycho-Analysis*, 43: 306–310.

Birksted-Breen, D. (2009). "Reverberation time", dreaming and the capacity to dream. *International Journal of Psycho-Analysis*, 90: 35–51.

Brenman, M. (1952). On teasing and being teased: And the problem of "moral masochism". *Psychoanaytic. Study of the Child*, 7: 264–285.

Britton, R. (1989). The missing link: Parental sexuality in the Oedipus complex. In: *The Oedipus Complex Today*. London: Karnac Books, 1989.

Chasseguet-Smirgel, J. (1991a). Sadomasochism in the perversions: Some thoughts on the destruction of reality. *Journal of the American Psychoanalytic Association*, 39: 399–415.

Chasseguet-Smirgel, J. (1991b). Review of *The Oedipus Complex Today: Clinical Implications*, ed. J Steiner. *International Journal of Psycho-Analysis*, 72: 727–30.

Coen, S. J. (1998). Perverse defenses in neurotic patients. *Journal of the American Psychoanalytic Association*, 46: 1169–1194.

Faimberg, H. (2005). Après-coup. *International Journal of Psycho-Analysis*, 86: 1–6.

Freedman, N. & Russell, J. (2003). Symbolization of the analytic discourse. *Psychoanalysis and Contemporary Thought*, 26: 39–87.

Freud, S. (1915). The Unconscious. *S. E., 14*: 159–215.

Freud, S. (1938). Splitting of the Ego in the Process of Defence. *S. E., 23*: 271–278.

Grinberg, L. (1987). Dreams and acting out. *Psychoanalytic Quarterly*, 56: 155–176.

Grossman, W. I. (1991). Pain, aggression, fantasy, and concepts of sadomasochism. *Psychoanalytic Quarterly*, 60: 22–51.

Hurvich, M. (2003). The place of annihilation anxieties in psychoanalytic theory. *Journal of the American Psychoanalytic Association*, 51: 579–616.

Rosenfeld, H. (1978). Notes on the psychopathology and psychoanalytic treatment of some borderline patients. *International Journal of Psycho-Analysis*, 59: 215–221.

Rosenfeld, H. (1983). Primitive object relations and mechanisms. *International Journal of Psychoanalysis*. 64: 261–267.

CHAPTER TEN

Discussion of the case of Mr. B

Terrence McBride

A dramatic narrative unfolds as Dr. Goodman describes the process of the analysis of Mr. B. A mother-child relationship that was characterised by pervasive elements of sadomasochism had been internalised and preserved within Mr. B's psyche. This became a central aspect of his internal object relations world which was revived, and aggressively defended against, in the transference-countertransference interaction between Mr. B and Dr. Goodman. The strength of Dr. Goodman's presentation lies in her description of both neurotic and characterologic features, each containing multiple aspects in combination with one another. This provides ample opportunity for an in-depth clinical study of the elements of sadomasochism in this case.

Mr. B was feeling desperate when he originally came to see Dr. Goodman for help. The precipitant was the break-up of a relationship, which was the latest in a series of break-ups. His complaints of feelings of sadness, despair, and emptiness, and fears of being invisible to others, were symptoms of his profound depression. His condition aroused deep concern in Dr. Goodman. He had suffered the same depression after the breakup of his marriage ten years earlier. His reaction marked the significance of separation and loss in his psychic functioning. However, it was the sadomasochistic nature of his object relations that predominated, which raised the question of the connection between the two. This would become manifest in the transference in Mr. B's unconsciously replicated sadomasochistic relationship with his preoedipal mother, and in Dr. Goodman's countertransference. Her countertransference became the primary source of information for understanding and interpreting the constantly fluctuating sadomasochistic dynamic in the analytic relationship.

A prominent aspect in this case is the mixture and interplay of both oedipal and preoedipal issues in the varying kinds and degrees of disturbance in Mr. B's personality. His symptoms seem to represent different levels of development. For example, his sadness and despair represent an oedipal capacity to mourn the loss of his relationship, but his sense of emptiness and fears of being invisible seem to indicate a sense of a defective preoedipal self/object structure. Throughout the case, Mr. B presents both a classical picture of instinctual dynamics, with characteristic defences against oedipal conflict, and regression from the oedipal stage to a fixation at the anal phase. At the same time, there is the appearance of a primitive internal mother-child object relationship that includes issues ranging from difficulties with separation and difference, and accompanying separation anxiety, to fluctuating sadomasochistic interactions with intense annihilation anxiety.

The major developmental task of the oedipal period is the navigation and resolution of the vicissitudes of oedipal wishes and triangular object relationships which involve complex feelings of love, competition, rivalry and lust. The terror of castration accounts for the relinquishment of oedipal strivings, and the repression of infantile sexuality with the passing of the Oedipus complex. A neurotic outcome of oedipal conflict results in symptom formation.

The most important characteristic of the preoedipal period is the almost total dependency on the primary maternal object for the infant's needs, affect regulation, and security. According to Greenspan (1977), the essential tasks of the preoedipal period are the establishment and internalisation of object relationships and the beginning of their integration into internal object and self representations. This contributes to a relative sense of constancy and to the capacity to separate from the primary object. The outcome is a sense of separateness from the real maternal object which permits the move from a dyadic relationship to the complicated triangular relationships of the oedipal period. The primary focus is on the early mother-child relationship, the nature of which determines the outcome. A pathological outcome of the preoedipal period presents a very different clinical picture from that of the oedipal period, including a lack of object constancy, splitting, and other developmentally primitive defence mechanisms, limited affect states, and a limited capacity for emotional relating to objects.

In Dr. Goodman's description of her understanding of Mr. B's internal psychic functioning, she juxtaposes several oedipal and preoedipal features which infer both instinct and object relations theoretical models. Some illustrations of the conflation of the psychodynamic forces of oedipal and preoedipal elements in Mr. B's psychic organisation are his "fear of annihilation/castration"; his "issues of autonomy and separateness ... coalesced around a regressive use of anal stage organisation"; and Dr. Goodman's "hypothesis about his idealising, searching for the phallic woman, [and] terrors about difference". Some examples of obsessional traits in Mr. B are his preoccupation with saving money, his almost ritualistic way of managing his feeling of being taken advantage of, his practice of making a list of necessary traits in the women he dated, his perfectionistic requirements for finding a potential partner, and especially the anal sadism aspect of his devaluation of women. Examples of preoedipal features are his need for care and nurturing, feelings of helplessness, wishes for merger, and fears of repeated disappointment, loss and abandonment, interspersed with powerful sadomasochistic fantasies.

The prevailing view today is that multiple theoretical and technical perspectives are necessary to understand, interpret, and deal with what Bolognini (2009) has referred to as "complex clinical cases" to describe the mixed psychopathologies of different developmental levels. Regardless of early deprivations and deficits, development progresses forward with a layering of new organisations on earlier ones. In the complex patterns of oedipal and preoedipal object relations there is no sharp distinction between them. Nevertheless, Novick and Novick (1995) state that it is important to distinguish oedipal from preoedipal disturbance because, as indicated above, the developmental tasks of each period are different, the nature of the object relations are different (dyadic part-object relationships versus triadic whole-object relationships), and the nature of the pathology is different. Each situation indicates a need for different technical/clinical strategies necessary for effective treatment. Regarding the interface within the oedipal and preoedipal periods, Greenspan (1977) addresses the analyst's "difficult clinical task of determining the developmental level of a patient's personality functioning" (p. 381). In his opinion, a way of understanding the oedipal-preoedipal dilemma is to view the periods between drives and object relations as two interrelated lines of development, each in interaction with the other, usually with one predominating over the other depending on the nature of the drive/object relations configuration. Throughout the clinical material the description of Mr. B's preoedipal world evokes a mother-child relationship in which the origins and functions of his sadomasochistic object relations were central and seemed to outweigh indications of oedipal dynamics. Of note is the absence of his father in the clinical material except for the one reference to him during latency.

While the Novicks (1995) say that sadomasochism has determinants from all levels of development, they present clinical evidence that it has its origins in the preoedipal experience of the mother-child relationship. Sadomasochism begins in infancy, is altered by each subsequent phase, and derivatives of each phase serve multiple ego functions with multiple determinants. In their view, a prime function of sadomasochism is the retention of the maternal object tie. It is an adaptive alternative to the child becoming aware of the maternal sadism and his internal conflicts about his own destructive wishes (p. 43). As such, the sadomasochistic relationship inhibits the separation process and interferes with the normal development of object constancy, one of the functions of which is the promotion of the capacity to separate. The child cannot do without the maternal object and must maintain the sadomasochistic relationship to retain the object and avoid the terror of separation and separateness. These views seem particularly applicable in Mr. B's case. In his mind, separation and separateness represented abandonment and/or annihilation. The enactments that would develop in the transference-countertransference interaction with Dr. Goodman indicate a connection between his sadomasochistic fantasies and his issues of separation and abandonment/annihilation in his preoedipal relationship with his mother. It should be noted that conceptually, separation anxiety (Fairbairn) and annihilation anxiety (Winnicott) are different. For Fairbairn (1943a), within a state of infantile dependent relationship with the mother, separation represents the inability to survive (pp. 275–277). For Winnicott (1956) an excess of the maternal failure of impingement "... produces not frustration but a *threat of annihilation*" (my italics), due to the interruption of the "going on being" of the infant (1956).

This reveals a deeper, more profound level of disturbance than issues of oedipal sexuality. The separation and annihilation anxieties that Mr. B defended against seem to predominate over his incestuous desires and fears of castration. Discussions of sexuality, including Dr. Goodman's reaction to his devaluing comments about the women he was dating, seem secondary to the countertransference issues of the mother-child struggles. His defences were directed primarily at the internalised bad objects of his infantile experience, within a fundamentally infantile dependent object relationship, rather than instinctual impulses. His early childhood need for comfort, safety, and merger in his relationship with his mother on the one hand, and the threat of damage to his maternal object and/or himself on the other, left him with an inner self in a state of depression, despair, futility, and deadness in his emotional existence. The sadomasochistic fantasies from his experience of his mother's sadism induced a fear of separation and loss which was unbearable. Mr. B's object relations conflicts between his sadomasochistic strivings and his fears of reprisals and loss predominated over oedipal issues. This highlights the primary area of Mr. B's disturbance.

The sadomasochistic motif is pervasive throughout the case. Dr. Goodman introduced this theme with the paradoxical title "Hurting Love." In Mr. B's internal world of giving and receiving pain, to be loved was to be hurt and to love was to hurt back. His entry into analysis triggered a profound transference regression to a terrifying object relations state with multiple images of internalised units of self and other. In this internal world, unconscious fantasy aspects of himself and his internal objects contained his conflicted experience of his masochistic appeal for maternal care, as well as the sadistic expression of his aggression for the trauma of his early experience of that care. His aggressive wishes toward his maternal object evoked a fear of destroying her and/or himself, and a need to protect the fantasy aspects of his internal mother and of himself. Given the reality of this area of Mr. B's inner life (a mixture of pleasure and pain, desire and indifference, love and hate, hurt and rage, and ultimately apathy and death), the metaphor of sailing through the waters of his infantile fantasy world was fraught with turbulence through the sadomasochistic storms that were to reemerge in the analysis.

Tellingly, Dr. Goodman begins her essay with the refrain of dread— "Oh no, not again"—to indicate the ordeal of her entry into the repetition of Mr. B's sadomasochistic struggle. This entailed issues of power and control, questions of who would hurt whom, who would attack whom, and who would annihilate whom. Dr. Goodman gives several examples of the ongoing struggles that ensued between them. One example describes her susceptibility at times to the regressive pull from Mr. B of wanting to merge into his sleepiness and the "agonising deadness" that it would produce in her. At other times she wanted to "force life" into him or had fantasies of "penetrating" him with the excitement that was missing in him. Once the regressive transference deepened, Mr. B's depressed mood gave way to a state of affective deadness which rendered him virtually unavailable for emotional contact. On a manifest level he used withdrawal, disavowal, and frank depreciation in his recalcitrant resistance to Dr. Goodman's attempts to engage him in a meaningful relationship. His devaluation of her, as with all the women in his life, contained the muted aggression of his "x"-ing out any relational value. The disdain and disregard that Mr. B expressed through his depiction of Dr. Goodman as a gasoline attendant, or a wooden Indian in front of a cigar store, was a depersonalisation of her. But as he regressed to a more primitive level of development it was the agonising effect of the deadness itself on Dr. Goodman that revealed its covert sadistic nature. Despite his devaluation of her, through her countertransference she was still able to discern, beneath the deadness, the deeper nature of the regressed world into which Mr. B had reverted. A need for connectedness to the maternal object/analyst was aroused in him which represented a paradox of dual function. Entry into analysis provided him with a refuge against the pain and desperation of the loss of his relationship with his girlfriend, which represented a return to the loving, nurturing mother/analyst. However, since the transference was a link to the object of the past, it also meant the entry into the dangerous infantile world of his own sadomasochistic urges and those of his internal mother/analyst. As a result, he had to control the depth of the attachment to his new object in order to keep in repression the core regressive sadomasochistic fantasies and their accompanying intense affect states. He had to keep Dr. Goodman at a distance "to prevent recognition of [the] direct connection with the original longed for and feared object" (Newman, 1999, p. 257).

The genesis of the sadomasochism in Mr. B's infantile world is significant because it reveals its roots and the process of its development. There are many factors that influence the outcome of early developmental experience. The meaning of any particular developmental experience may result from perceptions of the interaction with the parents based on the child's needs and may have little to do with the actual interaction between parent and child. On the other hand, there are strong indications of actual early mother-child struggles in Mr. B's experience with his mother. Mr. B gave Dr. Goodman examples of his early childhood experiences, one that was told to him by his aunt, of being "kept in his highchair until he had eaten what his mother wanted him to eat" and his memory "as a toddler [being given] an enema every three days if he was not producing a bowel movement". His aunt's witnessing the highchair event lends some credibility to the reality of his experience. Meyer (2011) cites Stoller (1975) who "... suggested that [the presence of] sadomasochism reflect[s] actual cruelty inflicted in childhood" (p. 317). Dr. Goodman refers to these as "screen scenes", similar to screen memories, of his experience of excessive severity of frustration and overstimulating aggression between him and his mother. To allay getting too caught up in the throes of the transference-countertransference interaction, Dr. Goodman used these screen scenes to anchor herself, presuming that he was conveying to her his experience of representations of his relationship with his mother.

Whatever the actual exchange between Mr. B and his mother, there are indications of force with multiple images of maternal sadism in the mother-child relationship in his unconscious mind. His state of infantile dependence on his mother for the satisfaction of his needs put him in a position of masochistic submission and surrender. Fairbairn (1946) asserts that the lack of maternal response to the child's need for love constitutes trauma. The consequent state of helplessness, frustration, and rage results in aggression. The Novicks (1995) extend Fairbairn's point by considering "the sadomasochistic fantasy as a whole" to be a derivative of aggression, continuously oscillating between externalising aggression in the form of a sadistic fantasy directed toward the object, and turning it against the self when it becomes the masochistic object of the object's sadism (p. 25). In addition, despite Fairbairn's assertion that aggression is provoked, there is a certain quality of innate aggression in Mr. B that seemed to contribute to the sadomasochistic interaction between him and his mother. The oral stage infant protesting his mother's efforts to make him eat, the rebellious toddler opposing her control by withholding his bowels, and the latency child rejecting the baseball glove because it wasn't the one he wanted, are all signs of an element of opposition on his part that infers a certain power struggle between Mr. B and his parents. This raises the question of a genetic predisposition on his part. But whether endogenous or provoked by his mother's intrusiveness and control, the screen scenes of her sadistic behaviour toward him (highchair imprisonment/enema impingement) indicate that his experience was traumatic.

Referring to the phenomenon of oscillation in sadomasochistic relationships, Fairbairn (1946) notes that masochistic surrender and sadistic retaliation alternate, depending on the prevailing mode in the interaction in any given moment (p. 44). Consequent to Mr. B's unconscious sadomasochistic object relations structure, the power of the fantasies created a corresponding interchange between him and his mother/analyst. The oscillation from masochism to sadism converted his helpless position into one of "triumph, mastery and revenge" (Stein, 2005, p. 780), and back again. This pattern was reflected in Dr. Goodman's countertransference experience through her own oscillating masochistic and sadistic fantasies between receiving and giving pain. Mr. B's oscillation between love and hate, sadism and masochism, and active and passive modes of interaction reflected the power struggles between them. The dynamic of the sadomasochistic interaction seemed to stem from frustration, rage, and sadistic provocation and/ or retaliation, each fueling the other. There were elements of both in each role. It is complicated by the fact that his mother, as well as being the object of his ruthless destructive attacks, was also the source of supplies for his need for nurturing, love, and protection. The split in his sadomasochistic world was the result of his need to keep separate the dialectical opposites of good and bad self, and good and bad object, which was necessary for protection against alternating attacks on the self in the masochistic mode and on the object in the sadistic mode. Racker's (1968) exposition of complementary identification with internal objects, in this case sadism, and concordant identification with the patient's self, masochism, is helpful for understanding the oscillation between the two. When Mr. B induced masochistic fantasies in Dr. Goodman, she was identified with his enduring masochistic self. When she had sadistic fantasies, she was identified with the internal maternal object in relation to Mr. B's victim self. This pattern of oscillation reflects the internalisation of the infantile sadomasochistic object relationship as a whole (Novicks' term, noted above) between Mr. B and his mother. Fairbairn (1946) suggests that relationships with internalised bad objects are usually of a sadomasochistic nature, *"with a bias on the masochistic side"* (p. 79, my italics). Regardless of the sadistic side of his struggle, Mr. B was basically in a masochistic position due to his helplessness vis-à-vis his mother.

A striking theme in this case is the way in which Mr. B's tenacious defensive manoeuvress against the anxiety of his sadomasochistic strivings were configured and manifested in the transference. Prior to coming to Dr. Goodman he was already in a regressed state due to the loss of his relationship. He had unconscious transference feelings from the beginning, despite his denials when Dr. Goodman raised them. Fairbairn (1951) explains that "the patient is not slow to sense that the therapeutic endeavour threatens to reproduce the situation against which his defences are mobilized" (p. 166). He also says that regression originates from unsatisfactory object relationships during the oral phase when the child does not feel really loved as a person in his own right by his mother and that his own love is not valued and accepted by her. This leaves the child fixated on the mother which is characterised by extreme dependence, and makes him vulnerable to the "regressive reactivation of his relations with her" (1941, p. 55). He refers to the spontaneous return of repressed bad objects as a phenomenon of the transference. Further transference regression was prompted by the transition from psychotherapy to the formal beginning of psychoanalysis. Within this deeper state of regression, a powerful unconscious sadomasochistic mother-child relationship was revived. The feelings of sadness, despair, and emptiness that Mr. B had expressed at the beginning of treatment seemed to quickly dissolve and give way to the powerful inner destructive forces within him that had dominated his infantile object world. These forces threatened to break through the repressive barrier against them. His symptoms were an indication that his usual defenses were wearing thin. The weight of his sadomasochistic wishes, fears of the threat of the retaliation or rejection by the object, the destruction and loss of the object, and/or the annihilation of the self, required intensified defensive efforts to regulate his anxiety and to maintain his fragile internal emotional equilibrium. This provoked intense unconscious anxiety which required him to redouble his repressive efforts against it, draining his mind of its life-giving affects. The purpose of this deeper level of repression was to maintain the sadomasochistic fantasies intact, necessary for sustaining the connection with the maternal object, and to protect himself against awareness of the longing, the pain, the hatred, and the dread that they contained.

This massive repression reduced him to the virtual affectless state that had an alexithymic quality that Dr. Goodman described as a state of "deadness" in her countertransference. This was in stark contrast to the sadomasochistic world against which it defended and which was alive and vibrant.

Referring to the concept of alexithymia in Krystal's (1988) theory of affect, the Novicks (1995) say that the sadomasochistic fantasy defends against the complete withdrawal from the object to a state some patients have described as "being dead" (p. 69). In McDougall's (1984) elaboration of the concept, she defines it in part as "... an incapacity to be aware of emotions ... with the defensive function of warding off deep-seated anxieties" (1984, pp. 390–391). In her reconstruction with her patients, she was able to find "... a paradoxical mother-child relationship in which the mother seems to have been out of touch with the infant's emotional needs, yet at the same time has controlled her baby's thoughts, feelings, and spontaneous gestures in a sort of archaic 'double-bind' situation" (p. 391). She asserts that these patients are "... unable to use normal repression [and] must instead have recourse to mechanisms of splitting and projective identification to protect themselves from being overwhelmed by mental pain" (p. 392). According to Grotstein (1986), repression and splitting and projective identification are not mutually exclusive. He reflects Fairbairn's view that repression is used as an instrument of splitting and projective identification. This is a different view of repression from what McDougall calls "normal" repression. It is a primitive repression which in Fairbairn's (1951) view originates in infancy before the emergence of the oedipal stage (p. 174). This repression is not directed against impulses but against intolerably bad internalised objects and the parts of the ego that seek relationships with these internal objects, as well as the memories and impulses associated with them (Fairbairn, 1944, p. 89). The intensity of these defences must reflect the intensity of the sadomasochistic fantasies. In order to secure safety against the multiple threats of these fantasies, Mr. B's original (oedipal) repression had to be augmented by these primitive mechanisms, characteristic of a more regressed state.

The prototype of Mr. B's relationship with his mother included a preponderance of projective identification. It was a manifestation of his regressed primitive state of mind. It pervaded the transference-countertransference interaction between Mr. B and Dr. Goodman. His infantile trauma constituted an experience of being overwhelmed which affected his ability to develop affect tolerance and stimulated the need to resort to the defences of primitive repression, splitting, and projective identification. The projective identification contained the unconscious feelings of the repressed state of his affective experience. Given his state of repression, the communications function of his use of projective identification provided Dr. Goodman with the only means she had to perceive and conceptualise the sadomasochistic aspects of his unconscious mind which were otherwise unavailable. Splitting was inherent in the process. In his state of dissociated deadness, these sadomasochistic elements of Mr. B's internalised infantile mother and of himself were split off and projected into Dr. Goodman. His denial of her as a whole person in his depersonalisation of her, and the oscillations between the sadistic and masochistic modes of interaction with her, are examples of his splitting.

The multiple functions of Mr. B's use of projective identification parallel those commonly identified by Ogden (1982): first, the original function of projective identification, identified by Klein, was from his need to ward off painful and threatening sadomasochistic fantasies and their associated affects. Through the evacuation of his sadomasochistic fantasies and their associated feelings he was able to keep these dangerous and intolerable feelings out of consciousness. Their intrusion into Dr. Goodman induced in her a state of mind similar to the one he had more or less successfully eliminated in himself from consciousness. A second function was to maintain a connection to the mother/analyst, at times merging with her and at other times distancing himself from her. A paradox of this was that while the function was to get rid of the unwanted feelings by projecting them into Dr. Goodman, it also maintained a link to her and to the feelings themselves. This affective link enabled Dr. Goodman to experience and interpret the feelings beneath his deadness and to provide a missing, and necessary, container function for his unarticulated sadomasochistic feelings and wishes. A third function was to control and dominate her as a means of his sadomasochistic attacks on her and at the same time to protect himself against the consequences of his attacks. Finally, a fourth function was to communicate his unconscious fantasies and feelings to her as a way to express his repressed sadomasochistic fantasy life and to make it known. This was a primitive, primary process mode of communication, from an inhibition of secondary process functions due to the regression. The overall function of his use of projective identification was to express, control, and master the trauma of his infantile experience, and thereby to provide an outlet as an alternative to consciousness or action.

Mr. B's use of the complex mechanisms and processes of projective identification, and Dr. Goodman's (introjective) receptivity to them, reflected his internal sadomasochistic fantasy world in the transference-countertransference relationship, which constituted a huge ongoing enactment. However, the roles were reversed. Mr. B enacted the role of his mother which put Dr. Goodman in a position similar to the one that he had been as a child (see Stein, 2005, p. 783). Her participation in the enactment as the object to his projections was inevitable. In this regard, her thinking was both shaped and constrained by his powerful influence. Through this means he exerted pressure on her to repeat the original mother-child relationship, inducing her to enact the complementary and/or concordant roles according to the mode of the original object relationship. The repeated enactments of Mr. B's devaluation of her interpretations, the underlying "covert" power struggle between them, his denial of any aggression in his attacks on her, and the helplessness and deadness that she would feel in reaction to his lack of response to otherwise scenes of excitement, stimulation, and passion, required her to tolerate and contain all the intense, painful, and at times even unbearable feelings, that he induced in her.

There were two levels of communication in Mr. B's use of projective identification: the manifest level which expressed very little of what was really going on in his unconscious mind, and the underlying level which expressed the true nature of his sadomasochistic internal world and the affects associated with it. This dual meaning was reflected in the paradoxical nature of the communication function of projective identification. It created a double-bind position for Dr. Goodman, referred to earlier by McDougall (1984), to force her to behave in a way that corresponded to his internal object world, as described above. This was the same double-bind position he had been in with his mother being reflected in the transference-countertransference relationship. It required her to alternate between submitting herself to the effects of Mr. B's projections in order to know and understand his sadomasochistic world, and then to free herself from the entanglements of them to recover and maintain her analytic role. This was a continuous process.

Up to the time that Mr. B announced his decision to stop his analysis after five years, not much appeared to have changed. He had begun to acknowledge some of Dr. Goodman's interpretations, but his complacency and recalcitrance seemed fairly static. No wonder she was shocked by his sudden announcement. The meaning of his involvement with the "short-haired" woman seemed a mystery that remained to be understood. But despite the precipitousness of his announcement, his agreement to continue, albeit at a reduced frequency, was a sign that he was receptive to her influence, in spite of his resistance. As a result, there were several interesting developments in Mr. B's psyche. Foremost, due to "the shock of difference", was his partial emergence from the state of primitive regression and the retrieval of some of his lost affect. His recognition of her "astonishment", along with perhaps a retrospective recognition of his earlier "knee-jerk reactions", opened him up to an awareness of her as a real person with feelings of her own, including her reactions to him as a whole person. At the same time this exemplified their separateness. Not unexpectedly, certain elements of the sadomasochistic nature of his object relations continued to exert themselves in the transference-countertransference interaction, but he was more emotionally present and engaged. The "deadness" was gone! The primitive level of his repression had lifted. This made Mr. B more accessible to insight and integration for a period of more collaborative analytic work. The resistance encountered appears to have been a more expectable amount. The other primitive defences of his previous state of regression, namely, his depersonalisation of her in the transference, his dissociation in the deadness of his repression, the splitting and projective identification as a way of communicating, seem to have dissolved. Higher level defences emerged in their place, for example a more developed level of repression, reaction formation, displacement, and isolation of affect. The residual sadomasochism appeared to be in somewhat sublimated form. Since one of the functions of projective identification was to banish his anxiety, it is not surprising that when he relinquished it, the result was intense anxiety. The question arises about the meaning of this anxiety. Was it from the preconscious recognition of his sadomasochistic aggression that he had repressed for so long? Or was it the emergence of castration anxiety that had been superseded by the annihilation anxiety of his preoedipal sadomasochism? Presumably Mr. B was able to integrate some of his sadomasochistic fantasies into his personality to some extent, resulting in their gradual mitigation and modification in his internal object relations. Winnicott (1950) states that "Patients who need objects for their aggression may desperately attempt to 're-fuse' the erotic impulse with aggressive drive" (p. 217). As a result, the object was not simply a "bad object" suitable for attack, but also the recipient of loving feelings. While there was a lot of talk about separateness and difference, there was also evidence of feelings of ambivalence which was an indication of whole-object relating. A fascinating phenomenon during this period was the nature of the condensation of Mr. B's preoedipal fear of separation and abandonment with his oedipal fear of castration which was noted at the beginning. The issue of "gaps" was a prime example. There was a definite shift in emphasis from preoedipal to oedipal conflict, which was most observable in his castration dreams, particularly the SS torture dream of being burned on his fingers.

The shift in Mr. B's psyche and the change in his conduct in the analysis toward Dr. Goodman seems sudden and dramatic. How can these changes be understood in clinical terms? Earlier in the analysis, Dr. Goodman had wondered about Mr. B's analysability and had had feelings of failure in the face of his formidable resistance. Given the pattern of interaction between them, traditional use of interpretation and insight did not seem useful for the most part. Newman (1999), among others, argues that "… it is how we manage the affects activated within us that eventually helps us to offer the patient an evocative awareness of his or her inner world known through our intense response to it" (pp. 192–193). By making herself available as the object of Mr. B's projections, Dr. Goodman allowed herself to be used by him as an object. This enabled him to return to the core traumatic experience of his relationship with the mother of the past and to experience it in the present within the transference-countertransference relationship. By adhering to the tasks of tolerance, containment, and maintaining a separate, integrated state of mind, even with the powerful pull of his forces of merger, she was able to manage his projections and to use them to know, understand, and articulate to herself the nature of that experience. It was the partial acting out that broke through her containment in the enactment that enabled him to recognise on some level that he was having an impact on her, as he had throughout the previous five years of the analysis. Whereas during the earlier extended sadomasochistic phase of the analysis, Dr. Goodman's subjectivity and personhood had gone unrecognised, the shift in Mr. B's psyche helped him to begin to experience the sense of mutuality that was the key to the intimacy that he both yearned for and feared. Writing about the arduous treatment of perversions, Eshel (2005) maintains that "… the psychic structure of the patient is influenced and changes, in the most essential manner, within the abiding, deep and sustaining connection with the analyst's psyche (p. 1093).

Finally, within the termination period, Mr. B's issue of separation and loss emerged explicitly, the issue that had brought him into analysis in the beginning. In spite of his protests, his difficulty separating was pronounced, at first symptomatically (migraines, nightmares, etc.). Then, there was a beginning acceptance of Dr. Goodman's interpretation of his ambivalence about needing her, and his struggle to relate to her interpretations about his resistance to acknowledging the meaning in his mind of their difference and separateness, as well as of the significance of the impending separation itself. One of the functions of his sadomasochism had been to maintain the illusion of no recognition of difference or separateness; that is, as a link to the early maternal love object/analyst and as a defence against separation and loss. It was through the working out and working through of his sadomasochistic conflicts through his analytic transference relationship with an actual "good object" that the return of the repressed bad objects could "… be made to serve a therapeutic aim" (Fairbairn, 1946). As Dr. Goodman became a whole object with real feelings in Mr. B's mind, she was transformed from a "wooden Indian in front of a cigar store" to the woman in the dream who was greeting him at the entrance to a museum, with all that that portends. Above all, Mr. B's experience in his relationship with Dr Goodman provided an alternative experience to the "hurting love" that he had endured in his relationship with his preoedipal mother.

It would seem that an indication for the termination of Mr. B's analysis would be a relative degree of separation from his attachment to his internal mother and the internalisation of the good analyst/object. The process of separation from Dr. Goodman would facilitate that.

This case is a tribute to Dr. Goodman's commitment and endurance. Thank you to Nancy Goodman for the opportunity to study and discuss her case, and to the editors of the book for the invitation to be a discussant of this very fascinating case.

References

Bolognini, S. (2009). Real wolves and fake wolves: alternating between repression and splitting in complex clinical cases. Presentation, Los Angeles Institute and Society for Psychoanalytic Studies, 9 May 2009.

Eshel, O. (2005). Pentheus rather than Oedipus: On perversion, survival and analytic "presencing". *International Journal of Psycho-analysius*, 86: 1071–1097.

Fairbairn, R. (1941). A revised psychopathology of the psychoses and psychoneuroses. In: *Psychoanalytic Studies of the Personality*. London: Routledge & Kegan Paul, 1986.

Fairbairn, R. (1943a). The war neuroses—their nature and significance. In: *Psychoanalytic Studies of the Personality*. London: Routledge & Kegan Paul, 1986.

Fairbairn, R. (1943b). The repression and the return of bad objects. In: *Psychoanalytic Studies of the Personality*. London: Routledge & Kegan Paul, 1986.

Fairbairn, R. (1944). Endopsychic structure considered in terms of object-relationships. In: *Psychoanalytic Studies of the Personality*. London: Routledge & Kegan Paul, 1986.

Fairbairn, R. (1946). Object-relations and dynamic structure. In: *Psychoanalytic Studies of the Personality*. London: Routledge & Kegan Paul, 1986.

Fairbairn, R. (1951). A synopsis of the development of the author's views regarding the structure of the personality. In: *Psychoanalytic Studies of the Personality*. London: Routledge & Kegan Paul, 1986.

Greenspan, S. I. (1977). The oedipal-pre-oedipal dilemma: a reformulation according to object relations theory. *International Review of Psychoanalysis*, 4: 381–391.

Grotstein, J. (1986). *Splitting and Projective Identification*. Northvale, NJ: Jason Aronson.

Krystal, H. (1988). *Integration and Self-Healing*. Hillsdale, NJ: Analytic Press.

McDougall, J. (1984). The "dis-affected" patient: reflections on affect pathology. *Psychoanalytic Quarterly*, 53: 386–409.

Meyer, J. (2011). The development and organizing function of perversion: the example of transvestism. *International Journal of Psycho-Analysis*. 92: 311–332.

Newman, K. (1999). The usable analyst. *The Annual of Psychoanalysis*, 26: 175–184.

Novick, J. & Novick, K. K. (1995). *Fearful Symmetry: The Development and Treatment of Sadomasochism*. Northvale, NJ: Jason Aronson.

Ogden, T. (1982). *Projective Identification and Psychotherapeutic Technique*. New York: Analytic press.

Racker, H. (1968). *Transference and Countertransference*. New York: International Universities Press.

Stein, R. (2005). Why perversion? "False love" and the perverse pact. *International Journal of Psycho-Analysis*, 86: 775–799.

Stoller, R. (1975). *Perversion: The Erotic Form of Hatred*. New York: Pantheon.

Winnicott, D. W. (1950). Aggression in relation to emotional development. In: *Through Paediatrics to Psychoanalysis*. New York: Basic Books.

Winnicott, D. W. (1956). Primary maternal preoccupation. In: *Through Paediatrics to Psychoanalysis*. New York: Basic Books.

PART III

CASE PRESENTED BY ANDREA GREENMAN AND DISCUSSIONS

CHAPTER ELEVEN

Eating for emptiness, eating to kill: sadomasochism in a woman with bulimia

Andrea Greenman
(I would like to express my appreciation to the late
Dr. Irving Steingart)

Mariah entered treatment in mid-life because of concerns about her bulimia and the impact this was having on her marriage and family. Daily vomiting since adolescence had eroded her teeth down to the gum line, threatening her health and shocking her into seeking help. Troubled by a sense of emotional vacancy in her relationship with her husband, she was continuously aware of him as a critical presence, and did not feel free unless she was out of his sight.

Initially, she began twice-weekly psychotherapy. After one year of treatment, she agreed to move into psychoanalysis, three sessions per week. At first, she would not agree to the fourth session, but, during her fourth year of treatment, she assumed a fourth hour. The process material I am going to present in this paper took place during this transitional year as we both began to develop an appreciation for the virulence of the sadomasochistic dynamic which marked her life and to enter actively into our relationship. I am grateful to Mariah for giving me permission to publish this material.

History

Mariah was born in a Latin American country, the only child of parents who emigrated shortly before the onset of war. Her father was absent for an extended period of time between her second and third birthday, travelling for a lucrative import-export business. Starting from when he returned home, when she was three, Mariah was regularly beaten by her father. Using his hands or a belt which was sometimes placed beside her at the table, he would beat her; most often the precipitant to the beatings was an angry interaction between Mariah and her mother over her refusal to eat. She felt her mother instigated the beatings and never attempted to stop or subdue the father. The beatings stopped when Mariah was around ten, for reasons which remain unclear, but angry, punitive interactions continued between her and her parents throughout adolescence.

Mariah experienced her father as a "cipher", someone who, with no mind of his own, was doing as her mother wished. Aside from these beatings, she had little contact with him. He owned his own business and would come home at the end of the day withdrawn and unavailable.

Mother was a bad-tempered, mean-spirited woman, who, immersed in her own egocentrism, forced everyone around her to cater to her idiosyncratic and unending needs. In the course of their present-day visits, she often expressed aggressive and critical comments about Mariah's clothing, taste, and family members. At the same time, what could also occur is that the mother might seem bereft and abandoned, expressing accusatory and self-pitying feelings. She was possessive, wanting all of her daughter's attention for herself. For example, Mariah made a visit to her parents' home in honour of her mother's birthday, bringing an expensive gift for the occasion. She spent the entire weekend with her parents, however made a brief telephone call to say hello to an acquaintance in a neighbouring town. Later in the day, she discovered her mother crying and when she inquired about the tears, her father accused her of not being sensitive to her mother's feelings by making the phone call. Couldn't she spend the entire time with them, for once?

Mariah slept in a crib in her parents' bedroom until age five. She remembers often being confined to her crib until very late in the morning while her parents were asleep, and may have been exposed to parental intercourse. She describes herself as partially existing in an imaginary world throughout much of her childhood, engaging in continuous daydreaming and interacting in her mind with an imaginary companion. She would come home to an empty house, feeling both lonely and relieved that her mother was not at home. She would do art work, by herself, feeling lost and empty.

She recalled, at the age of sixteen, lying in her mother's bed talking. When her mother tried to embrace her, she felt disgusted and suffocated, and couldn't wait to get away. As an adult, although a frequent flier, she would become claustrophobic if she could not sit on the aisle and also described a panic attack she had when scuba diving for the first time. She thought she was going to suffocate and die. Recurrent dreams throughout childhood of sinking and drowning in quicksand painfully reproduce her anxiety about being suffocated and annihilated.

After an awkward adolescence, with few friends, at the age of eighteen, she was a counselor in a summer camp and gained eighteen pounds in eight weeks. While at camp, she had an angry interaction with one of her campers, slapping the child. Subsequently, she was not asked to return. When she came home, she began her bulimic cycle, eating to excess, then vomiting everything she had taken in. She lost weight, began to buy her own clothing, and realised that she could gain social acceptance based on her appearance. Control of her weight now became a crucial tool, reinforcing the bulimia which persisted on a daily basis, even during her pregnancies, from age eighteen throughout her life.

She attended a local college, and met her husband almost immediately, marrying him as soon as she finished college. Mariah became pregnant with her first child soon after getting married.

She abused diet pills throughout these years of her marriage and in addition forged a prescription which she used for many years until given a warning by the pharmacist. She also shoplifted into her thirties and didn't stop until she was caught by a security guard. She was a compulsive shopper and withheld information from her husband about the debts she accumulated, into many thousands of dollars.

Process of treatment

Mariah was a chic woman who devoted much attention to her clothing, her hair, and her make-up, all of which were expensive and the height of fashion, yet simultaneously presented herself as sensible, someone who had her values and priorities straight in life; someone to whom her friends turned for advice. This created a favourable impression in me and I was pleased when we began working together. Initially, I found myself responding positively to this intelligent, attractive, and articulate woman. Her thoughts were complex and interesting, uttered in a highly expressive, even dramatic, tone of voice. I found this engaging as we met throughout the first few weeks of treatment. After several months, however, the first impression she had created of being a well related, personable woman began to shift and her intensely emotional presentation during sessions began to impress me as an attempt to distract both of us from contact with her inner world. Every time we met, I got the impression of a high-speed train, rushing toward one insight after another within the concentrated period of our meetings, leaving me with the feeling that I would have to speak up forcefully in order to get heard. I chose not to interrupt her, but for the most part simply to listen.

Based on the intense nature of what seemed to be her highly cathartic experience in our sessions, I would have expected to see dramatic change of some sort. However, this way of communicating persisted without change and over the next few months I found myself beginning to feel impatient with what seemed to be a static element in our relationship. It became apparent that there was no change in any of her life patterns, but rather an intensification of symptoms, and indeed, on my part, a frustrating awareness that there was no deepening, no connecting, no real relationship growing and developing between us. Mariah spoke so quickly and volubly during the sessions that she left little room for my comments, and although she expressed polite appreciation for those comments I did make, she seemed to work with them in only a cursory way. She did not express any curiosity about me or about my thoughts.

Although I was aware of this flat quality in our interaction, I decided against bringing this up at this early point in the treatment, because I sensed that she would find any comments addressing our interaction not only extremely wounding but also, more importantly, perplexing. She had earlier informed me that she left a previous treatment after several months because the therapist kept referring to their "relationship" and she could not understand the point of this. Although I felt constrained and restricted in my freedom of speech, I was aware of the thought that I would need to actively restrain Mariah in order to be heard. Even then, I felt, she would not be able to take my words in with comprehension.

Throughout the following months, Mariah related information about her history and current relationships with her parents, husband, children, and business partner. She drew a picture of herself as a displaced person, seemingly connected with many friends, relatives, and business associates, yet inwardly anxious, frightened, and withdrawn. She described herself turning to food, secretly, on a nightly basis to establish a warm, private, special place for herself which she could not find anywhere in relationships with people. Any feelings she expressed about me verbally continued to be super-rational in nature: I was nice, kind, and attempting to be helpful. However, over the ensuing months of treatment, it became clear that Mariah was intensely involved in binge eating on a nightly basis, gorging herself and then vomiting in an act that contained many emotions that she felt unable to label, identify, or acknowledge to herself, let alone articulate freely and directly in her relationships, including her relationship with me. The sense of constraint that was present for both of us, albeit in different ways, made it difficult for us to connect on a genuine emotional level, creating an atmosphere between us that I began to experience as arid and unreal.

Mariah would leave on frequent vacations, taking as much as ten days off every six weeks, cancel sessions on her return, and come back and eat, expressing shame about her bingeing and anxiety that she had angered me by leaving when we resumed meeting. She began to reveal to me the way she was living including choosing food over people, addictive eating, and anticipated punishment for these experiences. She told me how she kept a bag of sucking candies with her at all times, so that she could fill her mouth and create a private space for herself, feeling emotionally detached even while apparently engaged in working with her partner. The sucking candy in her mouth created a buffer for her and relieved her to some extent of the sense of impingement she felt each time her partner spoke.

Together with her use of food, she would develop an experience of a very cruel, punitive, and unforgiving other whom she saw both in me and in her husband, leading her to withdraw from contact or interaction. Since these experiences had not previously been revealed to anybody and were so alien from the way Mariah had initially presented herself, it confirmed my impression that her social façade was giving way as she became more genuinely involved in the treatment, and, after one year of treatment, I suggested that she enter into an analysis to which she readily agreed. However, she would only agree to increase the frequency of her sessions to three times per week as opposed to the four which I suggested. Although she stated that she could not ask her husband to pay for an additional session, it seemed clear that the more compelling issue was her need to assert her autonomy and protect herself from impingement by me by regulating the frequency of our interaction.

In the session following our agreement about the new procedure involving her use of the couch three times a week, Mariah told me a dream. She was Cleopatra, lying on her back on an elaborately orna-mented ceremonial barge, located at a fancy hotel, similar to the kind of place she stayed on her frequent vacations. She was about to begin a journey. Sitting behind her, at her head, was a dark-skinned man, who was both seductive and sinister at the same time. Her associations contained the thought that she was about to begin an analytic journey, lying on the couch, that seemed as though it would gratify and indulge her, but even though the man seemed to be sympathetic, she wondered why he was dark-skinned. I wondered with her if that indicated mis-trust of me?

The dream pointed out the way she used her involvement with self-care, personal beauty, and self-indulgence to bolster and protect her sense of self and solidify her sense of personal boundary, and marked a move into an intensification of her transference experience with a figure who sadistically and assaultively disregarded her needs. Her subsequent move onto the couch further intensified her transference experience. This dream eloquently condensed the critical conflicts which were to assume centre stage during this early phase of treat-ment, her continuous need to create a relationship with a sadistically violating object where she could experience herself as punitively beaten and assaulted, and her need to flee from that. I wondered if the dream was alerting me to her impulse to defensively flee from an intrapsychic engagement with the analyst by "vacating" the transference, for exam-ple, taking a vacation.

Many transference events indicated that she created an experience where she could see me as hostile, critical, and dangerously violating; judging her for a variety of self-gratifying behaviours: travelling, shop-ping, but especially about her eating. Repeatedly, this sadomasochistic relationship wove itself like a red thread throughout Mariah's experi-ence. As our attention became focused on this constellation both inside and outside of the transference, it became clear that this was, for her, a prime constituent of her behaviour. She would gorge herself on food, and then fear that this would lead to discovery and retaliation from her husband. She would procrastinate with work, and fear that her partner would be angry at her. She would take frequent vacations, cancelling multiple sessions, and fear reprisal from me. When she was late to a session, which she frequently was, she grew to understand that she wanted to anger me, and push me away. It seemed safer to have me angry with her than happy with her.

Mariah would voraciously and greedily take something in, then get rid of it, then anticipate criticism and rejection. She enacted these experiences again and again seemingly without the ability to reflect on her behaviour; indeed she even found a way to rid herself of insights gained in the sessions. After every session, Mariah would use the bathroom in the office suite. Ostensibly re-doing her make-up, she would spend as much as fifteen minutes in front of the mirror, oblivious to the needs of other patients in the waiting room, both "putting herself together" but also emptying her mind of the contents of the session. She would rid herself of any thoughts of me and leave with no memory of the session.

In a variety of ways, she refused to take me in and I felt that not only my analytic abilities but my very personhood was eradicated by her. In her presence, I often had the uncanny experience of feeling non-existent, an experience which at times filled me with rage and made me want to retaliate. At other times, I felt we were in sync with one another, working well together, and then found it painfully disconcerting when she would arrive half an hour late into the next day's session. Regaling me with tales of an errant taxi driver, or unexpected construction in the street, stories which she had told many times before, it was as though she had forgotten that I was the same intelligent partner she had confided in yesterday, but was now only someone who was dumb enough to be easily duped, who simply needed to be placated. At these times, it felt to me that, like Scheherazade, she was trying to distract me and also entertain me as long as possible so that she could delay the inevitable critical and punitive response for something she had done which was still outside of my awareness (binge eating? binge shopping?). Aware of my internal disturbance as an important source of information, it felt to me that she was trying to push me away as well as elicit a punitive response from me. I became the father who beat her.

Initially struggling with my own conflict over what I experienced as the distressingly aggressive feelings that she elicited in me, I found myself inhibited in my responsiveness because of a concern on my part that my comments would be experienced by her as critical and aggressively hurtful. My own wishes to confront her about her behaviour troubled me because of the sadistic countertransference feelings which occasionally surfaced for me and underlay our interaction, and I periodically felt helpless and enraged, without being able to address these feelings effectively with Mariah. This feeling may have lead me to be overly cautious in articulating my comments, and I think, had I continued to proceed in this manner, would at the same time have confirmed Mariah's fears that I, and our relationship, really were fragile and easily damaged by her aggression.

What was most instructive for me in working with Mariah, was the insight that it was inevitable that comments I made about her behaviour would be assimilated into her sadomasochistic fantasy, confirming her fears that I really was a persecutory, assaulting object, and that I, too, would have to accept and gain a level of comfort with my own sadistic impulses in order to work with her effectively. I learned to use my internal sadistic and masochistic affect as a signal about our relationship and as a powerful interpretive tool, rather than shy away from it. With this insight, the treatment moved into a new level of comfort and familiarity. We both gained greater freedom to acknowledge and speak openly with one another about these issues.

Mariah's sense of reality was insecure. Although never psychotic, her judgment about interpersonal interactions was fraught with so much anxiety, that her assessment of social cues and interpersonal affect was problematic. Her belief in the veridicality of these sadomasochistic experiences led her to experience intense anxiety as she became more deeply immersed in the transference. Because she had lost the security of seeing my face, which helped her in testing her fantasies against reality, she was often convinced that her fears of my hostility were not only real, but represented a mortal danger. Although there were indeed occasional moments of real tension in the room, her fears erased her ability to assess reality and left her engulfed with anxiety. Her fantasy that I would beat her was very real in her mind on a number of occasions. In addition, she feared that I might actually terminate treatment out of frustration and rage at the continuous roadblocks she put up. Conversely, she was so afraid of her own aggression that she felt the need to abase herself, or absent herself rather than let me know she was annoyed with me. What was most helpful in developing and facilitating an analytic process which sustained and deepened the treatment at this point were interpretations which repeatedly clarified for her ways in which she was an active agent in (re-)creating an experience of feeling persecuted. The sound of my voice, comforting for her in its sameness, helped to create an environment in which she could hear my comments as helpful and ultimately friendly, providing useful information to her about her need to create a context in which she could experience herself as being criticised and judged by me, as well as by the other significant individuals in her life.

Slowly and gradually her confusion about the locus of aggression within the relationship yielded to a greater clarity as she became able to own her own rageful and attacking impulses. Over the next years, she began to assess her projections and develop some understanding that these experiences were most often the product of her own internalised world. She became able to evaluate the reliability of her projections; while continuing to engage in sadomasochistic enactment, she began to develop the sense that because of some internal prompting, she was repeatedly motivated to initiate interactions where she could experience herself as being beaten, continuously re-enacting her childhood experience of being beaten by her father, incited by a mother who could not tolerate her daughter's needs for age-appropriate separation, differentiation, and individuation. With insight, she realised that beatings were the only form of love she had received from her father; that to her they were a sign she was noticed, that he cared. She realised that her ability to incite him to lose his temper made her feel powerful and special. Without the beatings, she feared that there would have been a deep emotional void in her relationship with him. With me too, her sense that she could experience me as angry with her made her feel that she mattered.

Mariah shifted into taking on the role of the violating aggressor. Once, she "forgot" her sunglasses, leaving them behind on the couch. Several minutes later, after the next patient had entered the office, there was a knock on the door; it was Mariah, interrupting the next patient's session to claim her sunglasses. What disturbed me most about the incident was not only the way in which she violated another patient's privacy, but her lack of concern for the other patient and failure to show remorse. When I raised this incident with her, I felt like the violating object, piercing through her bland denial.

As her trust in me deepened over time, she was able to acknowledge that within these sadomasochistic experiences, which often led to associations of sexual violation, she experienced a certain degree of excitement and control which gave her sexual pleasure, a pleasure she was unable to experience either autoerotically or in her sexual relationship with her husband. She experienced her husband's penis as a weapon that could be used to batter and abuse her. As she understood how she frequently turned pleasurable experiences into painful ones, she described the way she clenched her whole body during sex, attempting to create a sensation that was tense and painful, but gave her some pleasure at the same time.

Following upon several years of interpretive work, she was able to see herself as the agent of these sadomasochistic experiences, and acknowledge her own sadistic impulses, which gave her considerable relief. The following vignette dating from a period during her fourth year of treatment illustrates the development of her insight. On one occasion, she entered my office and placed her handbag on my desk, which was not her habit. When I spoke with her about this, which I experienced as a violation of my space, she responded with the following comments:

> Requests that you make are melded together with requests that my father made in the past; that my mother makes in the present. That I never acknowledge, or answer. So all of the rage that I see being heaped on me, time after time, just gets bottled up and has no place to go. So I'm constantly walking around in this state of suppressed rage.

Mariah beautifully captured here the reciprocal experience I often had with her; sitting close-mouthed in an experience of suppressed anger, feeling helpless because I could not find a way to speak with her without giving vent to my wish to hurt and penetrate her.

> And it's all because I see myself as powerless. I don't have to say nothing [sic]. I may sound foolish, but I don't have to say nothing. And what I'm covering up when I say nothing is not so much my anger, but the fact that I'd like to hurt the other person. And that if I let them know that I'm angry they'll see that I want to hurt them. That's what I'm covering up.

Her comments reflected the tensions both of us had been experiencing, the constraints against speech, the fear of our hurtful aggression, and the wish to pierce and violate.

(Analyst: Could you say more about that? What comes to mind about how you want to hurt them?)

First I was going to say I'd want to hurt them, but that's not it. I'd want to stab them. Then I thought what a sexual act it is—it's sort of penetration. I can't let the world know what a horrible person I am.

(Analyst: What thoughts do you have about the sexual connotation?)

The thing that came to mind was when my father hit me, I thought it was some kind of sexual act. Because I was aroused or because I enjoyed it which I don't remember doing at all. I remember being in pain or mortal fear. Somehow I have confused anger and striking out with sex and could have seen the sexual act as one of aggression. Something that somebody does to you out of anger. Because they want to own you. And they want to get inside you so they can control you—make you do and say and be exactly what they want you to be. So if I'm not able to have an orgasm during sex it is really a decision to protect myself, to not let go. To not give the other person access to me. To keep up a barrier. Not to let them take me over ... and so being hit actually felt like I was being raped. I don't know why I confused the two, but I definitely did.

Although Mariah speaks here of a sexual fantasy, and indeed her anxieties regarding penetration entered fully into her sexual life, the fears of violation went far deeper. Mariah's sense of self was so fragile that she feared she could be annihilated at her very core by her sexual partner's entry into her body, and feared that she might destructively attack her partner as well. I experienced just such an attack when she placed her handbag "in my space".

It's funny, my mind is wandering. I think it's too painful to stay on the subject.

(Analyst: Well, I think perhaps it's wandering away from what you felt you wanted to do to me.)

I don't know. Did I want to rape you? Maybe. If I have confused sexual aggression with anger, then that would be the ultimate form of punishment. Like the worst thing I could possibly do to someone. So when I want to think of what I would do to you, I can't think of you as you really are—because that doesn't make any sense. I have to think of who you are, this person sitting there, then you represent everything I would hate. A cold impartial, self-serving individual. I can't imagine who I am thinking about. Yeah, then I would want to get even with you. But how could I rape you? I don't have the equipment. But somehow it's the ultimate form of, I can't think of the word, not molesting but—violation. That's the word. It's the ultimate violation. It's like having no control over— someone taking away the thing that makes you you. And being totally frustrated. Being totally unable to stop them. Having no say. Being pinned down and violated. Did my father know what he was doing to me? No. Didn't matter what the reality was. It was my perception that mattered. So how do you heal and recover after something like that? I guess I just didn't. I just vowed never to let anybody in.

Mariah's decision to wall herself off out of fear of the destructive aspect of her sadistic impulses also defended against the wishes buried in her fantasy about penetrating me and served to keep her guilt-ridden and isolated. As she gained insight into her active role in creating and maintaining her sadomasochistic position, she became less guarded and began to think about how she had lived in a false world, warding off real emotional contact with people. Mariah began to speak about a deeper level of her emotional experience which involved conflicts over her sense of connectedness with others, rather than the more aggressive and paranoid experiences she had been immersed in up to this point. This shift marked the beginning of her ability to move beyond the sado-masochistic defence which prevented access to her deeper, vulnerable core self.

Her psychic space contained an exquisitely vulnerable core, which she felt she had no adequate means of protecting. Contact with other human beings left her feeling overwhelmed and threatened her with a sense of dissolution; she had no secure means of safely and reliably securing her sense of boundedness as an individual. Her reliance on binge eating, binge shopping and self-grooming were all methods of shoring up a very fragile sense of self and her repeated sadomasochistic enactments ensured that others would never get too close.

The following process material, culled from a series of sessions days and weeks apart during the fourth year of treatment, illustrates Mariah's movement through the threshold of sadomasochistic enactment into a deeper level of engagement with her fears of her own consuming sense of need and anxiety about loss of self and engulfment.

As mentioned earlier, the patient was wont to take frequent vacations, sometimes leaving and returning several times inside of two months. Each time she was about to leave, she withdrew from an emotional engagement with me days before her departure, and when she returned, she seemed to have lost the emotional thread of our work and it was as though we had to start anew. She did not voice any feelings about the interruptions in our sessions, and when I asked her, she denied that she had any feeling about it at all. I felt ignored and discarded, and realised that I, as the transference object, was being spit out and evacuated from her inner world, similar to the bulimic way she got rid of her food after a meal. It was easier for Mariah to get rid of me than to feel the emotions associated with loss of our daily contact. My countertransference fantasy was that when she left I was moved into a space where I was enclosed in an impenetrable bubble; it felt lonely, frozen, and isolated.

Oddly paralleling my countertransference experience, when she returned she would tell me about a sense of emotional vacancy she experienced during the time away. Not just a vacation in the sense we typically understand as a chance for rest, relaxation, and pleasure, her vacations constituted an experience of "vacating" the transference, and left her with a sense of internal deadness and emptiness since she had severed any internal connection with me. Often she would describe a deep sense of isolation from her husband as well. Despite the fact that I spoke with Mariah often about the impact of these repeated breaks, I felt that she never really "heard" me and noted again my annoyance at being disregarded and the sense that I would have to speak with her more aggressively in order to "pierce" her resistance.

There came a point when it felt increasingly urgent to "get through" to Mariah since her frequent breaks were threatening the very viability and integrity of the treatment. It became difficult, if not impossible, to establish enough continuity to make the work feel meaningful. I began to realise that I inhibited myself from effectively raising questions about her frequent breaks because to do so felt to me like I was pinning her down, sadistically limiting her autonomy, and even more, inflicting a beating on her, much as her father had beaten her for her refusal to eat. My fear of my own aggression led me to avoid confronting her and served to collude with the real danger that the treatment would be derailed. I realised that I had to confront her to preserve the treatment and that unlike her parents, my aggression was in the service of a battle to protect her growth and health and not, as with her parents, in a life and death struggle to destroy and eradicate her personhood. The following series of segments from sessions several days and weeks apart, will illustrate how the interpretation of this enactment moved the treatment forward.

She had been away for a couple of days, missing sessions, including a session which she cancelled on her return to the city when she returned for the following session:

> I'm just trying to think of where to begin. I had a great weekend at the spa. It was superb. A lot of it had to do with the fact that eating there was totally regulated. It seems that when I don't worry about food then I can just have a good time … every time I'm there it just seems like food isn't a problem. I realise now that it has to do with work. It has to do very much with being in situations where I don't have choices. It's funny, going up there the car gave this great shudder and stopped. We had to be towed. Nobody was upset about it because there was nothing we could do about it. On the way back home, we had to take a car service and I was sitting up front with the driver and the others were reading in the back. This driver evidently thought we were one big happy family. Every time I would start to read he would start talking to me. I started feeling really stressed. I didn't feel like talking to this driver for the whole two and a half hours. But you see, somehow because I wasn't thinking about food and hiding, my feelings were more accessible to me and I realised I was making myself feel trapped. As soon as I realised that, I thought I don't have to talk to him and then I turned around and talked to my friends in back. He then started focusing on driving and I said to myself, that was easy.

I heard the mixture of emotions in her comments, first the pleasure and sense of accomplishment she felt in freeing herself from an experience of confinement and intrusion. Yet at the same time I was also aware of the fact that she had cancelled the first session upon her return, and wondered to myself how secure the accomplishment was if she felt unable to protect herself from me, the intrusive analyst, confining her to show up for her sessions.

(Analyst: I wonder if there's an element of your feeling trapped in coming in here today)

It's funny, all I wanted to do when I came home was continue the good work and come in here and tell you how good I was and of course it didn't happen. From the moment I got back, it started, worse yesterday and definitely worse today; all I can think of is putting food in my mouth. I don't know which is worse, the sucking candy or the food.

Here I wanted to come in and tell you how proud I am with the way things are going and instead I'm telling you I'm messing up. I kept wishing that I didn't have to come in here anymore. I said if I'm making progress maybe I don't have to come in so much. It's as if I'm sabotaging myself. But then I come back and I feel like I'm in the position of being judged. (Analyst: Judged by me?) Yeah because obviously it was very important to me what you think of this week being away. I think I want to tell you how successful I was this week, so I could prove to you that being away was good for me, so you couldn't be angry with me for missing all the sessions. And I couldn't do it. I don't know if one thing has to do with the other but it's almost like I succeeded in the other direction. By not coming in here, I was out of control.

I wondered about the difference in her experience with the driver, yet her anxiety with me? Did she get rid of me in the absence?

Like I purged myself of you. Here I am, I got along so well without you. And here you are, you're gonna be so angry at me for getting along so well without you. But then if I don't get along so well, I'll still need you. It's almost as if by being a bad little girl I'm being just that— a little girl and you're my mommy and I don't want you to hit me.

(Analyst: For leaving me?)

Yeah, for running away from home. And now I'm back with my tail between my legs. And then I'm not going to be here next week too.

(Analyst: getting rid of me again?)

Right. So if I do something bad, like go away, I should go away and not have a good time. But if I go away and have a good time, then I have to punish myself for having a good time. I have to pay for it. This is my contribution.

The next day, Mariah came in with the following:

> I think I was very upset yesterday. I just felt extremely defiant. It felt to me like a battle of wills. It's like, either I do it your way or it's not good. I felt like I'm not going to change my life style just to accommodate you! When I started thinking about it, then I had really mixed feelings about it. First thing I said to myself was— I got up this morning, it was pouring outside and I said, do I really want to go in to my session in all this rain? Then I said, if I had a job in the city would I call my boss and say excuse me, I'm not coming in. If I had some god forbid life-threatening treatment would I skip treatments every few weeks? I guess it's a form of denial. I don't want to believe there's anything that serious wrong with me. As long as I keep looking at this as a dilettantish adventure, something to make me grow more as a person, instead of something essential to my health, I'm not really responsible …
>
> (Analyst: you know, there are some astonishing parallels here from your childhood,—I think you are repeating something. When a child refuses to eat, in some way, that strikes at the very heart of a parent's concerns about the child's health and growth and well being, and by doing that you were bound to get a reaction from your parents. In some important way, you were not only defying them and asserting your independence, but also forcing them to react to you. And in the same kind of way, whether or not you attend sessions strikes at the heart of our work here together. Without attending sessions, no real work can take place. So there's no way I could avoid addressing that I am concerned about your ability to grow and utilise your treatment. I believe that what happens in here is that a kind of tension builds up inside of you and you must get rid of that tension by vomiting me out, ridding yourself of me, but at the same time it cuts off a process that develops between us and interferes with our ability to do the work.)

This was an unusually long comment from me but an important one. I wanted to articulate the importance of the continuity of treatment and confront her defence against allowing the transference to grow and be present, so that we could work with it. At the same time, I anticipated that she would get angry with me for restricting her freedom.

> I guess the stress level builds up to a certain point. And I have to find some way of dealing with it. Which apparently is leaving here. My way of going away from some difficult feelings I don't want to address. Going away is the easy way out. It's something I didn't have the luxury of doing when I lived with my parents. I couldn't just go away. I guess I refused to eat because it was the only thing I had control over. But eventually they wouldn't allow me to do that because they wouldn't let me leave the table until I had finished EVERYTHING. But at least I had a little say. The one other area I had any control over was I guess my imaginary friend. It was sort of like an escape from unpleasant pressures. And my mother drowned him you know... I guess this is a pattern, not only in here but everywhere. When faced with any kind of anxiety, just, run. And it's so convenient to do it in here because I'm really just continuing a pattern that's been existing for a long time—I've been going away every month for at least a weekend. It was just a matter of continuing to do it. I guess in a way I look forward to breaks in the treatment ... it must be frustrating for you ... seeing it from your point of view, I would be frustrated also. It's hard for me to believe anyone would really care whether or not I got better. So by impugning all these bitchy motives to you it makes it easy for me to be defiant and treat you the way I treated my parents because never once did I believe that anything they did was in my best interest. They seemed more concerned with themselves and their own needs, than with me. There were so many selfish things that took precedence. So by attributing selfish motives to the people around me now I perpetuate that same defiant feeling I had toward my parents. It's like a dialogue that goes you're not interested in me any way so I'll just do what I want. I'll take care of myself.

Clearly our discussion had some impact on her. When she returned the following week after another break, she said the following:

> I was trying to think of where to begin ... It's been a strange week. I have to begin, like last Monday. Monday night, right after I had seen you, I was watching Prince of Tides on TV and in one part of

it, she's uh—they're away in a log cabin and she is sitting in his lap on a rocking chair. I think she fell asleep on him. They must've both fallen asleep. He gets up, and I became so aware of my feelings— what was he going to do now, because she was laying on him and he was stuck. What happened was nothing that I was feeling. He never felt afraid to move her. All of a sudden I realised that I wasn't afraid of getting close to somebody, because we had been talking about intimacy in here—I wasn't afraid of what I was revealing about myself—I was afraid I would be putting the other person in a position they didn't want to be in. That they'd want to get out—and they couldn't. I said to myself—my god—that's the reason I'm afraid to get close to somebody, because I'm afraid I would be smothering them. Because that's how I would feel, smothered. I would assume they'd want to get out, and they couldn't.

As she was speaking I could feel a tightening in my chest and a difficulty in taking full breaths. The intensity of the projective identification experience was such that there was a continual flow, back and forth between us, of images and sensations that made it hard for both of us to persistently sit with these excruciatingly physical experiences. I could easily understand her need to flee from an intense feeling of suffocation and restriction such as I was experiencing at that moment.

I keep coming back to these images. That time I described to you. I was a teenager, a Sunday afternoon, lying in bed with my parents. My mother just wrapped her arms around me and instead of reveling in the comfort of being held, I remember her smell made me nauseous and I couldn't wait to get free. It was the same thing I described when I had that panic attack of going scuba diving and I couldn't breathe. I had to get out. That's probably the reason I have to force myself to hug somebody. It's not a natural thing. I'm always pretending to myself that they enjoy my hugging them, but really I feel they can't wait to get out. I wonder how much of it is just me projecting my feelings onto other people.

I asked her if she understood why these feelings were coming up now.

I don't know. It was such a strange week. I was away, playing golf, having fun with family and friends, my husband and we were getting along well, and all I could think about was eating. I didn't know what was going on.

It started Monday, after our session? I asked.

Yeah, I don't remember what we talked about Monday—but it just jelled. I saw my getting close to somebody as an attack on them and I wanted to come in here and tell you and I couldn't because I was going away [she is crying and trying to restrain herself].

Why are you holding yourself back, I asked?

I'm embarrassed. I feel like a little girl, stupid and vulnerable when I cry. It amazes me because I didn't realise, I wasn't aware until I came in here how sad I am. I probably wanted to do this all week and I couldn't.
(You're feeling sad? ...)
I don't know what I'm sad about. It's like a—I feel that I'm missing out on a lot of love. I can't give it, and I can't get it. I seem to be punishing myself. I can't stop punishing myself. And I don't know what I did wrong. Punished myself for going away in the middle of my therapy and having a good time and I'm not sup-posed to.

I felt at this moment she was beginning to move away from her long-ings, from her consuming need for contact with me and I spoke. I won-dered if it was really something about the way she held herself back from me.

I was thinking about that, how this all relates to what's going on in here, how maybe I'm afraid to overwhelm you with all my need-iness, suffocate you and drive you away. If I didn't hold myself back, people would run away. You're just supposed to hold your-self back, not come on too strong. You don't let anybody know how much you like them or need them because they can't handle it. Why do I see myself as so strong and everybody else as so weak ... sometimes I feel that everything is changing and nothing's chang-ing at the same time. It's like emotionally I seem to be topsy-turvy and yet everything in my life continues on the way it always has.

I said that I didn't think that that was the case. I thought things were changing for her, and that one of the reasons this was coming up for her was that she had experienced me as holding on to her the way her mother had held her, when I spoke with her about her vacations.

> Yeah, something obviously frightened me. And yet I think I real-ised that I wanted what you were offering and I didn't want to run away... I think that what was unique about that insight on Monday night was that I always—it was the first time that I—somehow being close to somebody always meant them doing something to me. I never really saw myself as—almost like a preda-tor. It's a strange association, to view intimacy with attacking. And it became very apparent to me, just like people sit on each other's laps. I would never do that. I'd feel like I was too big, or too heavy. The other person would be too uncomfortable. Like the other per-son has no say. I'm afraid I would take this as a rejection. Not as a fact, as a thing. All of this is based on the assumption that the other person isn't pleased to have me there, sitting on their lap—hugging them—being close to them. They don't want me there. Now they have to figure out how to get away from me. It goes back to that lump of shit theory. I f you dump a lump of shit in someone's lap I don't think they'd be too happy.

Even as she spoke I was aware of a sense of anxiety, a worry that per-haps her needs *would actually be* too much for me. I realised that once again, I was receiving her projective identification.

> (Analyst: So if you stay around too long in here you're going to make me uncomfortable.)
> Yeah, I'm going to get on your nerves, complain too much, whine too much. You're going to be stuck with me. What if you want to get rid of me? .... you know it still all comes back to that assump-tion that I can't get rid of, that nobody really wants me around and they just put up with me.
> (Analyst: the memory of your mother?)
> Yeah it's a strange memory. Memory is usually visual, but this was a smell. It was part of that whole feeling of being smothered. Even my sense of smell was being smothered. I couldn't breathe, because if I breathed, I breathed her smell. I guess a very strange

memory—why would I find it so frightening? To have her hug me—I didn't feel like I was being hugged, I felt like I was being enveloped, imprisoned. I didn't see myself as having the ability to just get up and walk out of the bed. I didn't see myself as having choices. I was just stuck ... I don't know, somehow, it was like being pinned down ... I just felt like I was ready to gag (Analyst: gag?) which brings up throwing up and everything—why was I so nauseous? (Analyst: Ummm?) I feel like what I wanted to throw up were all the angry feelings I had towards her my whole life. Just throw up in her face! How miserable she had made me for my whole life! And now hugging me! It was totally obnoxious. Maybe that's what I do when I eat, get rid of all these angry feelings that I feel toward everybody.

(Analyst: I wonder if that's what you do when you leave on vacation. It's like vomiting me up—or getting rid of all the angry feelings you must feel towards me. If you stayed around, you might feel many more angry feelings towards me.)

Yeah, I'm the one who's pretending when I sit on someone's lap. It's really a cover up for a bundle of angry feelings. Otherwise why would I see it as an attack?

Importantly, Mariah was able to experience my intervention not as "pinning her down" but as a sign of caring containment on my part. She was able to consider the thought that I actually might want her to stay with me, rather than feeling consumed and suffocated by her neediness and wishing to be rid of her. What is noteworthy about this interaction was that it represented a turning point in the treatment. Where previously Mariah experienced any attempt to restrict her behaviour as a violating assault on her personhood, she was now able to tolerate my intervention and understand that my comments represented an attempt to sustain and reinforce our collaborative working relationship. In this moment, we broke through the sadomasochistic defence and were able to connect on a genuine level of intimacy. Much work remained to be done in what developed into an intense and lengthy treatment, but it was clear that now a friendship was developing between us. We were on the road to recovery. Shortly after this session, Mariah agreed to assume a fourth analytic hour.

CHAPTER TWELVE

Discussion of the case of Mariah

Steven Ellman

irst let me thank the editors for allowing me to comment on an extremely interesting psychoanalytic couple who are finding their way through a maze of sadomasochistic dynamics. The analyst in the couple is demonstrating some of the important characteristics of how to keep an analysis alive and relatively secure. To do this she has to withstand both internal and externally perceived attacks and she has been able to survive these attacks.

We enter Mariah's world most fully during her fourth year of treatment with Dr. Greenman. It is however, instructive to look at the earlier parts of the treatment to see how the analytic couple arrived at the period most fully described. We know from the history that Mariah constantly evacuated her mind and body through her use of pills and her daily bulimia. The evacuation was rarely complete and she had to rapidly propel ideas from her mind during her analytic sessions.

This view derives from Dr. Greenman's seeing Mariah as a "high-speed train, rushing toward one insight after another within the concentrated period of our meetings, leaving me with the feeling that I would have to speak up forcefully in order to get heard. I chose not to interrupt her, but for the most part simply to listen." We can easily see that Dr. Greenman felt full of Mariah's internal world and that Mariah at times left this world in Dr. Greenman's possession. Dr. Greenman notes that "she did not express any curiosity about me or about my thoughts." In my view she wisely decided against, "bringing this up at this early point in the treatment, because I sensed that she would find any comments addressing our interaction not only extremely wounding but also, more importantly, perplexing. She had earlier informed me that she left a previous treatment after several months because the therapist kept referring to their 'relationship' and she could not understand the point of this."

This brief vignette enables me to start to discuss the beginning of treatment with Mariah. There are two points (at least) that are illustrative in this short example. First of all, Dr. Greenman literally feels tied up; that is for her to speak she would have to use force to interrupt Mariah. Thus for several reasons, Dr. Greenman begins the treatment listening to Mariah and feeling that to be heard she would have to forcefully intrude on Mariah. Mariah is creating a world where Dr. Greenman is her audience and Dr. Greenman feels tied up and immobilised. While I will later maintain that Dr. Greenman is appropriately beginning the treatment in a way that allows her to enter Mariah's world, it is important to note Dr. Greenman's transference (or countertransference) to the therapeutic situation. As a second point, Mariah tells Dr. Greenman an important factor when she relates her previous experience in treatment. The previous analyst assumed that there was a two- person field but Mariah clearly wanted there to be only a one person field. (I have previously discussed this issue (Ellman, 2009) and what is clear is that while, of course, there is always a two-person field, it is the nature of the field that I am describing.)

The other person needed to be a retainer and a type of toilet bowl for the evacuated products of her mind. Frequently at the beginning and at other points in the treatment situation—points which usually involve sharp shifts in the transference—patients will want and need a mostly one-person field where the analyst is seen as receiving and at times reflecting the world that the patient is bringing to the analytic session. At the end of this beginning period of the treatment, Dr. Greenman takes an independent action and suggests that the therapy continue along the path of becoming an analysis. Mariah and Dr. Greenman agree on a three times a week format and Mariah moves to the couch.

Mariah was agreeable but also disappointed in the fact that Dr. Greenman was an independent entity. Mariah now had to take relatively extreme measures by leaving the treatment for extended periods of time. Now this may have been purely a transference manifestation where Mariah had to punish Dr. Greenman for existing independently (having her own thoughts, going away on weekends, having other patients etc.). It is also possible, however, that Dr. Greenman was found to have other independent movements even within the therapeutic situation and these needed to be firmly stamped out. The form of punishment on Mariah's part indicates that it was hard for her to accept prolonged contact as well as, paradoxically, any type of separation. It is hard to believe, for a non-analyst, that a woman of Mariah's age has not sufficiently developed object constancy, but clearly that was the case. Nevertheless, Dr. Greenman was able to provide a constant-enough figure so that Mariah could not actually destroy the object that she was attacking as well as testing.

Dr. Greenman has noted that when there was a failure on Mariah's part to make the other person inert, she frequently created a space for herself to defend against impingements that an alive environment might provide. Although this was an aspect of Mariah's functioning, Dr. Greenman's trust in the analytic process allowed the work to move to three times a week on the couch. Here Mariah was perhaps free for a rare opportunity to create and talk about her omnipotent, and at the same time sinister, Cleopatra fantasy (dream from the couch). The couch might have provided her freedom from any hint of affect that Dr. Greenman's face or body might have provided for Mariah. At the same time the couch often stimulates paranoid fantasies that are difficult to contain. Dr. Greenman maintained that the movement to three times a week and to the couch created "… intensification of her transference experience. This dream eloquently condensed the critical conflicts which were to assume centre stage during this early phase of treatment, her continuous need to create a relationship with a sadistically violating object where she could experience herself as punitively beaten and assaulted, and her need to flee from that. I wondered if the dream was alerting me to her impulse to defensively flee from an intrapsychic engagement with the analyst by 'vacating' the transference, for example, taking a vacation." Dr. Greenman does not highlight the obvious reference to Mariah as the beautiful Queen of the Nile. My first experience of a patient with this type of fantasy was a patient who was hospitalised and diagnosed as schizophrenic with classic catatonic symptoms. When she recovered from this state she reported that she had been Cleopatra with extraordinary powers—the power to topple buildings with her voice (hence she was mute).

Clearly Mariah needed to omnipotently control Dr. Greenman. Why not interpret this, and in addition interpret the idea that Dr. Greenman, who clearly was the sadistic dark-skinned man, was a projection that was then re-introjected as a sadistic threatening object? Dr. Greenman does wonder if the dark-skinned man indicated some mistrust of her but does not try to fully interpret this dream. Why not fully interpret the dream and point out the omnipotent-sadistic fantasy where Mariah is battling a dark-skinned rival who is trying to take away her powers? I will attempt to answer this question later in the discussion but for now I will be content to note that Dr. Greenman hit just the right note in her muted intervention.

Before discussing what I consider to be Dr. Greenman's exemplary treatment of Mariah, I will say a word about the patient's sadomasochistic dynamics. Although there is not a perfect correlation, patients whose main defensive structure involves splitting and projection (projective identification)—what Anna Freud might have called ego restrictive defences (1936)—tend to have strong sadomasochistic dynamics. Kohut began to write about this in his paper on narcissistic rage (Kohut, 1972). In this paper he illustrated the effects of an insult to a narcissistically vulnerable individual. His illustration reminds one of the quests described by Melville in Moby Dick when rage becomes all consuming and self-destructive. In my view the type of patient that Kohut wrote about was not simply narcissistically vulnerable but in addition used primarily defences that involved vertical splitting. (In addition in his 1968 paper Kohut suggests that narcissism can be treated if the patient has a stable sense of self. This is not true of patients who develop the type of rage he describes in his 1972 paper.)

Clearly Mariah's reactions do not reach these proportions but her environment is constantly fomenting the bad objects in her object world. She is being attacked, and attacking back, in small and large ways and her sense of vulnerability is constant. In addition one can feel her sense of revenge in leaving Dr. Greenman in a vulnerable state when she brings chaos to the analytic situation. This chaos (for example, her absences from treatment) can be seen as a type of revenge as well as a retreat from a situation where her sense of self is consistently threatened. Her unstable self-esteem and self-hatred had to be projected into Dr. Greenman, and when Dr. Greenman could contain these elements

Mariah's fragmented sense of self could begin to be sewn together in a less fragile state. In this description I am trying to picture an internal battle with bad objects consistently tormenting Mariah. These bad objects are frequently projected into Dr. Greenman and Mariah then appropriately (in her view) attacks these externalised objects. This constant oscillation can be seen in sadistic terms or one might say that the world is constantly a punishing one that needs to be fended off and attacked to survive. This however does not fully explain what I believe is Mariah's sense of satisfaction in frustrating and attacking Dr. Greenman. That sense of satisfaction is similar to the sexual excitement of pain that Freud has described. Thus in patients that utilise splitting as a main defence one often sees the world as filled with threat and potential aggression, however I suggest that sadism implies a sexualised excitement in this world view. While I feel this is present in Mariah it is not the main dynamic element.

The beginning of the treatment

Dr. Greenman is demonstrating some of the important characteristics of how to keep an analysis alive and relatively secure. To do this she has had to withstand both internal and externally perceived attacks and has been able to survive these attacks. To put the case into a clinical theoretical perspective I will introduce the concept of analytic trust, which in my view is largely derived from the work of Winnicott, Kohut, Bion, and Bach.

Analytic trust

Although it is my view that what I am positing is important for all analytic patients let me focus on two types of patients—narcissistic and borderline. Kohut posited that if the analyst maintained an empathic stance and "did not interfere by premature transference interpretations" that some form of either idealising, mirroring, or, in his later parlance, a selfobject transference would form. Kohut in his terms advocates that the analyst initially provide "forms of mirroring and echoing responses" (1968, p. 100) so that a form of the mirroring transference will firmly occur. In my interpretation, Kohut began to enable the analyst to enter the patient's world and Bach (1985, 1994, 2006) describes this entry in a more subtle, nuanced, and utilisable paradigm. Both caution against early interpretations and that for a long time it is a mistake to emphasise to a patient that his demands are unrealistic or not based on reality.

Following this logic we are not trying to assist the patient in reality testing or holding as a remedy, but rather we are trying to establish the conditions that allow the patient to develop what I will call a consistent and utilisable transference. Bach (1985) emphasises the idea of narcissistic states and in his concepts of anti-worlds explains the emptiness of the narcissist in terms of difficulties in agency. His writings have led me to state that what Gruness (1984) and I (Ellman, 1998a, 1998b, 1999) have called the affective interpenetration in the analytic dyad, is a crucial aspect of a patient tolerating ruptures in the treatment situation. The analyst must be able to feel the anxiety, turmoil, and psychic pain the patient is experiencing and be able to communicate this in such a way that it becomes a shared analytic experience. In my view this is the crucial aspect of the beginning of an analytic treatment, the ability of the analyst to facilitate affective interpenetration. This can be done in a number of ways: a simple synthetic comment allows the patient to know that the analyst is able to feel that two experiences have a certain affective equivalence. Thus, for the analyst to comment that this experience with your uncle seems to feel like what you have been describing with your fiancé, indicates that you have felt the affect in both situations and recognise the similarity in the two different situations. Synthetic comments also help the patient to begin to integrate a more unified sense of self. What Kohut called mirroring is really a form of marking (Gergely, 2004; Gergely & Watson, 1996) and the extent of the differences in the marking often give a clue to the depth of the narcissistic dynamics.

Early stages with some patients (narcissistic or otherwise) may require the analyst to tolerate a certain level of meaninglessness, or non-symbolic communication (Freedman, 1994; Steingart, 1995) in which he is not perceived or related to as anything like a whole object. Such patients often have limited ability to self reflect. This situation seems best described by terms such as narcissistic or self-object transference, during which, as we see it, the analyst often must accept the patient's transference but not interpret it verbally. At this point in the treatment the patient perceives and needs a one-person field in the analytic situation. Thus before a rupture can be repaired there must be a certain stability of structure so that the repair can be anchored and cohere in a stabilised configuration. Serious interpretations, and particularly transference interpretations, frequently cause ruptures and so this view is particularly germane to early interpretive interventions.

"Borderline" beginnings

Affective interpenetration often is more difficult with patients who need to destroy the analytic relationship. Each position that in some manner begins to develop a holding environment, frequently needs to survive a (borderline) patient's sense of rage, betrayal, or, in a less dramatic but perhaps more continuous sense, a patient's sense of being misunderstood. Bion's (1959, 1962, 1967) ideas about containment are implicitly present in various forms in both Winnicott's and Balint's (1968) formulations about treating the patient who, in Winnicott's terms, is not well chosen or is a typical classical psychoanalytic patient (Winnicott, 1960). Paraphrasing Winnicott I would say that surviving, rather than sidestepping or avoiding the destructive aspects of the analysand, is a necessary condition for a successful analysis to take place. One has to survive the patient's negative affect but in the course of survival it is crucial to be able to return the affect expressed in a manner that is detoxified (Bion's term).

In more ordinary language it is important to survive and talk about, for example, the patient's rage without moving away from it or being excessively retaliative. My assumption is that there is always some form of enactment (Ellman, 1999) that takes place around negative and destructive tendencies. With most narcissistic patients this is not a striking issue in the beginning phases of treatment. However as vertical splitting becomes more prominent in what many analysts would characterise as borderline experiences, there is a greater chance of containment being a central facet in the beginning phases of treatment. In treatments that I am alluding to the ruptures are externalised and frequently enacted and the first rupture that must be endured is one that threatens to destroy the analytic couple.

More dramatic splitting presents at least two different issues that lead to difficulties in the analytic situation. Frequently affect is quickly got rid of in some form of action or in a rapid negation, projection (for me the correct term is projective identification), or rapid oscillation to another state or sense of self and other. Here the interpenetration of affect is even more important, with the analyst not only being able to experience the affect but gradually to present it to a patient who has already left the affective state and clearly wants no part of this experience. Frequently this type of patient kills the affect with action that at times involves substance abuse and here it is particularly to re-experience with the patient the affect and experience that had to be destroyed. This has to be done gradually and in successive approximations.

A brief example: A patient wakes up in the morning and snorts cocaine, then when his agitation becomes too extreme starts to drink to calm down. He repeats this sequence several times a day. By the time he comes to treatment in the afternoon he is in a confused and altered state. Gradually within the treatment we are able to see how he empties out his mind, first with the aid of, and then even without the aid of, substances. Any topic that alters his self-esteem or brings him into conflict with others or is embarrassing is immediately negated, minimised, or contradicted in subsequent comments. When he passes by an experience and it is gradually brought back and he tolerates its return, then he is more able to endure the ruptures that he experiences in his agitated internal world. His repair had been attempted through substance abuse but gradually we are able to look at the role of substances that fragment his emotional life. It takes two years before he is able to tolerate these states and give up cocaine and alcohol (cigarettes are another matter). In this parlance, experiencing and returning affect to the analytic field is a crucial aspect of the long beginning of this treatment. He must endure the ruptures before he is able to begin to repair his psyche. He can only do that if we can tolerate his affect states within the analytic situation. When this same patient begins to rail about the meaninglessness of analytic treatment this too must be tolerated and returned to the patient. First directly, and then in synthetic form, so that the patient can see how he attempts to denigrate and demean many situations that threaten to produce aversive states for him. This containment, or the return of affect in general, is not interpretative in that it almost always deals with elements that do not go beyond what is consciously available to the patient.

Particularly with patients who use vertical splitting as a main defence it is important not simply to return affect but to understand and feel how difficult it is for the person to tolerate these states. To summarise, once reflection, echoing, synthetic comments, and containment achieve affective interpenetration, the assumption is that there will be more of a shared analytic field and a strengthening of analytic trust. This development will heal a rupture so that subsequent ruptures can be endured in less traumatic form. This strengthening of trust gradually leads to two inter-related somewhat "paradoxical" results; at the same time that the analyst is trusted and included in the analysand's world, both members of the dyad are more comfortable in being separate and both are slightly more comfortable in maintaining separate perspectives. If this separation can be tolerated it is the birth (or a strengthening) of a reflective self-representation within the analytic situation. When the patient begins to include me in their object world it is then that the possibility opens up to include aspects of the other within what may be the final part of the initial phase of analytic trust. Once the initial phase is experienced the analyst feels freer to think her own thoughts and these thoughts frequently drift towards transference interpretations.

For me to express my views on transference with a patient like Mariah would entail a longer discussion than is appropriate for this venue. Let me be content with several points about transference in the analytic situation. It is my view that within every theoretical perspective there is an avenue to escape the full manifestations of transference. I am positing that every position has characteristic ways of avoiding the full efflorescence of transference manifestations. Of course you will notice that simply in the way that I have stated this sentence I have presented a theoretical bias. It is my view that in most analyses, unless a patient experiences transference over some period of time, the therapeutic results from analysing transference manifestations will not be fully believed or internalised by the analysand. Thus the ideas of Brenner, Gill, and Kernberg about the rapid interpretation of transference does not allow the patient to fully experience the varied issues that are intimately tied to central transference themes (Ellman, 1991). The rapid interpretation of transference also has other meanings that I believe short-circuit the therapeutic process. More specifically the rapid interpretation of transference is frequently a signal to the patient that the analytic couple cannot tolerate this transference state.

In my theoretical matrix the key to an inclusive and empathic transference interpretation is to understand not only the dynamic and perhaps genetic meaning of the transference but also what Rapaport and Gill (1959) called the adaptive assumption. In the present lexicon why did the person view the conflicted alternative as the most adaptive possibility available to them. Now to be sure I am not talking about a conscious decision for the shape of the conflict but rather as the alternative that allowed the maximum possibility for psychological survival. The adaptive assumption is only one factor in the compromise formation of conflict formation but for the analyst to make an empathic interpretive response it is a crucial factor.

I have also found that the understanding of the adaptive function has led to transference meanings that I might have not understood or understood without the appropriate accompanying affect. A woman whose mother died when she was three and whose father had died several years before treatment began had severe hypochondriacal concerns (Ellman, 1999). She developed a strong idealising transference that I interpreted in terms of her wish for me to provide for her as her father had provided for her. A number of things were off about this interpretation but the primary factor was the timing and my lack of empathic understanding of how her maternal deprivation had totally sculpted the contours of her life. Gradually as the treatment was righted I was able to understand with her how her father became her joint parent and how her relationship with women was heavily influenced by the denial of her mother's existence. It was only when we were able to explore her desperate need for her father to be able to provide everything that mother and father could provide that we began to be able to understand her hatred of women and her envy of women who had a maternal presence. Her only friends were those that reflected her paranoid fears of women attacking her, and her projected fears of being attacked as an object of envy were frequently confirmed. As the transference analysis proceeded she could transform her desire for the perfect joint parent and begin to widen her range of friends and her movements in her world.

To turn to another aspect of transference I might ask why would I have provided a premature interpretation which intruded on her transference manifestations? Kohut (1968) writes about an analyst who in the beginning of treatment encounters a patient who is developing what he calls a twinship transference. She exclaims that the two of them are so alike and she posits that both came from a Catholic background. The analyst demurs and points out that he is not Catholic. She did not ask him whether he is Catholic but he had to insert an aspect of himself thus deflecting the transference. I would posit that her creation of him put in a state of narcissistic imbalance and in response to this imbalance he asserts an aspect of what he considered to be a realistic aspect of himself. In a similar way I could no longer accept the patient's idealisation (which in my view was not me) and I had to insert an aspect of "reality" to deflect or obliterate the transference. Prolonged transference states put the analyst in a narcissistic disequilibrium. Even idealisations at some point (unless enacted) have this effect since the analyst begins to feel the transference is not about them but is a creation of the patient.

Although I have focused on idealising transferences in writing about narcissistic imbalances, clearly the issues are more difficult in negative transference states. The uncooperative or disobedient patient is more often seen as unanalysable. The analyst does not want to receive or be filled with intense negative states since they are usually further from her or his self-image than are positive states. Moreover negative states usually bring up more intense conflicts related to hatred and destructive impulses. I recall vividly a schizophrenic patient who wondered how anyone could love me since I had no love in me—she said "your love had been shaken out of you". I thought consciously that her silly comment could not bother me (I had just married) but it led to a number of dreams where everyone was leaving, including my wife. Her statement(s) led to my forgetting an appointment and wanting to avoid her hateful transference that was a projection (projective identification) of her hateful internal objects. When I could finally contain her destructive fantasies her transference could progress to seeing me as a nursing mother with full breasts and milk. (This was only a bit easier for me to receive). In less dramatic form destructive thoughts are frequently put in us without our awareness and often the first clue to this occurring is that in one way or another we want to avoid the transference or aspects of the treatment in general. Frequently we accomplish this either by inserting an aspect of ourselves in the treatment that deflects the transference or by becoming particularly distant in the treatment. These types of therapeutic actions should alert us that something is happening that we only partially understand at best.

A further view of transference is that an analytic treatment can be viewed in terms of transference cycles (Freedman, 1994; Freedman & Lavender, 2002; O'Shaugnessy, 1981). Each cycle has a beginning and a movement into the next cycle. With patients whose main defences are ego restrictive (splitting, projective identification, etc.) early cycles may seem like the treatment is beginning over and over, since early forms of trust have to be regained. As the analytic pair moves through the cycles, analytic trust is strengthened and a true love develops between two separable subjectivities. The receiving of transference is a form of interpenetration of affect but the interpretation of transference begins a different process. As the analyst's interpretive efforts begin to stir, the analyst is formulating an experience that is different than the experience of the patient. The analyst's formulation is one that if useful will lead to a new pathway and the analytic dyad will be separated by the interpretive effort. As this separation is survived trust is increased and here the analytic third begins to be a presence. My Freudian view of the analytic third is the occurrence of the analytic parties accepting each other's lives outside of the analytic dyad. If things had been going well initially the dyad's focus was primarily on each other and self-object states prevailed. Transference interpretations can usefully disrupt these states and if survived and utilised, trust is strengthened. It is at this point that the vectors begin to equalise and intersubjectivity occurs between two separable subjectivities. In a brief review transference is seen as occurring in cycles and although transference is ubiquitous, it takes some time for transference to occur in interpretable form. The effect of a utilisable transference interpretation is two-fold: first, it should lead to new material not obtainable in other forms; second, it strengthens analytic trust since the patient begins to recognise that a relationship can survive different perspectives. The assumption is that when a useful transference interpretation is made, it of necessity presents a view of the patient that is different than the patient's view of himself or herself. Let me now return to Mariah. Clearly Mariah needed to omnipotently control Dr. Greenman Why not interpret this and, in addition, interpret the idea that Dr. Greenman as a sadistic dark-skinned man was a projection that was then re-introjected as a sadistic threatening object?

How does one answer this question, particularly when we note that Dr. Greenman's experience was one where, "she refused to take me in and I felt that not only my analytic abilities but my very personhood was eradicated by her. In her presence, I often had the uncanny experience of feeling nonexistent, an experience which at times filled me with rage and made me want to retaliate." Dr. Greenman felt inhibited and concerned that an interpretive response "would be experienced by her as critical and aggressively hurtful". In my view these responses by Dr. Greenman, while normal countertransference (in the old sense of the term), mask a deeper empathetic response. Mariah was filling her with her childhood trauma and asking her to endure it and to eventually help her understand what had happened to her. Dr. Greenman on the other hand feels that when she began to interpret, Mariah began to understand that the locus of her aggression was from her own internal world projected into the analytic situation. While I have no doubt that this type of clarification (I wouldn't call her interventions interpretations) were helpful I think that Dr. Greenman is closer when she says that "The sound of my voice, comforting for her in its sameness, helped to create an environment in which she could hear my comments as helpful and ultimately friendly." While it may have stabilised Mariah's internal world to understand where things were coming from, it was at least as helpful to know that they reach another mind where they are tolerated, contained, and returned with the destructive edge removed or at least attenuated. In my view this enabled her to become even more directly aggressive, feeling that she could trust that her aggression could be tolerated and understood. This enabled the analytic pair to reach a point described as a "deeper level of engagement with her fears of her own consuming sense of need and anxiety about loss of self and engulfment." It is at this point that two paradoxical feelings occur; the patient is feeling that she is making progress and doesn't want to come to treatment any longer.

Now this type of flight to health (or at least flight to some marginal improvement) is not unusual in a treatment and one can offer a variety of explanations for this movement. Here Mariah is actually thinking of the other and able to tolerate the pain that the other implies in her object world. She is in a position similar to Fairbairn's concept of love made hungry. Her bad love will infiltrate the other and smother them or worse. This is her conscious feeling and Dr. Greenman's conscious countertransference when Dr. Greenman experienced the "continual flow between us … and could easily understand her need to flee from an intense feeling of suffocation." At the end of this report Dr. Greenman relates that Mariah was able to experience her interventions "as a sign of caring containment on my part". So Dr. Greenman has, in my view, given us a narrative of her being able to get to the point of Mariah being able to utilise transference interpretations and experience some of her active fantasies (phantasies) in the transference. Up to this point most of what has been described has been Mariah's defensive attempts to survive with some aspects of a continuous, albeit perverted sense of self. Dr. Greenman has also survived in this difficult dance to form an analytic couple.

Here in this moving narrative Dr. Greenman has, in my view, related the difficulties in the movement towards a utilisable transference state. This movement might be described in Bionian terms as moving beta elements towards establishing alpha functions but this dichotomous view of the process does not do justice to Mariah's movement towards the capacity for object love. She is, certainly, some way from establishing this capacity, but she is on the path towards a new view of the object. In many ways her previous attempts hoped to quiet signs of life or evacuate her troubling objects and try to stem the tidal waves of persecutory affect that threatened to engulf her. Now she is moving towards a position that Freud (1913) described as a position of object choice where the love, or at least the concern, of the object is more important than the instinct involved in either pleasure or pain. Here it is important to again distinguish transference viewed as a ubiquitous function—in Brian Bird's (1972) sense of the term function—from interpretable transference. Interpretable transference depends on the development of analytic trust and at least the beginning of the path towards object love. Britton (1997) has described a patient who is not able to accept interpretations and more importantly cannot allow the other to think independent thoughts. While some may say Britton was not able to develop the right interpretive comments (a view expressed at a conference I attended) I would say that Britton understood in a deep way something that Bach has been writing about for several decades (Bach, 1985). Bach has written that for transference to be interpreted, "One must have two parties who experience themselves as separately alive and functional" (Bach, 1985, p. xiii). I would say that it is rare to wait to interpret until two parties are truly separate but at the very least there should be two parties that can at least allow for periods of separation and tolerate the frequent sadomasochistic reunions that will follow. Reunions where self-object ties are loosened frequently increase the capacity for love but also stimulate envy of the other. This envy which may have been defended against before now is seen as attacking a possession of another who is separate from and no longer under the control of the subject or patient. Thus in a reunion there is often some pleasure in pointing out lacks in the analyst or difficulties in the analyst's formulations. Frequently there may be pleasure evinced that the patient is actually feeling better when she/he is away from the analyst. This seemed to be the case with Mariah and I would hypothesise that she envied Dr. Greenman's capacity to soothe and had to attack and try to destroy this capacity. This is one example of the type of envious attacks that occur during reunions. I would almost see envious attacks as involving sadism (Ellman, 2000).

This brings me to a final point that is largely stimulated by Klein's (1940, 1945, 1946) and neo-Kleinian (Rosenfeld, 1987; Steiner, 1993) views on positions. Mariah's movement will not be a permanent one, there will be oscillations between her more object related experiences and times where the object will be evacuated or destroyed. In my experience (Ellman, 1999, 2009) good interpretations frequently lead to a break in analytic trust and, if tolerated, a subsequent movement towards a greater degree of trust that begins to include elements of object choice moving towards object love. These positions are found and lost during an alive analysis and they echo developmental periods where the object is lost and re-found. Freedman (1994) has proposed the concept of transformation cycles and I have suggested the idea of transference cycles. O'Shaugnessy (1981) has given a clinical illustration of what she called defensive cycles but in all these concepts there is a non-monotonic (where the curve moves in different directions) cycling that occurs. One might consider these movements regressions, but perhaps Winnicott describes it best in terms of his statements about ego-relatedness (Winnicott, 1958). His distinction of withdrawal and regression is equally important because the oscillation between analytic trust and its absence is the movement from an ego-relatedness versus a withdrawal from the other. Therefore what is being described is not only, or primarily, a movement to an earlier libidinal position but rather a movement away from contact with the object. Clearly this movement is rarely complete in either direction and here we need more ways to describe the partial transformation and incomplete movements of developing trust that occur during an analysis. It seems to me that Dr. Greenman has given us good illustrations to begin to conceptualise these transition points.

References

Bach, S. (1985). *Narcissistic States and the Therapeutic Process.* Northvale, NJ: Jason Aronson.

Bach, S. (1994). *The Language of Perversion and the Language of Love.* Northvale, NJ: Jason Aronson.

Bach, S. (2006). *Getting From Here to There: Analytic Love, Analytic Process.* Hillsdale, NJ: The Analytic Press.

Balint, M. (1968). *The Basic Fault: Therapeutic Aspects of Regression.* New York: Brunner/Mazel.

Bion, W. R. (1959). Attacks on linking. *International Journal of Psycho- Analysis*, 40: 308–315. Reprinted in: *Second Thoughts: Selected Papers on Psychoanalysis* (pp. 93–109). London: Heinemann, 1967.

Bion, W. R. (1962). A theory of thinking. In: *Second Thoughts: Selected Papers on Psychoanalysis* (pp. 110–119). London: Heinemann, 1967.

Bion, W. R. (1967). *Second Thoughts: Selected Papers on Psychoanalysis*. New York: Jason Aronson.

Bird, B. (1972). Notes on transference: Universal phenomenon and hardest part of analysis. *Journal of the American Psychoanalytic Association*, 20: 267–301.

Britton, R. (1997). The missing link: parental sexuality in the Oedipus complex. In: R. Schafer (Ed.), *The London Kleinians* (pp. 242–259). Madison, CT: International Universities Press.

Ellman, C. S. (2000). The empty mother: Women's fear of their destructived envy. *Psychoanalytic Quarterly*, 69: 633–657.

Ellman, S. J. (1991). *Freud's Technique Papers; A Contemporary Perspective*. New York: Jason Aronson.

Ellman, S. J. (1998a). Enactment, transference, and analytic trust. In: S. Ellman & M. Moskowitz (Eds.), *Enactment: Toward a New Approach to the Therapeutic Relationship* (pp. 183–203). Northvale, NJ: Jason Aronson.

Ellman, S. J. (1998b). The unique contribution of the contemporary Freudian position. In: C. Ellman, S. Grand, M. Silvan & S. Ellman (Eds.), *The Modern Freudians: Contemporary Psychoanalytic Technique*. Northvale, NJ: Jason Aronson.

Ellman, S. J. (1999). The concept of enactment: cutting edge or current fad. *Journal of Clinical Psychoanalysis*, 8(1): 9–61.

Ellman, S. J. (2009). *When Theories Touch: A Historical and Theoretical Attempt to Integrate Psychoanalytic Theory*. London: Karnac.

Freedman, N. (1994). More on transformation enactments. In: A. K. Richards & A. P. Richards (Eds.), *The Spectrum of Psychoanalysis: Essays in Honor of Martin S. Bergmann* (pp. 93–110). Madison, CT: International Universities Press.

Freedman, N. & Lavender, J. (2002). On desymbolization: the concept and observation. *Psychoanalytic Contemporary Thought*, 25: 165–199.

Freud, S. (1913). The disposition to obsessional neurosis: A contribution to the problem of the choice of neurosis. *S. E.*, 12: 313–326. London: Hogarth.

Gergely, G. (2004). The role of contingency detection in early affect-regulative interactions and in the development of different types of infant attachment. *Social Development*, 13(3): 468–478.

Gergely, G. & Watson, J. S. (1996). The social biofeedback theory of parental affect-mirroring. *International Journal Psycho-Analysis*, 77: 1181–1212.

Gruness, M. (1984). The therapeutic object relationship. *Psychoanalytic Review*, 71: 123–143.

Klein, M. (1940). Mourning and its relation to manic–depressive states. In: *Love, Guilt and Reparation, and Other Works, 1921–1945* (pp. 344–369). New York: Free Press.

Klein, M. (1945). The Oedipus complex in the light of early anxieties. In: *Love, Guilt and Reparation, and Other Works, 1921–1945* (pp. 370–418) New York: Free Press.

Klein, M. (1946). Notes on some schizoid mechanisms. In: *Envy and Gratitude and Other Works, 1946–1963* (pp. 1–24). New York: Free Press.

Kohut, H. (1968). The psychoanalytic treatment of narcissistic personality disorders—outline of a systematic approach. *Psychoanalytic Study of the Child*, 23: 86–113.

Kohut, H. (1971). *The Analysis of the Self*. New York: International Universities Press.

Kohut, H. (1972). Thoughts on narcissism and narcissistic rage. *Psychoanalytic Study of the Child*, 27: 360–400.

Kohut, H. (1984). *How Does Analysis Cure?* A. Goldberg & P. E. Stepansky (Eds.). Chicago, IL: University of Chicago Press.

O'Shaughnessy, E. (1981). A clinical study of a defensive organization. *International Journal of Psycho-Analysis*, 62: 359–369.

Rapaport, D. & Gill, M. (1959). The points of view and assumptions of metapsychology. In: *The Collected Papers of David Rapaport* (pp. 795–811). New York: Basic Books.

Rosenfeld, H. (1987). *Impasse and Interpretation: Therapeutic and Antitherapeutic Factors in the Psychoanalytic Treatment of Psychotic, Borderline, and Neurotic Patients*. London: Tavistock Routledge.

Steiner, J. (1993). *Psychic Retreats: Pathological Organisations of the Personality in Psychotic, Neurotic, and Borderline Patients*. London: Routledge.

Steingart, I. (1995). *A Thing Apart: Love and Reality in the Therapeutic Relationship*. Northvale, NJ: Jason Aronson.

Winnicott, D. W. (1958). The capacity to be alone. In: *The Maturational Processes and the Facilitating Environment* (pp. 29–36). New York: International Universities Press.

Winnicott, D. W. (1960). The theory of the parent–infant relationship. In: *The Maturational Processes and the Facilitating Environment* (pp. 37–55). New York: International Universities Press.

CHAPTER THIRTEEN

Discussion of the case of Mariah

Shelley Rockwell

An unsettling disjuncture is found in the opening lines of Dr. Greenman's eloquent and poignant paper. As the reader I found myself wanting to smooth over the discrepancies or ignore them, not quite able to grasp the actual reality of this patient— thus Dr. Greenman succeeded in recreating for her reader an experience of this patient's discordant reality. We learn in the opening lines about the patient's (Mariah) "concerns about her bulimia and the impact this was having on her marriage and family", which appears as a sensitive, civilised self-presentation—but in the second sentence we learn that her vomiting had occurred daily for perhaps more than twenty years and her teeth have eroded to the gum level, "shocking her into seeking help". Is it possible to be shocked after all these years of damage and does concern seem too mild or even an inappropriate word for her situation? In other words, the patient's concern seemed unconvincing to me. In addition, Mariah is "troubled" by the vacancy in her marriage and because her husband is "continuously … a critical presence, [she] did not feel free unless she was out of his sight." In total, a disturbing picture recounted by a patient who does not seem to feel disturbed, that is, in contact with what she has described to Dr. G.

Our resistance equals the patient's—we too, or at least I, found it hard to think clearly about the patient's reality, both external and psychic. This must be overcome in order to see that she is tormented from the inside with her drive to binge and purge, as well as in her real world with a husband who frightens her. I will attempt to address several issues in my discussion of this case material. First, the question: who is this woman—can we grasp her or trust we have a sense of who she is? What does it involve on the analyst's part to take her completely seriously? In addition I would like to discuss her confusion of identifications, with each parent as well as the parental couple itself, which may help us understand not only her sadomasochistic dynamic but also the disjuncture one feels in relating to her, finally contributing to the inevitable tenacity of her symptoms.

From the beginning we are able to follow Dr. G's experience with her patient. Although the analyst initially felt hopeful, engaged by this attractive seemingly articulate woman, this quickly dissipates. Because the analyst was well in touch with her own inner experience she was able to sense the patient's using of her in a peculiar fashion. The analyst is required to be unassuming, to listen and say nothing—to be a no-analyst analyst. Most importantly she is not to break in on her patient, but rather help her maintain a seamless undifferentiated couple/pairing with her analyst. The analyst makes a conscious decision not to confront this "high-speed train" treatment of her by the patient, imagining it would not only wound but would be "perplexing" to her patient. Dr. G established what Caper (1999, p. 154) referred to as a holding relationship which is in contrast to containment. She does not interrupt or interpret this transference. From this position of safety Mariah is able to describe in detail the world—both psychic and real—she inhabits; the bulimia has a special "retreat" feeling for her—allowing her to have "many emotions that she felt unable to label, identify or acknowledge to herself, let alone articulate freely and directly in her relationships." Leslie Sohn (1988) described the necessity of the analyst's presence for the maintenance of the patient's narcissism, that is, the crucial role of a not present-present, that is a non-intrusive analyst.

The "cathartic" nature of the sessions did not lead to emotional contact between Mariah and Dr. G, who noted that her experience with the patient was "arid and unreal". Dr. G's capacity to feel and process this about her patient was crucial, and the pivot on which the treatment depended. In essence, the patient had established an atmosphere, a "transference as a total situation" (Joseph, 1989) in which manic excitement (catharsis and high-speed train) alternated with vacancy and absence. The empty space was created by her frequent weeks off, and her nightly private bulimic sessions. In essence, Mariah established a massive projective identification, extremely concrete and somatic, as well as manic, with her analyst which allowed her to escape direct experience of her inner world. I will develop this idea as I go along with my discussion.

General observations

Mariah described to Dr. G that she kept a bag of "sucking candies with her at all times, so that she could fill her mouth and create a private space for herself, feeling emotionally detached even while apparently engaged in working with her partner." This candy-sucking solution seemed striking as it allowed her (in fantasy, omnipotent) control over a "sweet object in her mouth kind of feeling", thereby dodging the panic and smallness that relating to a separate object would bring. The soothing sensations in her mouth might help her titrate the cruelty she felt was always in the air with her object; thus a concrete/somatic effort (sucking candy) countered an emotional anxiety. The sucking appears to have the same function as the bulimia, but on a micro level operating in the hour between patient and analyst, as if the patient were always saying to her analyst: I have everything I need right here in my mouth and I don't need anything from you, thus projecting into her analyst her own need and deprivation.

I am interested in picking up how from the beginning Mariah created a dual communication with her analyst, that is, I am afraid of your intrusion or contact with me and to protect myself (i.e., by sucking candy) I egress on you, becoming in the same action both victim and aggressor. This reminded me of the feelings stirred up by young children who continue to use a pacifier. When playing with this child the adult is tempted to pull the "binkie" out of the child's mouth, as we are aware that although this sucking may be serving the purpose of "holding the child together" it is also a block to our relating to him/her. The child is distracted and garbled, remaining cut off and immune from us—which stirs our aggression. The action of sucking candy enacts Mariah's victimisation by her object; she masochistically protects herself *and* simultaneously attacks the analyst's ability to make contact with her. The "danger" with Mariah is that when her aggression is not interpreted the analyst might feel she too has enacted this conflict in becoming the patient's victim.

Mariah brought a dream to the session following their decision to increase the treatment from two to three sessions weekly. In this dream, as Cleopatra, Mariah floats on a barge surrounded by comfort and luxury, all-powerful, while "sitting behind her, at her head, was a dark-skinned man, who was both seductive and sinister ... [yet] seemed to be sympathetic".

This dream figure raised the question: what are the analyst's motives for suggesting more contact—are they dark, frightening, erotic, or, more ordinarily, sympathetic? Who is really more powerful, the dark man who sits behind or the white woman in front who lies on the couch? The patient's associations indicate that she expects her analyst to "gratify and indulge her", thereby imagining the analyst's role as masochistic and submissive.

A significant development in the treatment occurred when Dr. G was able to accept the inevitability of the patient's transformation of her interpretations into sadomasochistic exchanges. This required that the analyst "gain a level of comfort with my own sadistic impulses in order to work with her effectively. I learned to use my internal sadistic and masochistic affect as a signal about our relationship and as a powerful interpretive tool, rather than shy away from it." We see that the "intrapsychic [had] become interactive" (O'Shaughnessy, 1983) and that it was essential the analyst facilitate a "self cure" (Sodre, 2000) before interpretive work could be possible.

Not surprisingly, and perhaps concurrently, Mariah began to face her reliance on being "beaten" as a sign of love from her object as well as on the power and excitement it provided her. She could acknowledge her desire to hurt others ("to stab them") which she wished to cover up. A bit later, Dr. G wrote that the patient could accuse her of being a "cold impartial self-serving individual" and that she [the patient] would want to "get even with" her. Mariah continuously encountered feelings of being violated and powerless, and continuously attempted to rectify this horrible imbalance. The reality of the patient's sadomasochistic inner world had gained more hold and substance in the actual transference and counter transference of the analysis.

Clinical material: the spa

Dr. G's description of Mariah's return to her sessions after one of her "vacations" took my breath away with its provocative quality. This spa weekend, she told her analyst, was superb and wonderful because "eating there was totally regulated". I found this disparaging of her analyst—she seemed to say that spa life is so much better than my sessions with you. And secondly, Mariah complained, perhaps accused, the analyst of not providing what the spa does—regulation. The staff are able to do for her what she cannot do, control what she eats so that she does not have a problem, does not have to worry. In general she conveyed that the "spa" really knew how to take care of her in contrast to her analyst.

Mariah's description of her car ride to the spa provided a break in the manic state in which she began her hour, as "the car gave this great shudder and stopped ... we had to be towed." This description of a breakdown and her dependency on an object to rescue her, although "nobody was upset", introduced a more accurate sense of her psychic situation. This more difficult situation was further developed "on the way back home" as she must now face a "driver [who] thought we were one big happy family ... [and he] would ... talk to me." Her arrogance and contempt toward the driver/analyst who thinks he/she has something to say that might be worth the patient listening to, was evident as she now must face the return to her analysis, after a manic flight.

I think when Mariah said that she could not face talking to "this driver for the whole two and a half hours" that there may be a reference to the amount of time in her three analytic sessions, as they, too, total two-and-a-half hours in a week. Remember that Dr. G introduced the hour with her determination to confront her patient about these breaks in the treatment. The analyst did indeed have something to say, and we can't help wondering if the patient sensed this; she has pushed her analyst too far, and something *must* be said to her. Her solution was "easy": she told her analyst she simply "turned around and talked to my friends in the back." In other words when the talk gets too difficult, Ms. M is well-prepared to turn her back on her analyst.

Later in the session, after the patient had attempted, unconvincingly, to convey pride in her self-rescue, she worried that the analyst would "judge" her and be "angry with me for missing all the sessions". I found it a relief that the patient could approach the reality of damaging, that is, angering and devaluing, her analyst. The patient said, "By not coming in here, I was out of control." This seemed exactly right, but this insight does not stick, cannot be used, as we soon see.

In the last part of the hour the patient released a storm of self-abnegation, she is a "bad little girl ... with my tail between my legs" whose "mommy" may want to hit her. In the middle of all of this false "intense feeling" there is the announcement: "I'm not going to be here next week too." Mariah had deftly turned her back on the analyst, making it clear that the talk or "insight" is empty. It feels to me that the patient is pushing her analyst into a sadistic response, thus enabling the patient to continue in the false role of victim to her analyst. Unfortunately the patient's manoeuvreing covers over more genuine feeling, involving abuse, abnegation, and hateful fury.

Mariah's sense of omnipotence and self-delusion is made more clear in the next day's session: "If I had some god forbid life-threatening *treatment* [here she has made a slip and must have intended to say *illness*] would I skip treatment every few weeks ... I don't want to believe there's anything seriously wrong with me." Can we take these words seriously? Mariah has told her analyst that she feels the treatment is in fact a life-threatening disease. Thinking this through, is it a way of saying that the analyst is making her ill, that without the analysis she might be well? I thought she felt in a panic about the analyst's desire to be a "big happy family" with her—she feared the analyst's desire for her. This projective identification is what Sodre (2004) called disidentification, allowing Mariah to escape and lose contact with her greedy and devouring wishes. She can indulge these needs and desires alone at night when she is in control of the object's ingestion and expulsion, or safely at the spa where the staff will take charge of her need-desire problem and the analyst is left behind to pine for her patient. Mariah's need to keep herself unintegrated and deeply split is a focus in the analysis; this attempt at "cure" feels like an illness to the patient—you are making me worse!

The analyst does confront her patient's treatment of the analysis as a "dilettantish adventure" (remember the Cleopatra dream): "whether or not you attend sessions strikes at the heart of our work together ... I am concerned about your ability to grow and utilise your treatment". The patient responds somewhat defensively, but reveals her inner dialogue: "It's like a dialogue that goes you're not interested in me anyway so I'll just do what I want. I'll take care of myself." Dr. G has just given

Mariah an impassioned statement reflecting her concern and interest in her patient—Mariah bats it away, obliterating the words she has just heard from her analyst, thereby attempting to maintain her victimisation by the analyst.

A fairy tale—Prince of Tides: smothered and smothering

The next section in this treatment description picks up the feelings which underlie Mariah's vacancy behaviour. After returning from her break she recounts a scene from the movie *Prince of Tides* where the protagonist, Tom the Prince, holds his psychiatrist (who is also his sister's psychiatrist) on his lap while they both sleep. He wakes, is startled and begins to move as though to get up, looks at her (Dr. Susan Lowenstein) and instead relaxes back into the chair. The scene fades, with the two of them in a seemingly sleepy, peaceful state. Mariah remembered the film differently: "They must've both fallen asleep. He gets up ... what was he going to do now, because she was laying on him and he was stuck." In my view it was Tom's ability to look at Susan and see the real Susan (in contrast to his original archaic objects, Mother and Father) thereby reassuring himself, which allowed him to relax and be with her. Mariah is unable to "see" her real object (a concerned analyst) and its distinction from the internal projected objects of her childhood past and present. She is fiercely intent on making a concerned good analyst into a persecuting, sadistic object, thereby (the paradox) forcing Dr. G into submitting to this role as a masochist.

Mariah continued and came to the idea that it is her fear of "smothering" the other person: "I would assume they'd want to get out, and they couldn't." The analyst reported that she "could feel a tightening in my chest and a difficulty in taking full breaths." I thought Dr. G could be receptive to the patient's desire to smother and restrict her, an identification with the patient in relation to her own mother.

Mariah recounted as a "teenager, a Sunday afternoon, lying in bed with my parents. My mother just wrapped her arms around me and instead of revelling in the comfort of being held, I remember her smell made me nauseous and I couldn't wait to get free." All is topsy-turvy: it *is* the psychiatrist/mother/analyst who needs to be held, *not* the child, patient. Mariah's understandably (healthy!) revulsion to what appears to be an incestuous situation with her mother is deeply engrained— her primary object, far from being good in any ordinary way, was, and is, exploitative, invasive, and consuming of her daughter. Mariah's description of her mother is harrowing: she demanded her daughter eat every single bite, she was not allowed an imaginary playmate or a phone call with a friend, and the third object/father is only a cruel appendage of this monster mother. In other words, there is no way out, no gap, no separation possible between mother and daughter. Mariah's desperate eating, sucking behaviour makes sense, how can she exist on her own over a night, over the week-end—she must flee as though to a hospital, otherwise she might fear a breakdown in the face of separation.

We see that Mariah flips quickly and frequently between being the smotherer and the smothered (thus the sadomasochistic interplay). Up to this point in the treatment it looked to me as though the analyst has had to bear being the aggressor, the patient her victim, but it seemed this had begun to open up a bit as Mariah could better acknowledge her need to possess the other, even to be the "predator". She is "always pretending to myself that they enjoy my hugging them, but really I feel they can't wait to get out." Mariah cannot imagine her object having a reality different from her own. She is able to describe her fear that the analyst may "want to get rid of" her as she, the patient whines, complains, gets on the analyst's nerves—the analyst as victim.

Mariah does not understand the full extent of her enslavement to the mother/internal object and its very disturbing and panic-inducing nature. She again described her mother's frightening, smothering smell and conveys the primitive level of her anxiety; she cannot differentiate from her mother—to be caught in the smell of the other is to be infiltrated like an infant with no boundary/skin between them. Mariah's angry wish to throw-up in her mother's face is, as she said, revengeful, but it is also a desperate effort to push the mother away, to find space between them in defiance of their mutual desire to merge. Mariah cannot trust that she has the capacity—nor, she fears, does her object—to exist as two separate beings. This dilemma is endlessly played out in the bulimia, as she must reassure herself she can completely possess and then reject her object; the coming and going in her treatment is a kind of whole body enactment of the bulimia.

Discussion

In standing back I observe that the clinical material has an *incestuous and all-consuming atmosphere* with scant sense of the outside: no real live children, husband, friends; parents are primitive and archaic with no ordinary human qualities. Mariah had succeeded in wrapping herself around her analyst so there is no breathing space. Paradoxically, she had also succeeded in being an *"on the run" patient who does not need* her analyst, and who, like Tom, is able to enact the exciting fantasy in which he does the holding for his psychiatrist and also manages to leave her bereft and missing him. This reversal of roles replicated Mariah's relationship with her original object, a mother who was clingy and possessive of her daughter, the child's needs thwarted in order that her mother's could be met. The fathers in the film, and in Mariah's childhood, were both violent and minimally involved with their children, deferring to a seductive and consuming mother. Mariah is caught, still the child of a mother unable to feel concern who instead possesses and exploits her daughter. She cannot stop running or "vacating" because it is necessary that her analyst feel this split-off neglect and abandonment, the ensuing desperate, needy longings which the patient cannot feel for herself. She alternates between her desire to fall into the arms of her mother/analyst and the panic this creates which necessitates action: she runs away. We see her yearning to masochistically submit to mother/analyst *and* her need to run (as did her Father), leaving an abandoned weak object behind.

Mariah's uncanny capacity to be victim and perpetrator at the same time is related to a *complicated series of identifications*, not in a normal sense but as part of an extreme and pathological series of moves. These processes can be followed as we think about Ms. M's *use of space* in relation to her analyst.

One day Mariah walked into the office and "placed her handbag on my desk, which was not her habit ... which I [Dr. G] experienced as a violation of my space." Mariah very quickly turned the discussion into what was being, and had been, done to her: "rage being heaped on me ... walking around in a state of suppressed rage ... see myself as powerless." And later her wish was to "stab them ... what a sexual act it is—it's sort of penetration. I can't let the world know what a horrible person I am." Although it may be right that the patient was involved in a sexualised and retaliating attack on her analyst, I thought there was another possible explanation. Mariah may be communicating her identification with her mother: her violation of the analyst's space brought her mother into the room, or more simply she *is* the mother and the analyst *is* the little girl. Little girls (like Mariah) have no private space apart from their mother, she has "identified with the aggressor" (A. Freud, 1937). We see in this action with her handbag that Mariah is "Cleopatra", a queen surrounded by underlings, or the privileged guest at a luxury spa. In this seemingly minor gesture she takes over the analyst's space and essentially her analyst's identity. It may feel in the moment to Mariah that her analyst's desk belongs to her, is hers to use however she pleases. This is further developed by Dr. G in another vignette:

> Once, she "forgot" her sunglasses, leaving them behind on the couch. Several minutes later, after the next patient had entered the office, there was a knock on the door; it was Mariah, interrupting the next patient's session to claim her sunglasses. What disturbed me most about the incident was not only the way in which she violated another patient's privacy, but her lack of concern for the other patient and failure to show remorse. When I raised this incident with her, I felt like the violating object, piercing through her bland denial.

Mariah seemed to feel, even to believe, that this space was hers, and she owed no apology or concern to her analyst or another patient. Her handbag and sunglasses are little bits of herself strewn around whereever she chooses. Again this seemed to be evidence of Mariah's introjection of her analyst in a total and concrete way. Whose office is it? She feels she can come and go as she pleases, it must belong to her. We see in relation to Dr. G, as with her mother, there is no permissible separation of identity. Importantly, it is the analyst who is left feeling as though she had done the violating—Mariah had successfully cut off her feelings of envy and smallness in relation to her analyst's possession of an office, an identity, and a capacity to understand, which the patient does not control. Instead the analyst feels she is small and powerless and in the grip of a powerful figure; if she does protest (become strong) she will injure a fragile innocent child.

Mariah's fantasy, which I think of as a massive projective identification, is also played out in her bathroom ritual. She used the analyst's office restroom for as much as fifteen minutes at a time, surely inconveniencing both her analyst and other patients. The analyst is left to feel intruded into and invaded; if she interprets the patient's mistreatment she will become the harsh, violating, "slapping" other. Mariah is highly skilled at inducing her object (i.e., the pharmacist, the security guard, business partner, husband, and analyst) to slap her, as she herself had done to a child when at age eighteen she worked in a summer camp. This must have been a time when her capacity for projective identification had broken down and she was at the mercy of her own impulses. During this period she gained eighteen pounds, frightening her into bulimic activity.

Theoretical considerations

I would like to suggest that Mariah's functioning is dominated by her pathological identificatory processes, involving both directions, that is, projection and introjection. She is able to insert herself into the other, taking the object over possessively as well as absorbing her object, becoming the other through incorporation.

By way of a quick review (following the work of Leslie Sohn (1988) and Ignes Sodre (2004)) I will highlight some psychoanalytic thinking (a sampling only) on identification. Sodre wrote:

> Freud's discovery, in "Mourning and Melancholia" of the process through which the ego unconsciously identifies with the intro-jected bad object (the rejecting loved object) thus becoming a victim of its own superego, was one of the most important breakthroughs in psychoanalysis The idea that when the individual feels "I am the worst person in the world" they may in fact be unconsciously accusing somebody else whose victim they feel they are, but who through a pathological process of introjection and identification, they have "become" ... (that is) the subject seems to have "become" the object. (p. 53)

In essence I am suggesting that Mariah has "become" her Mother (invasive/suffocating), at times her father (on the run/slapping), and at other moments the parental couple (the two directions combined into one)—who, as we understand, are not themselves separated but operate as a unit subsumed under the mother. As we observed in the clinical material, Mariah's identifications have been at the centre of her treatment, putting her analyst under enormous pressure to enact these processes with her.

Henry Rosenfeld wrote further on this fascinating topic.

> Identification is an important factor in narcissistic object relations. It may take place by introjection or by projection. When the object is omnipotently incorporated, the self becomes so identified with the incorporated object that all separate identity or boundary between self and object is denied. In projective identification parts of the self omnipotently enter an object, for example, the mother, to take over certain qualities which would be experienced as desirable, and therefore claim to be the object or part-object. Identification by introjection and by projection usually occur simultaneously. (1964, p. 170)

And returning to Sodre's paper:

> I will suggest that such states of pathological identification imply the excessive use not only of violent projections but also of concrete, pathological introjections and that this mode of functioning also relies for its 'success' on the massive use of manic defenses. (p. 55)

> The central characteristic of the use of 'projective identification' is the creation in the subject of a state of mind in which the boundaries between self and object have shifted. This state can be more or less flexible, temporary or permanent. (p. 56)—(involving) motives ... (and) also modes of functioning ... as well as wholesale concrete introjection of the object. (p. 57)

These ideas are also developed by Leslie Sohn in his paper "Narcissistic organization, projective identification and the formation of the identificate" (1988).

> To me it appears that in the narcissistic organization, an identification by projective identification has taken place; the process of identification starts the narcissistic organization: that is to say, by becoming the object, which is then felt to be within the possession of the self. (p. 277)

Further on he wrote:

> This consideration of the narcissistic organization ... is so different from the ones discussed by Freud and Melanie Klein, as we

have an unbalanced situation with *introjection kept at a minimum,* and a maintained split in the ego with its consequent disposal; it is because of this considerable difference that I dislike the term identification in this context—I would prefer the term identificate. (p. 278)

In reading Sohn on this point I think he is referring to the lack of normal introjection in these patients. We do see evidence of massive and incorporative introjection which does not provide the ego with what Klein called a "focal point" that works against splitting and does not require a merging of self and object. (Italics are mine.)

Identification is a central aspect of normal development. Freud wrote in his paper "Identification" in "Group Psychology and the Analysis of the Ego" (1921) that "Identification is known to psycho-analysis as the earliest expression of an emotional tie with another person" (p. 105). And Melanie Klein wrote:

internalization is of great importance for projective processes, in particular that the good internalized breast acts as a focal point in the ego, from which good feelings can be projected on to external objects. It strengthens the ego, counteracts the processes of splitting and dispersal and enhances the capacity for integration and synthesis. The good internalized object is thus one of the preconditions for an integrated and stable ego and for good object relations. (1955, p. 312)

Both Freud and Klein describe identification as a form of, as well as the outcome of, good relations between self and object. In turning to Mariah, we can see that there is little evidence of what could be called an ordinary "emotional tie with another person" or what Klein called the good internalised object that allows the projection of good feelings onto the external object. Rather, her relations are essentially sadomasochistic—there seems to be no interaction free of this virulence. I hope I have been able to show in Dr. G's excellent clinical material how the sadism was continuous between patient and analyst. Tracing the very slippery slope between the victim and victimiser is extremely challenging. In the very act of interpretation meant to rescue the analyst from her masochistic position, she becomes the sadist.

Mariah "takes over" Dr. G's desk, office, the subsequent hour of another patient, the bathroom—usurping time and space, thereby revealing her concrete and massive *introjection* of her analyst: what is yours is mine, I am now you. We see her omnipotence and grandiosity, reflecting her mania. The patient simultaneously *projects* her weakness, including dependency and envy, into the analyst, succeeding in getting a hold on her mental functioning. The analyst is pressured to stop being the analyst (there is already one very confident analyst in the room!) and to feel like a sadist, or weak, or envious or whatever. One's *separate identity* is momentarily (we hope) lost and we will feel disturbed, perhaps inhibited in our functioning; the internal work of righting ourselves and remembering "who is who" is crucial in these situations. (Sodre, 2004)

Conclusion

Dr. Greenman has provided a beautiful and moving case study of a patient who is severely narcissistic, but more specifically gripped by her pathological identifications, what Sohn has called the "identificate" which is in contrast to those identifications that are more flexible and integrated within the ego. This reader's confusion in the opening lines of the paper reveals a patient deeply at odds with herself. The analyst's job, to find out who she is at any given moment and to make contact with that experience, is daunting. We see—because the victim-victimiser roles shift so quickly, even imperceptibly at times, and that like the combined parental couple, they often exist at the same time—the analyst will always be "wrong" (by which I mean caught on one side or the other of the sadomasochism). Nevertheless it is the following of the patient's movements between her identificates which is necessary. It is only with this kind of work that the patient can begin (her struggle here with Dr. G) to believe in the possibility of a good object not taken over by her sadistic and masochistic drives. Mariah appears to be holding very tight to her earliest objects, to the point that the analytic "cure" feels to her like its own kind of illness. As analysts we must keep in mind not only who the patient is at any given moment but who we are as the object of our patient, which includes our commitment to psychoanalysis as a method of growth and development and not one of illness and destruction.

References

Caper, Robert (1999). A theory of the container. In: *A Mind of One's Own*. Routledge: London and New York.

Freud, A. (1937). *The Ego and the Mechanisms of Defence*. London: Hogarth Press and the Institute of Psychoanalysis.

Freud, S. (1917). 'Mourning and melancholia'. *S. E., 14*: 237–258.

Freud, S. (1921). 'Group psychology and the analysis of the ego'. *S. E., 18*: 65–144.

Joseph, B. (1989). *Psychic Equilibrium and Psychic Change: Selected Papers of Betty Joseph*, M. Feldman and E. Bott Spillius (Eds.). London: Routledge.

Klein, M. (1955). On identification. In: *The Writings of Melanie Klein*, vol. 3, *Envy and Gratitude and Other Works*. London: Hogarth Press (1975).

O'Shaughnessy, E. (1983). Words and working through. *International Journal of Pyscho-analysis*, 64: 281–289.

Rosenfeld, H. (1964). On the psychopathology of narcissism: A clinical approach. In: *Psychotic States*. London: Karnac, 1965.

Sohn, L. (1988). Narcissistic organization, projective identification, and the formation of the identificate: In: *Melanie Klein Today: Developments in Theory and Practice, vol. 1*. London and New York: Routledge and Tavistock.

Sodre, I. (2000). Florence and Sigmund's excellent adventure: (On Oedipus and us), presented at the English Speaking Conference, London.

Sodre, I. (2004). Who's who? Pathological identifications. In: E. Hargreaves & A. Varchevker (Eds.), *In Pursuit of Psychic Change: The Betty Joseph Workshop*. Hove and New York: Brunner-Routledge.

CHAPTER FOURTEEN

Trauma, archaic superego, and sadomasochism: discussion of the case of Mariah

Léon Wurmser

This very impressive case and treatment study confronts us with issues that are very frequent in our practice, but not often presented in such a dramatic and graphic form. There were several elements in it and questions that struck me especially:

1

One is the massive **depersonalisation** that affects much of the experience both of patient and analyst—the pervasive absence of self-feeling in the perceptions of self and world, as if they said: "I do not feel this (or anything) to be real although I know it is." One could talk about estrangement as a dominant quality of transference and countertransference. She feels "emotionally detached while apparently engaged working with her partner" (it is not clear who is meant here by "partner"), and the analyst notes "the flat quality in our interaction". She "began to think about how she had lived in a false world, warding off real emotional contact with people." In regard to the frequent absences and interruptions, "she denied that she had any feeling about it at all", but would "tell me about a sense of emotional vacancy"; the "vacations ... left her with a sense of internal deadness and emptiness

213

since she had severed any internal connection with me. Often she would describe a deep sense of isolation from her husband as well." The therapist "felt ignored and discarded"; "when she left I was moved into a space where I was enclosed in an impenetrable bubble; it felt lonely, frozen and isolated"—a very good description of depersonalisation in the countertransference. Dr. Greenman adds: "I felt she never 'really' heard me and noted again my annoyance at being disregarded ..." and the urgent need to "pierce" her resistance and "to get through to her".

Concomitantly with such depersonalisation, goes the sense of discontinuity and its factual repetition time and again by the disruptive "acting out", similar to what a patient of mine kept complaining about: "It is a profound discontinuity: that nothing good can be held onto."

Who is not remembered and perceived as a continuous self forgets himself and thus his inner continuity—in a poignant image drawn by Sheldon Bach (2001): "... a person's specific memories and experiences are like individual beads that can achieve continuity and gestalt form only when they are strung together to become a necklace. The string on which they are assembled is the child's continuous existence in the mind of the parent, which provides the continuity on which the beads of experiences are strung together and become the necklace of a connected life" (p. 748)—and with that of an identity. Typically, the contents of the therapy sessions are being forgotten or estranged from one time to the other: "I don't remember what we have been talking about last time."

The same metaphor is used by another patient, in connection with her emotional distance toward her lover. She relays how she succeeded for the first time, while reaching a climax, in staying in her sensations both with him and with herself: "You have to imagine it that way, as if the feelings were to correspond to pearls, and they had been laying scattered on the table, each one for itself wonderfully beautiful, but unconnected, and it was so as if in this experience they were strung on a thread: suddenly they were joined together" (communicated by Dr. Heidrun Jaraß, a psychoanalyst in Regensburg, Germany, with whom I have been working continually and intensively since 1988).

The experience of meaning and of time grows out of a sense of connectedness of experience, and this in turn grows with the remembrance by and of the other in one's own inner life. Clinical experience has taught us that there is an intimate relationship between chronic depersonalisation/derealisation and chronic, unconscious shame (as I extensively described in The Mask of Shame, 1981). There appears to be a deep, clinically observable parallelism: just as massive unconscious guilt tends to lead to chronic depression, massive repressed shame is likely to lead to chronic depersonalisation. To what extent is this borne out by the observation of Mariah?

In his beautifully written and important book, Disappearing Persons—Shame and Appearance, Benjamin Kilborne (2002) stresses the central role of the feeling of shame for this disturbed sense of identity and inner discontinuity. He quotes Milan Kundera: "Shame is one of the key notions of the Modern Era ... we enter adulthood through the rebellion of shame" (p. 70). Crucial to the understanding of the link between shame and identity is the polarity of fantasies of appearance and anxiety over disappearing (p. 5). This polarity and its inherent dialectic shape our identity: "To imagine what we are looking at, to imagine ourselves looking and being looked at while looking—all seem essential to our sense of who we are, and to some confidence in the continuity of our lives" (p. 70). In reverse, it means, as one of Kilborne's patients states: "You could say that you are without an identity when you can't recognize in others what you can't see in yourself. Without an identity you can't make a connection"—and we may poignantly add the reverse: without a connection and relationship you can't create an identity (p. 32). This discontinuity of being seen and seeing oneself is preeminently rooted in the shame created by the soul blindness of others, paramount of course by the parents' soul blindness. Kilborne speaks therefore of "their [his patients'] overpowering feeling that they are unrecognizable, that there is no place for them as themselves, that consequently they are struggling against both fears of recognition and fears of being not-seen ... [In the transference] they repeat the sense of being doomed to be invisible, while longing for recognition" (p. 26).

2

What is the relationship between these two—depersonalisation and shame—and the sadomasochistic symptomatology? Again, clinical experience shows that one of the functions of induced suffering, like cutting, bingeing, or vomiting, can be attempts to pierce the wall of not-feeling, but are in themselves so circular as to only engender vastly deepened shame, and hence lead to more depersonalisation. Dr. Greenman writes, the patient "express[es] shame about her bingeing" upon return from her frequent vacations. "Without the beatings [by her father], she feared that there would have been a deep emotional void in her relationship with him. With me too, her sense that she would experience me as angry with her made her feel that she mattered." The therapist speaks about Mariah's "exquisitely vulnerable core, which she had no adequate means of protecting." I think here she speaks about extreme vulnerability to humiliation and shame. She goes on: "Contact with other human beings left her feeling overwhelmed and threatened her with a sense of dissolution; she had no secure means of safely and reliably securing her sense of boundedness as an individual. Her reliance on bingeeating, binge shopping and self-grooming were all methods of shoring up a very fragile sense of self, and her repeated sadomasochistic enactments ensured that others would never get too close."

All this could be put in terms of a self that is very profoundly threatened by shame. She actively brings about various forms of self-abasement and self-degradation in order not to have to suffer them passively, suddenly, and helplessly. The "inner deadness and emptiness", as well as the "impenetrable bubble" are thus above all defences against traumatic and traumatogenic shame—the former in the form of traumatising humiliation, the latter as a reaction to trauma more generally. I also think that the inhibition of the analyst from questioning the patient about the disruptive breaks or communicating her own anger may have been an intuitive reaction to her preconscious awareness of how sensitive Mariah was and is to being shamed. Every "penetration" by an interpretation, especially of the transference, let alone of the countertransference, would be experienced as a very dangerous humiliation.

In narcissistically very vulnerable and seriously traumatised patients, transference interpretations quite generally can be quite ill tolerated. Fischer and Riedesser stress in their in their standard textbook of psychotraumatology (2003) the required caution with direct transference interpretations. They tend to stoke the great affective pressure even more (p. 212):

> The concentration upon the here-and-now, be it in the framework of affect-activating therapeutic approaches or in an exclusive "transference analysis", is contraindicated in trauma patients. The past subverts the present without its being recognized or named. The therapist fails to help his patient in the differentiation of past and present. Psychotherapy with trauma patients that is restricted to

the here-and-now of the therapeutic relationship runs the danger of being retraumatizing. It does not allow the patient to experience the therapeutic work relationship in optimal difference to the past and potentially exposes him to an unmitigated reexperiencing of the destructive experience. (p. 225)

On the other side, a mere reconstruction of the past without reference to the actual life situation and the transference relationship also fails the optimal difference and becomes an intellectualising and rationalising preoccupation with the past (ibid.).

Returning to Mariah, we might ask: Could we perhaps also understand the frequent breaks in the treatment as a manoeuvre to avoid painful shame—shame about closeness, shame about intense feelings of any kind, shame about dependency, shame about penetrating interpretations or clarifications, shame about revealing her own overwhelming feelings, especially her sadomasochistic fantasies?

Especially masochistic fantasies of all kinds are usually felt with extreme embarrassment and therefore very carefully hidden.

3

Usually, such severe psychopathology is rooted in massive traumatisation. Fischer and Riedesser define, trauma "as a vital experience of discrepancy between threatening situational factors and the individual's abilities of mastery, a discrepancy that is accompanied by feelings of helplessness and unprotected exposure and thus effects a lasting shock in the understanding of self and world" (p. 82); they reject therefore the term "*post*traumatic stress disorder" and replace it with "*(basal) psychotraumatic stress syndrome*" (pp. 46, 372). Trauma is an ongoing process, not simply an external event (p. 46), and they distinguish shock trauma from cumulative trauma.

There are, of course, many forms of traumatisation, but of special importance is what we may call "soul blindness" and "soul murder": "*Soul blindness*" is a systematic, chronic disregard for the emotional needs and expressions of the child (or, more generally, towards other people), a peculiar blindness to the individuality and hostility to the autonomy of the child (or one's fellow). It shows itself as the peculiar dehumanisation of the other person, as that what Francis Brouček (1991) has called "objectification" and postulated as the core of the shame experience. Put differently, soul blindness is a severe form of lack of empathy. As to "*soul murder*", Shengold (1989) defines it as "the deliberate attempt to eradicate or compromise the separate identity of another person ... depriving the victim of the ability to feel joy and love as a separate person" (p. 2). It stands "for a certain category of traumatic experience: instances of repetitive and chronic overstimulation, alternating with emotional deprivation, that are deliberately brought about by another individual" (p. 16). The first term refers to something that is too little, the second to something that is too much; yet they cannot be clearly separated and belong also clinically closely together. Also, trauma and inner conflict are complementary concepts.

In Mariah's case we find it, manifestly and consciously, throughout her childhood in both primary relationships, foremost to her father in strong physical abuse, accompanied by sexualisation, another cause for shame, and emotionally to her mother who seems to have related to the child with deep ambivalence and a lot of double-bind messages.

We may also define trauma as an overwhelming, unsolvable external conflict between self and environment, that leads to a conscious, but unsolvable inner conflict. The affects battling each other overwhelm the capacity of the ego to master them, a failure that leads to the split between the groups of ideas, to the act of making the connections unconscious, about which Freud originally spoke (Breuer & Freud, 1893/1895). Dissociation and even hypnoid states remain important concepts for the understanding of the traumatic genesis of the severe neuroses.

Severe, repeated traumatisation means that every emotional experience resonates as if it were the recurrence of the trauma. It leads to the standstill, usually partial, of affective development: the differentiation, verbalisation and desomatisation of the emotions are blocked, as Henry Krystal has so well described. Thus in traumatisation, by definition, the feelings, once roused, very rapidly become overwhelming, get out of control, are global ("dedifferentiated"), beyond symbolisation ("deverbalised"), and are being experienced, as if they were physical ("resomatised"). These three concepts of dedifferentiation, deverbalisation or hyposymbolisation, and of resomatisation represent, according to Krystal, affect regression (Krystal, 1988, 1998).

But there is something else of great importance, especially in recurrent traumatisation in childhood: these affects tend to appear in sexualised form. Sexualisation is an archaic defence set up to regulate affect. The affect flooding, combined with this very primordial defense by sexualisation, leads, however, to an overwhelming sense of humiliation and embarrassment: not to have any control over one's own emotional life is just as shaming as the loss of sphincter control, if not more so. Aggressive wishes are then being used to reestablish control, a form of further archaic defence to deal preventively with a spiraling out of control, an important way of turning passive into active. In this connection it is also very important to see not only the passivity towards the outside, but, at least as essential, the ego's passivity vis-à-vis the affects, the drives and the lashings by the superego (Rapaport, 1953).

The result of such severe disturbance of affect regulation is an archaic equation we typically encounter in the intensive, long-term treatment of the severe neuroses. The following five states and contents are equated: 1. overstimulation by something on the outside which is being experienced as traumatic, as intolerable, and to which one feels helplessly, passively exposed; 2. overwhelming, but usually contradictory feelings, the sense of bursting, "I cannot stand it anymore", the traumatic state (that inner state of passivity); 3. something devouring, consuming, that is, the imagery of orality, like rapacious animals or elements (fire, floods); 4. sexual excitement; and 5. aggressive fantasies and of violence, even cruelty (Shengold, 1989). Each of the five may be an entrance point into the equation (Wurmser, 1993, 2000, 2007).

Dr. Greenman's case study states: "... she frequently turned pleasurable experiences into painful ones." This is the response to the reverse: that she learned to turn painful experiences into pleasurable ones, in the very early and powerful form of defence by sexualizstion (Wurmser, 2007, "the alchemist's dream" in the case Elazar; Fraiberg, 1982; Novick & Novick, 1996a, 1996b).

Losing control over the affects, the collapse of affect regulation, and the conflict between global, but opposing affects, is indeed a primary danger, evoking a most profound sense of helplessness, of "fragmentation" and "splitting", and thus deepening in circular form the basic anxiety and shame; it is not even necessary theoretically to resort to fears of abandonment, rejection, castration, or self-condemnation to explain this anxiety. All these latter dreads simply give the necessary concrete and specific form, rooted in personal history, to those overwhelming, repetitive, traumatic experiences.

4

Overriding in Mariah's consciousness is the archaic superego: an implacable inner judge that is being either experienced as coming from the outside, or provoked there, in an active re-enactment of what had been suffered passively, in other words: turning passive into active, or in Kleinian parlance: by projective identification. "… she would develop an experience of a very cruel, punitive and unforgiving other whom she saw both in me and in her husband, leading her to withdraw from contact or interaction." So much in her behaviour can best be understood as a provocation of punishment: "Many transference events indicated that she created an experience where she could see me as hostile, critical, and dangerously violating; judging her for a variety of self-gratifying behaviours: travelling, shopping, but especially about her eating … her continuous need to create a relationship with a sadistically violating object where she could experience herself as punitively beaten and assaulted, and her need to flee from that". "… she was trying to push me away as well as elicit a punitive response from me. I became the father who beat her … It seemed safer to have me angry with her than happy with her." To elicit the figure of the tormenting judge on the outside, under her active stage management, was a powerful defence against suffering it incessantly from within.

How can we understand psychodynamically this archaic, totalitarian superego which is ubiquitous after severe and prolonged traumatisation?

In the severe neuroses (and they are almost coextensive with severe and chronic traumatisation in childhood), we deal on the one side with wishes insisting on their absolute fulfillment and equally global affects, in particular the manifold, overwhelming anxieties, but also rage and shame and guilt (and others), that involve similar claims for absoluteness. On the other side, the defensive processes trying to protect the self against the overpowering dangers from without and within are equally absolute, equally radical and all-encompassing. And ultimately, the conscience and the "ideal demands" become the leading representatives of this inner absoluteness, and with that we have those fatal vicious circles, the repetitive patterns (also Wurmser, 1996, 1999, 2000). Inner polarity in its entirety is then marked by such absoluteness. "Abyss calls the abyss" (Psalm 42.8)!

The just-described archaic equation of traumatogenic affective storms, sexualisation, and aggression is in turn again very deeply frightening and humiliating, calls for equally global defenses, and eventually to massive counteractions by the superego, in the form of pervasive and global forms of guilt and shame: "... and conscience, turned tyrant, held passion by the throat" (Ch. Brontë, *Jane Eyre*). A very central part of such an overweening superego is the omnipotence of responsibility: "It is in my power to prevent all these disasters. If they recur, my guilt is total."

The archaic superego manifests itself by pervasive, internalised, global guilt feelings and shame. These may be conscious or unconscious, with a strong sadistic, that is, sexualised component. Psychodynamically, the prominence of broken reality, both experiential and observable, can, therefore, not only be understood as the outcome of <u>defense against traumatisation</u>, but at the same time also as *defence against superego pressure*, or, more precisely, against *contradictory superego demands*— like opposing values and ideals, commitments and loyalties, and especially shame against guilt (*shame-guilt dilemmas*: Wurmser, 1981, 1993, 2000, 2007). Confronted with these antitheses ("intrasystemic superego conflicts"), the individual feels powerless, even fragmented: "torn asunder".

The archaic defences most prominently dealing with the overstimulation inherent in trauma appear to be in Mariah's case above all: sexualisation, turning passive into active, and identification with the aggressor (=turning against the self). It is this transmutation of the trauma and its overexcitement that we encounter in the severe sadomasochistic symptomatology, the character of all her outer and inner object relations, and of course particularly dauntingly in the archaic superego.

Both the wish to penetrate and the fear of being penetrated directly reflect the penetrating quality of the physical and emotional traumata. Stabbing, penetration, piercing—these are excellent metaphors for the doubleness of passively suffered trauma and their active repetition, for traumatic overstimulation. The depersonalisation acts as a protective shield against such penetration.

5

The feeling of shame in its multi-layeredness and depth is prominent among the frightening affects induced by trauma. What is this original link?

One root may indeed be *massive shaming* as part of the trauma, and that seems to be a self-evident connection, and certainly easily inferred in the way Mariah had been mistreated. But there is far more that we uncover in our analytic work.

Very commonly it is *the shame about the intensity of feelings* in general, the great anxiety to express them, and the anxiety of inner and outer loss of control. It is so often the premise in the family, supported by cultural prejudice, that it is a sign of disgraceful weakness and thus of vulnerability, to show, or even just to have, strong feelings. This causes a very strong tendency to be deeply ashamed. The body, especially sexuality, may be far less strongly shame inducing than this alleged weakness of having strong feelings: feelings of neediness, of longing, of tenderness, of being moved, of being hurt. Many look then for a partner who is an *anti-shame-hero*: someone emotionally untouchable, impenetrable, invulnerable, a disdainful ruler. Looking for the acceptance by such a figure and merger with him or her would remove the shame of feeling and wishing too strongly, but it means an almost incorrigible masochistic bondage, and a renewed and deepened sense of disgrace (Wurmser, 1981, 2011).

Third, shame is caused by the experience that one has not been perceived as a person with the right for one's own feelings and will. The *"soul blindness"* of the other evokes the feeling of great worthlessness; the contempt by the other expressed by disregard for one's own inner life is matched by self-contempt (certainly quite prevalent in Mariah's case). Analysis itself may be shaming and thus inadvertently repeat the traumatogenic shame. There are many ways of doing this: sometimes it may be the silence to a question, sometimes a sarcastic comment, often direct drive interpretations, and, what I see particularly in my supervisions in Europe, the unempathic, forced relating of every aspect to transference (see above). All this can be felt to be "soul blind". Incomprehension and tactlessness are experienced as a renewed deep insult and shaming.

Fourth, typically in severe traumatisation in childhood and as already described, sexualisation is deployed as an attempt to regulate affects. Both the flooding with affects and the very archaic defense by sexualisation lead to an overwhelming feeling of shame. On an additional frontline of defence, aggressive wishes, impulses, and fantasies are thrown in as means to re-establish control; they should stop the further tumble in that regressive spiral.

Fifth, every kind of excitement turns, as affect regression, into overexcitement and overstimulation, and this inevitably leads to a crash, to a very painful disappointment. This traumatic, passively experienced process is again and again turned around into something actively re-enacted. How so? It happens in that way that every joy, every gratification, every expectation, everything good has to be broken off and changed into something negative and bad. It may seem as if it were unconscious guilt that would make it appear as if one did not deserve to be successful. This may certainly contribute. But that dangerous, mortifying, shame-laden excitement appears to be more important: "It is too dangerous to sense pleasure and joy; it will be abruptly taken away or it will become unbearably intense and totally unfulfillable." Thus the inner judge, the archaic superego, has to prevent all pleasure. I think this is most central in Mariah's development and clinical state and also being continually re-enacted in the form of those "breaks".

Closely connected with this is a sixth reason, already briefly mentioned: that of the *intrapsychic passivity*. David Rapaport (1953) wrote about the passivity of the ego. Often, what appears as if ordained from the outside, is in truth an inner passivity in regard to affects and drives, but also, and no less so, a passivity vis-à-vis the threatening and hammering superego. There is not only profound anxiety about being helplessly delivered to these inner powers, but also shame for such *inner ego-passivity*. Outer victimhood is very often its externalisation: a repetition on the outside in the vain attempt to resolve it within.

6

Reading Mariah's history I was wondering about its transgenerational aspects. There are vague references to the background: "emigrated shortly before the onset of war". Had they emigrated from Europe to Latin America in order to escape from the Holocaust? Or from Latin America to the US before some war there? In the former and likelier case, it seems to me inescapable to assume that the family's traumatisation by persecution, mortal threat, terror, and extermination would be of enormous, albeit strongly denied, presence behind the phenomena described in the study of case and treatment. If my conjecture is correct, the entire case study needs to be understood in that light: this would be the cardinal psychodynamic fact around which the entire psychodynamics revolve. Not to mention that this would be a grave omission, and not to deal with it as a central issue would express pervasive denial (Grubrich-Simitis, 2008).

7

Finally, especially in the treatment with so severely and chronically traumatised patients as Mariah, particularly if my surmise of the connection with the Holocaust is borne out, we may have to resort to a framework different from the one that is solely based on the theory of technique, and hence on the "analysis of transference". It is a difference of the philosophical vantage point.

As psychoanalysts we usually go out from the a priori assumption that inner life can best be understood by seeing all the inner processes as incessantly standing in conflict with each other and continually also complementing each other in spite of their contradictions. Without this philosophical presupposition, psychoanalysis would be unthinkable. It is being used and is useful in every moment of our work.

But it is not the only one. There is a second a priori presupposition: that all these insights are only truly mutative if they occur in the matrix of an emotionally intimate relationship, a deep trustful togetherness that far transcends intellectual insight. Here Buber's philosophy of dialogue appears to be particularly helpful. In no way should it supplant the understanding by conflict, it should only complement it. In other words, the intrapsychic and the interpersonal or relational way of understanding are dialectically bound to each other. One without the other does not do justice to the complexity of our work. The more severe traumatisation there is as background, the more important is the real relationship in treatment (Grubrich-Simitis, 2007, 2008). This is, of course, particularly true in families of the survivors of the Holocaust and of other genocides.

This is an inescapable conclusion from work that is as difficult and demanding as that so skillfully carried out and so well described by Dr. Greenman and others who work with survivors.

> The innateness of the longing for relation is apparent even in the earliest and dimmest stage … It is not as if a child first saw an object and then entered into some relationship with that. Rather, the longing for relation is primary, the cupped hand into which the being that confronts us nestles; and the relation to that, which is a wordless anticipation of saying You, comes second. But the genesis of the thing [*das Dingwerden*] is a late product that develops

out of the split of the primal encounters [*Urerlebnisse*], out of the separation of the associated partners—as does the genesis of the I. *In the beginning is the relation [Im Anfang ist die Beziehung]* [my emphasis]—as the category of being, as readiness, as a form that reaches out to be filled, as a model of the soul; the *a priori* of relation; *the innate You [das eingeborene Du]* [emphasis Buber]. In the relationships through which we live, the innate You is realized in the You we encounter: that this, comprehended as a being we confront and accepted as exclusive, can finally be addressed with the basic word, has its ground in the *a priori* of relation. (Buber, 1947, pp. 38–39)

References

Bach, S. (2001). On being forgotten and forgetting oneself. *Psychoanalytic Quarterly*, 70: 739–756.

Breuer, J. & Freud, S. (1893–1895). Studies on Hysteria. S. E., 2: 1–251.

Brontë, C. (1847, in 1994). Jane Eyre. In: *The Brontës. Three Great Novels*. Oxford: Oxford University Press.

Brouček, F. J. (1991). *Shame and the Self.* New York: Guilford.

Buber, M. (1947). *Dialogisches Leben.* Zürich: Gregor Müller Verlag. (W. Kaufman (Trans). *I and Thou*, pp. 77–79).

Fischer, G. & Riedesser, P. (2003). *Lehrbuch der Psychotraumatologie* (3rd, revised edition). München: Reinhardt.

Fraiberg, S. (1982). Pathological defenses in infancy. *Psychoanalytic Quarterly*, 51: 612–635.

Grubrich-Simitis, I. (2007). Trauma oder Trieb—Trieb und Trauma: Wiederbetrachtet. *Psyche*, 61: 637–656.

Grubrich-Simitis, I. (2008). Realitätsprüfung an Stelle von Deutung. *Psyche*, 62: 1091–1121.

Kilborne, B. (2002). *Disappearing Persons: Shame and Appearance.* Albany: State University of New York Press.

Krystal, H. (1988). *Integration and Self-healing: Affect, Trauma, Alexithymia.* Hillsdale, NJ: Analytic Press.

Krystal, H. (1998). Desomatization and the consequences of infantile trauma. *Psychoanalytic Inquiry*, 17(2): 126–50.

Novick, J. & Novick, K. K. (1996a). *Fearful Symmetry: The Development and Treatment of Sadomasochism.* Northvale, NJ: Aronson.

Novick, J. & Novick, K. K. (1996b). A developmental perspective on omnipotence. *Journal of Clinical Psychoanalysis*, 5: 131–75.

Rapaport, D. (1953/1967). Some metapsychologial considerations concerning activity and passivity. In: M. M. Gill (Ed.), *Collected papers of D. Rapaport*, (pp. 530–568). New York: Basic Books.

Shengold, L. (1989). *Soul Murder: The Effects of Childhood Abuse and Deprivation*. New Haven, CT: Yale University Press.

Wurmser, L. (1981). *The Mask of Shame*. Baltimore: Johns Hopkins University Press.

Wurmser, L. (1993). *Das Rätsel des Masochismus. Psychoanalytische Untersuchungen von Gewissenszwang und Leidenssucht*. (The Riddle of Masochism. Psychoanalytic Studies of the Compulsion of Conscience and the Addiction to Suffering) Heidelberg: Springer-Verlag.

Wurmser, L. (1996). Psychoanalytic trauma, inner conflict, and the vicious cycles of repetition. *Scandinavian Review, 19*: 17–45.

Wurmser, L. (1999). *Magische Verwandlung und tragische Verwandlung. Die Behandlung der schweren Neurose* (Magic Transformation and Tragic Transformation. The Treatment of Severe Neurosis). Göttingen: Vandenhoeck & Ruprecht.

Wurmser, L. (2000). *The Power of the Inner Judge*. Northvale, NJ: Aronson.

Wurmser, L. (2007). *"Torment Me, But Don't Abandon Me". Psychoanalysis of the Severe Neuroses in a New Key*. New York: Rowman & Littlefield.

Wurmser, L. (2011). *Scham und der böse Blick. Verstehen der negativen therapeutischen Reaktion*. Stuttgart: Kohlhammer.

PART IV

CASE PRESENTED BY RICHARD REICHBART AND DISCUSSIONS

The primitive superego of Mr. A: sadistic revenge fantasies, arousal and then masochistic remorse

Richard Reichbart

It is hard to remember the feeling I had treating Mr. A fifteen years ago or to convey the texture of those early sessions. Mr. A could be tedious in the extreme and so consistently repetitive as to lead me to often roll my eyes as he lay on the couch. In fact, the beginnings of sessions for years were more or less the same with his stating in almost the exact same words how he did not want to be in treatment, how I was out to hurt him, how he could not possibly say anything new, how he wanted to leave. At the beginning of his treatment, the sessions would only be different after an obligatory forty minutes of this diatribe. Over years, the obligatory time was gradually reduced to half an hour, to fifteen minutes, to ten minutes, until eventually fourteen years into treatment, it would be only a sentence or two about how he was still not comfortable coming to see me. At the same time for years of early treatment, he was anxiety-provoking, frequently threatening suicide at the end of sessions (which at one early point led him to arrange a noose for himself in the basement of his parent's home, a basement to which he often retreated to stare for hours at the fish in the large fish tank which he tended there) and often begging me, pleading with me, to "let him go", to just give up on him. I think I benefited from a certain naïveté: he was an early psychoanalytic case and I was

229

overjoyed to have anyone on the couch. And despite what often struck more experienced psychoanalysts as something approaching psychosis about him (I was told by one analyst to whom I presented the case as a candidate that he was a "very sick" man and told repeatedly that he would make a poor control case), I found myself plodding along with him day after day, year after year, tedium after tedium, only to find years later somewhat to my own surprise that this marginal individual, this self-made outcast had fashioned a life for himself, married, become a loving if conflicted father to two children, and gained some understanding of his emotions and his fears.

But things were hardly promising at the beginning. Mr. A, twenty-six years old, appeared in speech and affect tighter than a drum. He was hunched, his face expressionless, and he gave off the impression of not wanting to notice anyone or to be noticed. When he sat on a waiting room chair, staring downward, he seemed as if sitting on a New York subway train the kind of person to whom one might instinctively give a wide berth. He exuded suspicion of others, everything in his face and body saying, "Stay away from me. Don't talk to me." Indeed, for ten years Mr. A reported that he feared coming to the waiting room and preferred to enter just a moment before the session from his car in the parking lot. He avoided eye contact with anyone he met in the street and certainly with other patients. For that matter, he also did not let register obvious things in his environment. It took him fifteen years to realise that there was a large watercolour of tiger lilies on the far wall of my consulting room, beyond where I sat, one of the first things one might ordinarily see on entering. It was useless information to him: each time he entered he looked sideways at me and made his way to the couch.

For that matter, there was not much information that Mr. A could impart about himself because he did not remember his early childhood at all. His memories seemed to begin around adolescence and they were traumatic. It was almost as if at the symbolic moment of his Bar-Mitzvah, Mr. A had decided to leave civilised society rather than journey into responsible manhood; and that was the way he thought of his development. When adolescence came, right after the Bar-Mitzvah, Mr. A, who described himself as having until then friends who were "normal" (although in fact he never spoke of them), changed his friends, becoming involved with a sadistic boy whom he idolised and whose ways he tended to follow. The reasons for the change no one knew but it became clear that one of them was that Mr. A believed that as an adolescent his breasts had become enlarged, making him look feminine which then became symbolic for him of the fact that normal kids would not have anything to do with him. From that moment, he avoided taking off his shirt, refused to go swimming in his family's pool, gave up swimming entirely although he enjoyed it, and changed his friends. For six years in treatment he continued to believe that he had enlarged breasts; and only after fourteen years was he able to remark to me, "What was I thinking when I thought I had breasts?"

Another reason for the change after his Bar-Mitzvah was that Mr. A felt he could not view the world in what he considered a "normal" way, meaning loving or accepting. Instead, he believed the world was cruel and terrifying and that in ways unknown even to his family, he himself was warped. For that matter, he took distinct sadistic pleasure in his own and the world's harshness. The "normal" ways of the world—any view that the world was at all beneficent—were disdained for being as fatuous as cotton candy.

Before I proceed further in this history, however, I do not wish to give the impression that Mr. A told me details of his history directly. On the contrary, he told me things in dribs and drabs over many months and many years. For years Mr. A would omit telling me of an event from his past that he knew was crucial, because he was embarrassed or felt that what he had done was terrible. Then when he had reached some internal point when he felt that it might be safe to tell me about the event, he would say that he had something important to tell me but could not. After often months of this, he would tell me a portion of the event but leave out a crucial part, something I might extract if the story he told was clearly incomplete, and at other times, something of which I remained entirely unaware for additional months or years. This tendency to withhold with its teasing quality was not just a defence: it was a sadistic aggression, designed—albeit sometimes unconsciously—to mislead and frustrate me.

There were many events to which this process applied, almost all sexual in nature. Mr. A eventually told me that his adolescence was all but haunted (my words not his) by his mother's seductiveness toward him. When he began treatment, he described his mother with reverence and awe as the strong parent who had established her own business. He thought of his father in contrast as weak and spoke of him with disdain. By the time of his adolescence, his parents' roles at home had apparently changed from his childhood: his mother who formerly had done the housework now did very little. His father, whose work hours were less demanding, did all the cooking. Typically, when Mr. A was an adolescent, his mother came to the dinner table in her underwear. The table was glass, and Mr. A would become obsessed at looking at her crotch; his interest in her was particularly aggravated when at the end of the meal, she pushed her chair back and relaxed with a cigarette, crossing her legs. In the evening, Mr. A would also go to his mother's bedroom, where she would lie in her underwear, and he would sit on the bed while she helped him with his homework. His mother had been an elementary school teacher, but this process of help from her was fraught with mixed feelings by Mr. A. He could not take his eyes off of her, always wondering how much of herself she would expose; and he believed in part that she wanted him to look at her. (As it was, Mr. A had great difficulty in school; he appears to have some degree of dyslexia—so that his mother helped him by actually doing much of the work. How much of this learning disability was created and not just aggravated by knowledge itself becoming sexualised as a conse-quence of his mother's efforts was never entirely clear. Suffice it to say, however, that by the end of treatment, Mr. A was able to learn without hindrance; his job performance and his responsibility for the welfare of others at his job were dependent upon this improved reading and understanding.)

When his parents were out of the house, Mr. A would enter their bedroom, remove his mother's frilly underwear and put on her panties. He found this tremendously exciting and would masturbate. Some-times he would take his mother's underwear and dispose of it because he was afraid his ejaculate on it would be discovered. Other times, he would just return the underwear to the drawer. He was somewhat con-vinced that his mother was aware of his activity because, after all, her underwear disappeared from time to time.

Often after dinner and his having been helped with his homework, his parents would retire to their bedroom from which a strong odour then emanated, making it obvious that they were smoking marijuana. This whole procedure infuriated Mr. A: he felt he had been allowed to be aroused by his mother only to have her then go into the bedroom with his father behind a closed door. At one point, Mr. A discovered that there was a marijuana plant growing in the backyard. Indeed, Mr. A as an adolescent began to indulge himself heavily in pot to the extent that he became a dealer, never mentioning his activity to his parents. His pot smoking was so intense, getting high every day for years, that for much of his early treatment he was convinced that his inability to recall his childhood reflected brain damage that he had done to himself. Ultimately as an adolescent, he was arrested for having marijuana and put on probation. At that time, the marijuana plant disappeared from his parents' backyard.

But his activities with his friend Ralph reflected Mr. A at his most self-hating, dangerous, and sadomasochistic. Ralph, Mr. A, and his friends, for whom Ralph was the ringleader, were constantly smoking pot at Ralph's home. Mr. A was enamoured of Ralph. He disguised from Ralph and his new made friends that he was Jewish (his last name was not obviously Jewish) and joined in their anti-Semitism. In fact, at the beginning of treatment, Mr. A was ashamed of being Jewish. Mr. A got particular pleasure and fear sitting behind Ralph on his motorcycle, which Ralph tended to ride at dangerous speeds. At these times he became aroused but also was terrified. In addition, Ralph would often do sadistic things to animals, with which Mr. A would assist or of which he would be an approving audience, the most vivid being setting a chicken on fire. At the time Mr. A thought that this was funny and indeed could not describe it without laughing in session at the appearance of the chicken. At one point, after smoking pot and drinking with Ralph and his friends, Mr. A became so intoxicated that he passed out; it was unclear whether Mr. A had let himself be penetrated by Ralph at this time because much of the remembered activity involved reference to sex from the rear with animals. Mr. A's other intimate friend, in his mind, was his own dog, to whom he felt tremendously attached and which he would not hurt. Often in the transference, he would think of me as this dog. This childhood pet had passed away but his parents acquired a new dog at the beginning of his treatment with me. Although the new dog was a female, Mr. A, who was given the privilege of naming it, gave it a male name to which his parents acceded.

During early adolescence Mr. A also had an experience with a dentist to whom his mother took him regularly and this figured frequently at the beginning of treatment. Apparently, his dentist would place his tools on Mr. A's lap as he was seated in the dental chair. Mr. A would find himself aroused at the same time as he was in pain and had to have his mouth open. Whenever the dentist had occasion to get a new tool, Mr. A would find his penis touched. Mr. A did not tell his mother, who brought him to this dentist so that he ended up returning over and over. At one point, Mr. A had an emission which frightened him. As a young adult now, Mr. A had related experiences with his barber. He was terrified of going to this barber apparently because he found himself becoming aroused. He insisted on having his hair straightened from its curly state which he thought was ugly (his mother's hair was straight) and he parted it down the middle. The barber to whom he had been going for years was a man, also anti-Semitic, to whom he pretended he was not Jewish. In addition, he pretended to the barber that he was married when he was still single so that the barber would not mistake him for a homosexual. Making an appointment with the barber and actually going were fraught with anxiety, because he feared that the barber, like the dentist from his childhood, would sexually seduce him. Mr. A would procrastinate over and over and worry obsessively about it.

In fact, any new activity for Mr. A was fraught with anxiety; and he often found himself gagging when he contemplated doing something new. More particularly, any sense that he was motivated by aggressive or sexual desires that he found unacceptable (sometimes as a consequence of some observation I might make to him) resulted in his beginning to gag uncontrollably. In addition, such pleasure whether anticipated or experienced, often resulted in Mr. A subsequently coming down with a severe migraine. Although Mr. A evinced the desire to have a relationship with a woman, the only sexual relationship he could recall at the beginning of treatment involved one with his cousin, of whom he was very fond. They had sex in his grandparents' home in Florida when he was an adolescent which appears to have been interrupted but not discovered by his grandfather. This experience served Mr. A, who was very much in love with her, to come out of himself, despite his discomfort with the incestuous wishes which he associated with his love for her.

Despite his evident confusion about his body, his fear of sexuality, and his sadomasochistic desires, Mr. A yearned most of all to have a fulfilling relationship with a woman and to get married, and he all but begged me to help him make this possible. Of course, the eventual process of dating was as anxiety-filled as anything else. The thought of a woman's vagina filled Mr. A with disgust; he would gag at the mention of it. He could not bear to look at a woman's vagina, indeed refrained from doing so when he was first married for fear he would gag. For that matter, he had tremendous difficulty kissing a woman or touching her at all. Kissing was experienced as disgusting. At the same time, however, once married he more than once found himself kissing a friend's spouse full on the mouth "unintentionally" in the process of saying goodbye. Indeed, at his own wedding, when his mother kissed him they kissed full on the mouth despite himself, which very much upset him. My sense is that his mother was in the habit of kissing him in this fashion when he was a boy.

Mr. A hated his younger sister. During his childhood, he felt that she got all the attention. She spoke volubly and continuously. Mr. A was quiet. She would have screaming fits to which his mother would respond, while Mr. A would not protest his mother's actions. The constant screaming between mother and daughter simply resulted in Mr. A isolating himself in his own room. Mr. A was afraid of his sister getting out of control just as he was afraid of his mother. At the same time, Mr. A evinced envy that his sister as a child was able to talk back to his mother and perplexity (accompanied by more envy) that his sister as an adult appeared to be the best of friends with her mother despite their earlier animosity toward each other. He remembered that as a teenager his sister had friends who came to the house and he did not, which also inspired his envy. Even as a child, Mr. A could recall that whenever he was at the dinner table, he refused to accept a plate of food if it had been prepared initially for her, although it was the same food. He wanted his plate prepared specifically for him.

His mother's hysteria was marked, although at the beginning of therapy Mr. A had difficulty recognising the extent of her difficulties. She had been a teenager herself when she had Mr. A and must have been an inept mother in many respects. Although she was competent in her business, she would become hysterical whenever her husband had to leave the home overnight for business. She would have to be called and reassured often by her husband; and if possible her husband would have to drive inordinate distances in order to be at home and then return early the next morning to his business meetings (often hundreds of miles away) rather than staying overnight at a hotel. Whenever something made her anxious, her husband would immediately attend to her and to her crying and screaming fits. Her hysteria occupied the attention of the entire family. Mr. A felt his needs were forgotten not only by his mother, but by his father in his father's desire to attend to her. Not once does Mr. A recall his father confronting his mother when she became hysterical.

However, despite his mother's hysteria and self-involvement, Mr. A felt he received more attention from his mother ultimately than from his father. His father never spoke about feelings and became obsessively involved in practical details, evincing little interest in Mr. A's life and not taking him to any activities. In contrast, his mother was the sports fanatic in the family; his father knew nothing about sports nor did he apparently care for them. Thus, it was Mr. A's mother who brought him to his baseball games as a child, remained there to root for him and talked about sports with him in general. She was the one who would turn on the television to watch sports games. And in fact Mr. A was not only talented in sports but felt a sense of wholeness and competence when he played that he experienced nowhere else in his life. Unfortunately, at the time I began to see him (although this has since changed) he was so isolated that he could not get himself to take part in these activities: he was too anxious about meeting new people.

Mr. A's fear of and identification with his mother were monumental. He saw her as powerful and frightening. She personified his superego and he could not interact with anyone without hearing his mother's disapproval inside himself. The fact was that he felt that the only person to whom he could be emotionally close was his mother, and that they had an exclusive and sexualised relationship. Thus, any effort to get close to me was fraught with danger as was any effort to get close to a woman other than his mother, much less to make friends in general. On the one hand, he feared that if he did these things, he would incur his mother's wrath and she would no longer protect him; on the other hand, he felt doing these things made him disloyal to his mother. Mr. A's power lay in his belief, on some level, that his mother preferred him sexually to his weak father. At the same time, when Mr. A became anxious, he acted exactly as his mother did, becoming hysterical, forgetting about everyone else in his world. He feared anxiety so much that he avoided doing the simplest things or he procrastinated.

As one can imagine, Mr. A's isolation was also so great because he was constantly envious and competitive with potential male friends and felt frightened of his sexual desires for any woman he might meet. Once he became married, when he met a woman he liked, he tended to avoid her for fear that his sexual fantasies about her would lead him to get out of control. If he met a man with a wife or girlfriend, he immediately found himself silently derogating the man, criticising his ability to make a living or his inattentiveness to his wife or his qualities as a parent, all in the service of a fantasy that he would displace the man and be a better husband to the wife (as he believed on some level he had done with his mother). As a consequence of his projecting his sexual wishes, his competitiveness, and his animosity onto new people he might meet, he became so anxious that he often avoided stepping out of the house entirely or, if he did so, he could not take part in the social give-and-take necessary to establish new relationships. In this regard, it should be mentioned that Mr. A had little nuance in establishing a relationship: he often completely mistook somebody's kidding of him as open hostility, often missing entirely the import of what was said, while at the same time managing in his own attempts at joking to say tremendously aggressive things without realising it. Lastly, it should be mentioned that Mr. A committed the most striking malapropisms without any awareness of doing so and often in the service of trying to say something in the vernacular—a marked contrast to a certain formality and stiltedness of his speech in general. In a way, I could observe Mr. A careen like a man frightened of his internal urges over which he has limited control (not unlike an uptight drunk), one moment saying the most aggressive things unintentionally, the next being unusually formal, in effect viewing every encounter with another human being whether stranger, friend, or loved one as a mine field.

Sadomasochistic ideation, arousal, revenge, remorse

Mr. A's background does not necessarily prepare one for the sadomasochistic fantasies that permeated his thoughts and interactions with me, when he felt safe enough *not* to be repetitive and boring. The fantasies were brutal, and perhaps the best way to indicate them is by selecting a number from various sessions, before I provide a more in-depth look at some process. For example, he becomes concerned that his five-year-old daughter would see his penis, and then he fantasises that he would like her to suck his penis, and then that she should die (in part so she could not tell anyone). He then wants me as punishment to slowly beat him to death over five hours, and then because I have a conscience, I would commit suicide. He wishes I never tried to save him, because he is an evil person. He wants to say: "Fuck you." Or again, he is attracted to a pretty woman at a party, whose husband is there, and who reminds him of his mother. He starts to get aroused in session at the thought that he would like to strangle her by the neck, holding her up before everyone as he does so. His wish is for revenge, and that is what is exciting—to make his mother suffer for humiliating him. Or another time, he thinks about getting revenge on his mother, telling me—very late in the treatment—of the vibrator that he discovered in her bedroom as a teenager. He would like it to be a hair curler, to get her in her vagina with his "too hot" penis and scar her—prevent her from ever having sex with his father: "Burn her. Brand her." He has the image of having her cry out in pain, and then he has the same fantasy about doing that to me.

Then, a month later, after a number of sessions in which he realises I am a "nice man", and I am not becoming aroused at his fantasies, which angers him, he struggles with thoughts about his masochistic child-hood friend Ralph. He has thoughts of sucking Ralph's penis. He was attracted to him. He wants me to be a "mean mother fucker" like Ralph. Then he himself wants to be "evil and a loser, the best loser there is." He now has the fantasy that he will become aroused, naked, and handcuff me to my chair. He will rub his penis against my chest and ejaculate on me. I will worry about his putting his penis into my mouth and I will wonder "What's going on here." In the next session, he elaborates fur-ther: he will cut off my testicles and penis and eat them like franks and beans, and I will be seated at the table with him, with my penis cut off, wondering what he is doing. He laughs about this.

Too quickly, in many of these sessions, the tables would turn and his sadism would transform to equally cruel self-punitive masochism, which would preclude working through his feelings. At other and later times, Mr. A would be genuinely upset and wish to understand why he became aroused at such awful ideation. Two things became clear as time went on—he needed to have his penis in effect acknowledged and his manhood accepted (because he was so castrated psychologically by his parents) and he was very reluctant to give up the excitement of his sado-masochistic arousal (despite his hatred of it). He literally lived for those arousing moments. It was very important for me in the transference to acknowledge his manhood while not endorsing his sadomasochism.

Some process

Here is an example from a session twelve years into treatment which indicates how primitive Mr. A's wishes remained and how punitive his superego, in this case as he tried to negotiate having a male friend, actu-ally a paternal uncle. Despite the fact that this uncle and his wife had lived around the corner from Mr. A as he grew up as a child, his parents had never visited them nor invited them into their home. Now, many years later, Mr. A was making an effort to befriend this uncle who had, with his wife, made some overtures toward him. This was fraught with difficulty for Mr. A because he sensed that his parents (particularly his mother) would disapprove; and the difficulty was aggravated by the fact that the uncle and his wife seemed to accept Mr. A's children much more readily than his own parents, and in fact seemed easier to be with generally. Thus, Mr. A felt very guilty that he liked his uncle. When his uncle suggested they go fishing together (one of the few activities that Mr. A had once done with his father but which his father no longer pursued) Mr. A's trepidation about accepting became major. This was aggravated, unbeknownst to me, by the fact that his uncle had told him he would teach him how to fly-fish, which Mr. A had always wanted to do.

He began one session by continuing to talk about how afraid he was to go with his uncle and to enjoy it, because he would give himself a terrible migraine if this happened—just as he was afraid to go out with male friends in general for this reason. He then fantasised that his uncle would rape him and force him to have anal sex; and then he fantasised that I would do the same thing to him, that it would hurt because my penis was so big. I wondered to him about his need to think of anal sex only as so painful or of my penis as so big. He then fantasised that I would hold his penis, at which point he reported feeling nauseous. He said that he would ejaculate and his ejaculate would go so far up that it would hit the picture on the wall above his head, and that as a result I would be compelled to throw him out. He then fantasised that *he* would force me to have anal sex. At this point, he became accusatory towards me and said that this was not helping him, why was I letting him go on like this. He threatened to kill himself by leaving the session and walking in front of a car. Or he would simply cancel his trip with his uncle. He will have to cancel it because he now envisions that when his uncle takes him fly-fishing, his uncle will touch his hand to teach him how to cast and will stand behind him. He contends that I will throw him out. I ask him, "Why?" He is convinced he has done something to offend me. He is convinced that I want to hurt him. I state that this is his fantasy: "Why would I be offended?" I say that he hasn't done anything to hurt me; it is all a wish, a fantasy. He is convinced that if he ejaculates here, I will throw him out. I ask, "Why?"

As I indicated before, this was hardly the first time that he had articulated sadomasochistic thoughts and then become anxious about doing so. Thus, when he continues to say that, if not now, at some time I will surely have had enough of him and will get rid of him, I tell him that it is clear that he would prefer not to work this through so that he doesn't have these thoughts. He would prefer for the thoughts to remain with him all the time and prevent him from making male friends, and sustain his view of himself as a victim. (I had made these interpretations before, but perhaps never all of a piece, and not when the immediate possibility of a friendship—after all, he tended to avoid friendships—was so compelling.) When he comes in the next week, he says that he was surprised because he looked at himself in the mirror and realised that he does not have such a bad body. "What was I thinking when I thought that I have breasts?" he says. He then talks about his uncle at some length and has fantasies that if he embraced him, he would get aroused. I make an interpretation that underlying his fantasies seems to be his wish that people notice his erection, and that he wants me to admire his erection. His need for this is a consequence, I say, of the fact that his mother denied that he had a penis, when she appeared to him in undress, as did his father. He wants me to acknowledge that he has one. He is silent. Tears stream down his face. After a while he is able to speak: he says that he wishes that he had had a father like me.

Six months later, his mother died precipitously from cancer. It was an awful death, aggravated by the fact that his mother was angry and hysterical throughout and to the end denied she was dying. But her death had the curious positive effect, after his initial shock and mourning, of releasing Mr. A from his internal sense that his mother was all-powerful. At the same time, his mother's passing also led to another disappointment: Mr. A had fantasied that, with his mother gone, he and his father might share their loss together and that his father might draw closer to him, but his father remained as distant as before. Thus Mr. A felt more dependent upon me than ever. At one point, he became very angry at me because I was to be gone for two sessions on a brief break. He said it was not fair for me to leave and then went on:

> I had my psychotic mother, my father that couldn't put a sentence together, my sister that was off the wall. No wonder I was always so attached to animals. [He laughs.] I'm hoping that you will have a puppy when you come back here. I would never establish close

feelings to you because I'm out to be hurt and disappointed. Now I think of you as a dinosaur with a long tail. I'd like to pet the iguana. [He laughs again.]

Very often I don't even feel my own wife is a friend. I am always in a state when I really don't know you, and I'm never willing for you to know me. I am never getting to know my wife and children. I am never having some type of equality with the other person because I am always having a competitive nature. It's what seems to fit here, a recreation of a dysfunctional relationship but now with my therapist. I don't know how to change all that.

How do I love the dinosaur? All day long I've felt tired, I don't know how to sort this one out. I don't know how I fit in the room. [He sighs] I must be pretty mad at you. ["That's an understatement," I say] Yeah, ain't that the truth. I'm so mad, why do I come back? Just a return of the anger, just more firewood. I do think you're right. I never really acknowledged how pissed I must be. And because I didn't get my way. And because I can't create a relationship in my mind. And because I can't feel good here all the time. I do recognise there have to be limits. Certain things are up to me to change.

A month later, when I confronted him about his fantasy that he would come to see me forever, he said:

I really don't know what to do. I think I am still in shock, about earlier this week. I really do have the idea that I should be with you until you retire, forever. And now that it has become clear that I have to get out of here before that, I don't know what to do. My first desire was then to just leave. Kind of all or nothing, I know. I mean I came to therapy because I wanted to get married, to have a child, to have a home ; and I've gotten all that. And I know that really I am very lucky. That there are many people who don't have these things. But I don't want to leave you. I feel I cannot do things without you. That I won't know what to do.

I suddenly got a vision of you as Santa Claus. I feel embarrassed because I thought of you like a Daddy, like a Santa Claus. [I asked: "Why are you embarrassed?"] Because it is as if I am a child talking to you like a daddy. I want you to take care of me and protect me and give me things.

My father always made me feel everything was my fault. That it was my fault when my mother lost control. He blamed me. I would be afraid he would take out the belt. I don't remember it; but my sister says he sometimes hit us. I just remember being afraid. He blamed me, instead of blaming my mother for being out of control; and I always thought I had done something wrong. Now, anything goes wrong and I think it is my fault. When my son doesn't stop crying, I think it is my fault.

I'm blaming my parents. The fact is that my father just didn't care. I had a mother out of control and my father didn't care about me. It is as if I were invisible. I just grew up thinking I didn't exist, that no one cared. That's the thing about seeing you; I think you care. I know you care. And I hate you for it. [I ask, "How come?"] I hate you partly out of habit; I expect you to be like my parents, like my father. That would be easier; that's what I am used to. I know how to be angry. But I hate you because you care; and because then you will leave me. That's why. And because I will have to leave here.

He goes on to lament the fact that we are moving toward termination. Near the end of the session, I ask: "What kind of person would I be, if I kept you attached to me, the way your mother kept you attached? If I did not help you grow into the kind of man you can be?" He replies: "I know. You are not that kind of person. But that means that at some time, I will have to grow. That you will not be able to be my Santa Claus."

Countertransference

Mr. A's very graphic sadistic ideation and wishes expressed during the treatment toward me rarely—as far as I could discern then and even in retrospect—had a pronounced emotional effect on me, although he was usually convinced I was disgusted and appalled by them and that I must hate him for them. I believe I was less affected than he imagined for a number of reasons. For one, although in his interpersonal dealings, he could be emotionally cruel, he never acted sadistically in a physical way (despite his experiences with animals when he was a teenager). In fact, much of my work involved helping him to distinguish between sadistic wish and action—he might wish with sexual excitement to strangle his mother or cut my penis like a sausage and eat it, but they were wishes only. In his primitiveness and his failure to make a distinction between wish and action, he thought of himself as supremely evil and was harshly punitive toward himself. My recurrent job then was to challenge this primitive superego by pointing out to him that his sometimes gruesome wishes were wishes only and did no harm. If anything, I thought of his extreme statements as representing his anxiety which he dreaded experiencing and tried to pushed away by dressing it up in ghoulish, exaggerated, and extremely sadistic (and sometimes masochistic) disguise, not unlike donning a Halloween costume to scare others.

In this regard, countertransferentially, I had learned as a child not to react to the exaggeration of consequences which my own mother favoured as a defence against her own anxieties (a tendency to spread the "wealth" of anxious feelings by trying to get others to suffer them in the same fashion—something of a "Chicken Little" or "the world is coming to an end" variety). Admittedly, my mother did not accompany this defence with the sadistic ideation that Mr. A expressed. Nonetheless, I think my childhood experience gave to me a certain "stalwartness" (to which I will return) in the face of Mr. A's frequent onslaughts and helped me to think of them as his need to rid himself of his anxiety. Further, my childhood experience with my at-times hysterical mother also provided me with decided empathy for what Mr. A had suffered in his own mother's even more extreme hysterical reactions which had permeated the entire family and had traumatised him growing up. Countertransferentially, however, I had considerably more difficulty with another defence of Mr. A's: his constant need, time after time, year after year, to say the same thing over and over and to bore me, to which I alluded at the beginning. I experienced this as much more of a sadistic attack on me than any of his graphic depictions of sadism (which had the ironic virtue of at least being lively). At times, I tried to satisfy myself with my own fantasies of writing a paper called "Boring You to Death" which would highlight the sadism behind being boring: the wish to suck (note the oral imagery) the enjoyment of life out of the envied, lively "other" and to have the "other" experience the same deadness that the patient experiences. In my judgment, it was not only that this boringness was Mr. A's defence against anxiety and feeling in general, but that it had an active, aggressive dyadic component. Under this assault, it was hard for me not to experience resentment toward Mr. A for wasting my time and devaluing my attempt to help him (remember I did not know that ultimately the outcome would be positive) and, at other times, to find—despite myself—that I vengefully responded by barely staying awake or in some instances actually nodding off, although recovering in a few moments without (apparently) being detected.

To return to my being "stalwart" in the face of Mr. A's sadism and primitiveness, such stalwartness came at a price. Feeling compelled to be an unadorned and matter-of-fact symbol of reality for Mr. A when he indulged in his exaggerated sadistic reactions—with their hysterical tinge—I experienced the need to be stalwart as a confinement and a burden. I found that Mr. A responded best to matter-of-fact, almost concrete, ways of saying things, without nuance. When I intervened in this manner I spoke to that part of him that reacted as a child who needed to know that the world was not as dangerous a place as he feared, and for whom nuance would confuse rather than comfort. For example, it was much more useful to say in a concrete way, to Mr. A, that he brought his mother into the room (or into his relationship with his wife) than to talk about the nature of his internal processes more abstractly. Rarely could I relax into the type of allusions or speculative thinking that might touch my work with another patient. For much of the treatment, there seemed to be no room for poetry or grace or embellishment in what I said. In part, this was because some of the references (given Mr. A's inability to educate himself) would have been obscure to him and then would have distracted from the import of what I said, but also because he seemed to require and respond to unadorned directness. Perhaps the only exception to this was that Mr. A could respond and incorporate a remark by me in which I was cuttingly facetious about some manner in which he was withholding or cruel to others, such as when he procrastinated repeatedly on getting his wife a birthday present she had requested (one of her few open requests), and I remarked when he persisted in a clearly transparent excuse, "Nice guy." (This brought not a defensiveness on his part but laughter followed by somewhat penitent acknowledgment of his motivation to hurt by withholding.)

Another reason for the direct and matter of fact approach was that, although Mr. A's imagined sadistic scenarios were not in danger of taking place, he too often acted emotionally cruel toward his loved ones—his children and his wife and then, in turn, himself. Often he was in danger of emotionally sadistic or un-thoughtful parenting (and he would actively plead to me for help with it when he recognised it), and I was conscious of the need to try to ameliorate or guard against an ongoing problematic interaction which, if it developed further, could permanently affect his children. (Perhaps this also reflected the fact that I treat young children as well as adults—something of which Mr. A was aware because he saw children in my practice—in fact, he would sometimes wish that he could play with me as they apparently did.) When someone truly does not know, because of the deficits in his own parenting, how to act and seeks counsel in the course of analysis, it seemed to me to require more than a typical hands-off psychoanalytic approach. Often, Mr. A was tremendously grateful for the most rudimentary child rearing remarks—I tried to avoid elaborated "instructions"—and he believed implicitly in the wisdom of what I might comment upon, all of which I took as testament to the fact that he really had little clue about what was appropriate parenting. For example, when I suggested that his infant girl, who cried when placed face-forward in an infant carrier might be more comfortable if facing towards him, where he could also hold her, he was amazed that the crying ceased. (To his credit, Mr. A, upon the birth of his first child, hired a wonderfully maternal older woman, who babysat a number of children in her home, and who patiently taught him, as well as his wife, how to parent in very fundamental ways. Mr. A's attachment to her was very great; she represented the mother he had not had.) Clearly, when his children were younger, Mr. A idealised me as a nurturing parental figure (after all a figure he had never in reality had). I became a kind of magical bulwark against his fear that he would be aggressive toward his children. During his youngest child's infancy in particular, it did not seem the right time to challenge this idealisation, nor did he yet have sufficient evidence of, or confidence in, his own nurturing abilities.

Later on, when treatment was winding down, it was much easier for me to be myself. He was no longer so literal-minded nor so frightened of his aggressive thoughts. Curiously, his tendency toward malapropisms had very much disappeared by that time although I had never once addressed it directly nor corrected him when he made a mistake. I always felt that the ego-blow that would result from pointing out his mistakes or looking at them as psychodynamically determined—which they undoubtedly were in part—would discourage him from speaking freely. These were his attempts at being less rigid, more spontaneous, and more intimate and if I treated them as "slips of speech" deserving investigation, as one might with another patient, I felt it would have been counterproductive. It should not come as a surprise, perhaps, that as a consequence of helping him to achieve a less rigid superego, he began to speak with more nuance himself and to respond to more nuance from me.

Conclusion

This was a remarkably successful psychoanalysis despite the initial seemingly grim prognosis of others. The final healthy turning point came when Mr. A was able to seek out a job where he had true responsibility. For years, he had a position, of which he was initially very proud because it had a "scam" quality to it, in a major company where the employees constantly billed clients for hundreds of hours in which they did nothing. It did have one virtue: it permitted him to come to see me during the day, because no one at the company cared that he was unavailable. Gradually, it came as a revelation to him that his very work was destroying him with its boringness and encouragement of deceit. In a sense, his superego—so rigid in some ways, so lax in others—became gradually modulated and continuous in both directions.

Near the end of treatment he also spontaneously remarked that he could not believe how much he constantly feared that I was going to seduce him the way the dentist had, and that he realised now it was all in his mind—that in fact he had wanted to seduce me.

As to my role in his life, and the extent to which I was compelled to make suggestions to fill the deficits he had, I certainly was like a parental figure for him. Not infrequently he said, as therapy drew to a close, that I had saved his life. He often fantasised at that time that he would bump into me when he was out with his children and his wife, so that I could see them. It was as if I had been the father he did not have and the grandparent his children never had. Still, five years after the end of his treatment, I have on four occasions received phone calls on my answering machine very early in the morning, when he is in his car on the way to work. He lets me know that he is doing well and thanks me. In the last one, he called to tell me that his daughter had just had a Bat-Mitzvah. He was so overwhelmed with gratitude toward me—remember too that his reaction to his own Bar-Mitzvah had marked his turning away from health in his own adolescent development—that he kept on repeating into the phone, "Thank you, Thank you, Thank you."

CHAPTER SIXTEEN

Discussion of the case of Mr. A

Sheldon Bach

I want to thank Dr. Reichbart for allowing me to discuss this interesting case, for being so open with us about his countertransference thoughts and feelings, and above all for sticking with this very challenging patient for so very many years. As I read this case with its remarkable and moving outcome, I kept feeling that there was a great deal in it from which all of us could learn.

Most obviously there seemed to be a lesson in humility, for Dr. Reichbart was at the beginning of his career and, although he rightly turned to more experienced analysts for help, he was told that the patient was very sick or quasi-psychotic, which may have been correct, and that he would make a poor control case, which was certainly wrong. For I think that Dr. Reichbart might well admit that the many years he spent with Mr. A have been both enormously instructive and rewarding for both of them. How this came about makes a fascinating story.

The story begins with Dr. Reichbart taking on a patient whom he finds tedious, boring, and consistently repetitive, so much so as to often lead him to roll his eyes as the patient lay on the couch. The patient would arrive just moments before the session began because he was terrified of sitting in the waiting room. He would then spend most of the session repeating how he did not want to be in treatment, how the analyst was out to hurt him, how he could not possibly say anything new, and how he wanted to leave. At the end of the session he would frequently threaten suicide, or plead with the analyst to just give up on him, to "let him go", as if he were enthralled or enslaved.

Now if you type "boredom in the countertransference" into the PEP-Web search engine, dozens of articles on the subject will appear. For the most part they all seem to agree that boredom in the countertransference is a sign that the analyst is defending himself in some way against something important that is going on between him and the patient. This is not necessarily a bad thing; sometimes momentary self-defence is the only way to stay alive or to not give up at certain times in a very difficult treatment. And of course it is perfectly comprehensible that fifteen or twenty years ago Dr. Reichbart would have been unclear about how to proceed, because it is hard to believe that any beginning analyst would have known how to treat patients like this one without the help of a supervisor who had had long experience treating psychotic, borderline, or other challenging patients in psychoanalysis. It is a great credit to Dr. Reichbart's strength, natural instincts, psychoanalytic talent, and downright doggedness that he nonetheless persisted with this case for so many years only to find, as he so touchingly puts it, that to his own surprise this marginal individual, this self-made outcast, had fashioned a life for himself, married, become a loving if conflicted father to two children, and gained some understanding of his emotions and his fears. So how now, with the ease and great advantage of hindsight, might we try to understand what was going on?

I believe that, in general, because his clinical and theoretical training had presumably been with "neurotic" patients, it was rather difficult for Dr. Reichbart, as it is for most of us, to really grasp and comprehend the extremely primitive level of pathology at which Mr. A was operating. Two small examples:

> Mr. A seemed unable to remember his childhood at all. This is a rather common symptom with challenging patients, not primarily because the childhood memories have been repressed or suffered from childhood amnesia, but because they have never really been constructed as memories in the first place. Living in a constant state of cumulative trauma generally precludes the construction of a reliable memory history, as it also precludes the laying down of a reliable, continuous, and well-regulated sense of self. In the course of a satisfactory analysis, as we can see in this report, the

challenging patient begins to construct not only a continuous and better regulated sense of self but also, along with it, a continuous narrative story of his own history and the history of his family. (Bach, 2006)

Again, Dr. Reichbart wonders at Mr. A's need for concrete, matter-of-fact responses and his inability to deal with poetry, grace, or embellishment. This again is a common symptom at this level of pathology and implicates his relative lack of reflective self-awareness that might allow him to get outside of his own subjectivity (Bach, 1994, 2006) and the relative absence of a transitional area (Winnicott, 1953) in which poetry, allusion, speculation, and uncertainty can co-exist with concrete reality. These deficits of course limit his ability to have enduring relationships, and also undermine his ability to play, whether with partners and children or in the analysis. The ability to play, as we have learned from Winnicott (1971), is essential not only to engage in an authentic analysis but also to live an authentic life. But at every step of the way we can recognise and empathise with the patient's persistent but not totally successful efforts to create or to provide himself with the "normal" transitional attachments that were lacking, as when he masturbates in his mother's underwear while she is gone (Kohut, 1971), or when he becomes tremendously attached to his dog.

So we have, at the beginning, a patient in a state of extreme anxiety, with a fragmented sense of self and a constant fear of being attacked and annihilated. He barely manages to get to the sessions at all and, while in session, he constantly repeats the same stereotyped words and phrases as if to reassure himself and to reassert: *I AM, I AM HERE, I EXIST, you cannot hurt me, you mean nothing to me, it's just ME, ME, ME.* To this Dr. Reichbart responds with boredom, as if he were being left out of the picture and psychologically annihilated, which is exactly what is actually happening; but it is only the patient's pre-emptive counterattack to his own terrible fears of annihilation, and his repetition in the transference of what had been done to him. As a child and adolescent the patient was not recognised by his mother as a separate person with his own needs and identity; this left him feeling not only castrated, as Dr. Reichbart notes, but also with a confused identity (breasts) and a deep feeling that he was not really human. It is one of Dr. Reichbart's many accomplishments that in the course of this treatment Mr. A began to feel more like a human being who could once more rejoin his cohort and become part of the mainstream of life.

Developmentally, we are seeing here what Gergely (2000) regards as the earliest stage of the infant's development, when the baby prefers to gaze at the same thing, over and over and over again, in the course of the establishment of a sense of self, a sense of "I AM". Later on, when the self becomes reasonably consolidated, the infant then prefers to gaze at novel objects and to engage with the larger world.

This strong sense of self, a boundaried and delineated ego, had, for many reasons, never been adequately developed by Mr. A. First, his mother had constantly impinged on and violated his boundaries, both sexually and otherwise. Second, she had never recognised his psychological existence as a separate, stand-alone person. For these and other reasons, the first part of the analysis was devoted to Mr. A's establishment of a strong-enough sense of self and a sufficient degree of analytic trust (Ellman, 2007) that would enable him to allow Dr. Reichbart. to enter the picture at all. This first part of the treatment was promoted by Dr. Reichbart's faithful and consistent presence as a non-intrusive, non-retaliatory part object or narcissistic object (Kohut, 1971), without any existence of his own other than holding and allowing Mr. A to experience what he had never been able to experience before, namely, being alone and reassembling himself in the presence of a benevolent and receptive other (Winnicott, 1958).

The second phase of the analysis is ushered in by the sadomasochistic fantasies. I agree with Dr. Reichbart that this starts when Mr. A "feels safe enough not to be repetitive and boring", that is, the establishment of analytic trust, but I also feel it happens in conjunction with the establishment of a personal sense of self that feels strong enough to confront another person for the first time without fearing total annihilation. That this first confrontation with the Other takes place in a sadomasochistic modality is, in my experience, absolutely normative and par for the course. If we think about it developmentally, this is analogous to the anal phase or the "terrible twos", when the child is beginning to confront the Other and establish boundaries of dependence-independence and dominance-submission between self and other, but this time it is happening to a grown-up adult. The patient is moving from using the analyst as a part-object to seeing him as a whole object with separate needs and existence, from the paranoid-schizoid position to the depressive position. At this point he must learn how to regulate pain-pleasure and dominance-submission without losing his hard-won sense of self, and I believe that Dr Reichbart has it exactly right when he says that the patient "needed to have his penis in effect acknowledged and his manhood accepted", although I might word it more broadly as having his self acknowledged and his existence accepted.

I also see the patient's reluctance "to give up his sadomasochistic arousal" in a wider way. This patient had a major problem in affect regulation because it is largely the environmental mother who teaches affect recognition and regulation to the child, and this mother was unable to recognise her son's personal affects or to hold and transform them. She could barely contain her own emotions and overly sexualised their interactions so that the patient never learned to recognise, hold, and modulate his own feelings. Sadomasochistic or sexually and aggressively tinged feelings enlivened him because they were the only kind of aliveness he experienced from his mother, who herself had never been able to feel alive in a consistent and modulated way and thus couldn't teach this to her son.

If the choice is between having perverse or sadomasochistic fantasies or activities and experiencing psychic death, the perversions will always win out. Remember that his mother had her own major problems with separation anxiety and abandonment, and that her own fear of psychic death was constantly warded off by her hyper-sexuality, her affect outbursts, her use of marijuana, and her use of her husband and the patient as narcissistic objects. All this is to say that this patient was not going to give up his sadomasochistic arousal until he had some other forms of enlivenment available, that is, until he could begin to use the analyst and/or a partner as a whole object who could provide more appropriate ways of relating and feeling alive.

Of course the sadomasochistic fantasies are in themselves quite fascinating. They parallel in many ways the fantasies of the Marquis de Sade, and I refer you to the paper that I wrote in 1972 with Lester Schwartz about the Divine Marquis that includes an extended discussion of the function and meaning of such fantasies and their relation to masochism and anal sadism (Bach & Schwartz, 1972). Without repeating that close analysis, I want to make only two points:

1. That the patient's sadomasochism is part of his struggle to begin relating to another person, while at the same time trying to hold himself together and not fall apart or totally submit and lose himself as he did with his mother and again with his friend Ralph. I believe it very possible that Mr. A had a psychotic breakdown in early adolescence, not because of the pot smoking but because that is what typically happens to such patients when the hormonal upsurge threatens their

already highly precarious ego structure. This period of hypothesised breakdown might include not only the many years high on pot but also the friendship and adventures with Ralph and the quasi psychotic experiences with the dentist and the barber. At issue here is the very integrity of the mind and body, as evidenced in his overwhelming concern with *le corps morcelé* or the body in pieces: castration, separation and death, as Lacan (2002) describes it.

2. The other point that I made some time ago (Bach, 1991, 2002) is that these sadomasochistic fantasies are specifically contractualised to ward off the most extreme separation anxieties, of the very same kind that his mother suffered from. In these fantasies, the masochist is unconsciously saying to his partner:

> "You can do anything you want to me—I will submit to anything. You can beat me with whips or interpretations, so long as you don't leave me."

The sadist, on the other hand, is proclaiming to his partner:

> "No matter what I do to you, you will never be able to leave me, and we can live in this timeless world where you participate in my omnipotence!"

Since sadism and masochism are invariably found together, although one may be conscious and the other unconscious, what we have here is an oscillation between two poles: between the fear of total loss and the total denial of loss. This oscillation can only be resolved by the slow process of building whole-object relationships in which love and hate can be integrated, and in which the binary, either-or vision of loss can be replaced by a sense of process. This involves mourning and working through the original distortions in the fabric of the ego caused by early lack of recognition and lack of object constancy and the dysregulation of affects, particularly of the pleasure-pain continuum.

Mr. A's mother lived in constant fear of abandonment and total loss; she was unable to give him the security that comes from connection to a constant attachment object that nevertheless recognises you as separate person. He became attached to an object that caused him pain. The typical result of an early attachment to the Mother of Pain is that pleasure becomes aversive or feels unreal and not genuine; the only thing that feels familiar and real are situations of pain. When these patients come to analysis, the early years of the analysis reproduce this situation of mutual painfulness.

Mr. A's first solution was either to withdraw from attachments completely or else to attempt attachments in the sadomasochistic way that I have described. Working with Dr. Reichbart, he learned for the first time that one can become attached to a person who consistently recognises and accepts you for who you are, and yet himself remains a separate and differentiated person. This is a lesson that we must all learn over and over again, and one for which we may join the patient in saying to Dr. Reichbart: "Thank you, Thank you, Thank you!"

References

Bach, S. (1991). On sadomasochistic object relations. In: G. Fogel & W. Myers (Eds.), *Perversions and Near-Perversions in Clinical Practice* (pp. 75–92)New Haven: Yale University Press.

Bach, S. (1994). *The Language of Perversion and the Language of Love.* Northvale, NJ: Aronson.

Bach, S. (2002). Sadomasochism in clinical practice and everyday life. *Journal of Clinical Psychoanalysis*, 11: 225–235.

Bach, S. (2006). *Getting from Here to There: Analytic Love, Analytic Process.* Hillsdale, NJ: Analytic Press.

Bach, S. & Schwartz, L. (1972). A dream of the Marquis de Sade. *Journal of the American Psychoanalytic Association,* 20: 451–475.

Ellman, S. (2007). Analytic trust and transference love; healing ruptures and facilitating repair. *Psychoanalytic Inquiry*, 27: 246–263.

Gergely, G. (2000). Reapproaching Mahler: New perspectives on normal autism, symbiosis, splitting and libidinal object constancy from cognitive developmental theory. *Journal of the American Psychoanaytic. Association.,* 48: 1197–1228.

Lacan, J. (2002). [1949]. The mirror stage as formative of the I function as revealed in psychoanalytic experience. In: *Ecrits* (pp. 75–81), Trans. Bruce Fink. New York: Norton.

Kohut, H. (1971). *The Analysis of the Self.* Chicago, IL: University of Chicago Press.

Winnicott, D. W. (1953). Transitional objects and transitional phenomena— a study of the first not-me possession. *International Journal of Psycho-Analysis*, 34: 89–97.

Winnicott, D. W. (1958). The capacity to be alone. *International Journal of Psycho-Analysis*, 39: 416–420.

Winnicott, D. W. (1971). *Playing and Reality.* London: Tavistock Publications.

CHAPTER SEVENTEEN

Discussion of the case of Mr. A

Harriet I. Basseches

"Mr. A could be tedious in the extreme and so consistently repetitive as to lead me to often roll my eyes as he lay on the couch." These words, used by the analyst to convey the early sessions with the patient, caught my attention immediately, alerting me to the possibility of sadomasochism. I am appreciative of having the opportunity to comment on Dr. Reichbart's case. It is a beautifully written description of a long and successful psychoanalysis with a very difficult patient. There is much to learn from this psychoanalysis, which would offer the consideration of many aspects of psychoanalysis in the clinical setting. As the sadomasochistic fantasy life, the sadomasochism as revealed in the treatment in the transference-countertransference interaction, and the sadomasochism in the patient's behavioural life, all come alive, these elements help to shed light on the way they seem to intertwine with certain seminal environmental and developmental points in the life story of the patient. To tease out the sadomasochism, existentially, might lose the precious interconnections with these other aspects of the situation. In describing the treatment, Dr. Reichbart emphasises the slow emergence of both historical recollections and fantasy life, bringing to mind both the natural flow of an analysis and also the possibility of withholding by the patient. The fantasy life is almost

255

exclusively centred on harsh and extreme sadomasochistic material expressed in a variety of contexts.

Detail, however, is mostly absent from recollections of childhood. Nevertheless, in the course of the unfolding treatment, a picture does form of an emotionally charged home atmosphere, with the patient, whom Dr. Reichbart calls "Mr. A" often depicted as a neglected and isolated witness to the interactions among other family members, including loud exchanges between an envied younger sister and the mother, and between a mother and a father who seemed to minimally acknowledge the son, Mr. A. That picture of isolation, however, does not quite jibe with other descriptions that emerged in the report of the analysis. These include Mr. A's closeness with his mother in early childhood as well as later, and his shadowy connection with his father. With regard to his father in particular, one wonders if there was a need by the patient to emphasise the minimal involvement of the father perhaps for conflictual reasons. Taking the following recollection more as an exemplar of an important conflictual attitude of the patient toward his father than as concrete confirmation of the father's attitude toward the son, Mr. A acknowledges (albeit incidentally, in making a very different point) the father taking an interest in going fishing with the son. However, the patient focuses on the father's not doing so more than the once reported. A father who takes his son fishing, even once, is not devoid of interest in that son. Further, the father characterised by the patient is weak and ineffective, at least in later years when he is doing the "woman's work" of cooking. Here too, one wonders if there is some wish to minimise the father's abilities, for example, as a good provider, an idea suggested by the fact that the family had a family pool, a sign of some financial affluence. (This came up incidentally in the context of Mr. A describing his discomfort with displaying his body in adolescence, suggesting his self-consciousness at a time when his secondary male characteristics would have been more noticeable. Mr. A described being no longer willing to swim in the family pool despite his talent as a swimmer, highlighting his misery and negative feelings about his physique, and downplaying his own ability—his being a good swimmer— and his father's—providing a family pool.)

The role of the mother in the household, too, seems to have shifted in later years, as described by the patient, not only changing from homemaker to business woman, but also from attentiveness in a positive sense. The attention changed from her going to the ball games of

Mr. A to a threatening kind of attentiveness. The later attention from his mother, as reported by Mr. A, became oversexualised, overstimulating, exhibitionistic, and at the same time, intrusive and infantilising (over homework sessions for the dyslexic Mr. A, conducted on mother's bed, while she was scantily clad).

The "later years" when the parental reversals occurred seemed to coincide with puberty and adolescence for Mr. A, following his Bar-Mitzvah. With a striking convergence of events, it is at this time that his sadomasochistic fantasies seemed to burgeon and his entire modus operandi in life seemed to change. There are arguments supportive of illness onset beginning in adolescence. Certain illnesses, schizophrenia, for example, often have onset in adolescence, underscoring that adolescence is a vulnerable time; it is also true for this case that the family dynamics and activity seemed to mark a discontinuity of roles and expectations coincident with Mr. A's adolescence and his strong shift in behaviour. Nevertheless, it still does seem unlikely that his constellation of troubles could have hatched full-blown only with the onset of adolescence. Specifically, the following nodal points could have been sources of possible vulnerability preceding the adolescent crisis. We do not know the age difference between Mr. A and his envied younger "off the wall" sister nor how he handled her birth and subsequent intrusion into his world. Perhaps his sibling rivalry and envy and accompanying experience of a sense of neglect by the parents have distorted his male identity development. Depending on his age at the time of her birth, it likely would have had an impact on his oral and anal development, his nursing, feeding, and toilet training. We do not know about his experience of control over his bodily toileting functions, nor his masturbatory history. Any and all of these factors could have had profound influence. Further, the nature of his identifications with his mother and, especially, his father would have determined the kind of oedipal resolution that he carried out of his latency and into his approach to adolescence.

There are a few recollections reported that might clarify the earlier developmental situation. The point seems at least suggestive that the sadomasochistic imagery did not spring fully formed in adolescence. I hear in the report the premise that everything was relatively tranquil in his development until adolescence. This is because the Mr. A described in the report invites the perception that this surging sadomasochistic fantasy life, plus withdrawal from previous relationships to join in new delinquent-like sadomasochistic relationships, all began with the Bar-Mitzvah.

Symbolically, the Bar-Mitzvah, for the thirteen-year-old Jewish male, marks the transition from childhood to joining the adult male community. (In reality that does not actually happen, at least in most Western cultures, until sometime later in age.) There is an old funny story of the reluctant boy in the days and weeks approaching his Bar-Mitzvah being encouraged by his parents to persevere with his preparation because he would receive many presents. The boy was so excited by the prospect of the presents that when he stepped up to read from the Torah, he began: "Today I am a ... fountain pen." While noting the phallic symbolism of the popular Bar-Mitzvah gift, one is also struck by the central question, why the need for bribery. There is the implication that perhaps for some boys there can be a fear and reticence accompanying the prospect of greater maturity. Increased sexual and aggressive potential carry not only the promise of power, competition, and excitement, but also greater responsibilities, ethical challenges, and the fear of failure and/or the dangers of success. There sometimes is needed a push to impel him out of childhood forward through puberty/adolescence towards manhood; in other words, the movement from boyhood to manhood is not without ambivalence. In the case of Mr. A, his identity crisis and confusion could have been the precipitant of his shift or it could as well have been his defensive retreat brought on by his anxieties under the pressures of adolescence. It seems that something tipped the ambivalence forcefully onto the negative side and him into a regression, presumably at the same time that his physical development—on track with the "raging" hormonal changes of puberty and adolescence—continued forward.

Of course, by my use of the term "regression", I expose my bias that his difficulties could not have just started at that point. By regression, I am referring to the idea that Mr. A was returning to earlier modes, potentially from a more advanced level of development, that is, backing off from the promise of moving toward attainment of a genital level, and regressing to earlier fixation points at all levels of psychosexual development. And I say "all levels" because I seem to hear evidence in Dr. Reichbart's report of the sadomasochism described and enacted in the treatment of oral, anal, and phallic ideation. Moreover, added to the clear evidence of bodily confusion and gender identity issues—all early concerns—as well as object choice confusion and anxiety, there also seems to be evidence of both negative oedipal and positive oedipal issues intertwined and threading through the confusion and the anxiety. To all these must be added the presence of perverse fetishistic behavior (masturbatory activity in the mother's bedroom, with the mother's underwear). Before leaving this set of ideas related to the onset of Mr. A's manifest illness, I have some further thoughts about Mr. A's adolescence. In the literature on adolescence and on adolescent breakdown, Laufer (1976) brings to our attention the organising importance and centrality a person's masturbatory fantasy has to future sexual and personal identity. Peter Blos (1962) points out that "[m]asturbation assumes pathological features whenever it consolidates regressively infantile fixations" (p. 162). Laufer and Laufer (1984) emphasise the close link between body image and ego functions, especially perception and reality testing. In young people for whom adolescence does not create a developmentally progressive platform, their masturbatory fantasies and behaviours do not function as trial actions leading toward acceptance of mature genital function being incorporated into their body image. Instead, not only does genitality appear dangerous, but the pre-phallic regressive fantasies, even if accompanied by self-disgust and self-disapproval, offer powerful satisfactions that are inhibitory to forward development.

For Mr. A, his fetishistic masturbatory activity involving his mother's underwear further distances his sexual functioning from adult resolution. Greenacre (1953, 1969), following Freud, studies fetishism to suggest that the fetishist is, at the same time, trying both to deny and to proclaim the existence of the female phallus in the form of his selected fetish of a concrete symbol of the fantasy. In Mr. A's case, this knowing and not knowing is presumably about his mother's genital equipment, the mother with whom he seems most strongly to identify. One posits that his wish to confirm his genitalia and his confusion over his own equipment vis à vis the female, stands in the face of the knowledge that he likely would have acquired early, with the birth of his sister, and later with his fascination with his mother's genitals. All this is under the terrifying spell of major castration anxiety, despite the reassurance that holding his own penis in masturbation could have provided him.

I want to add two more points from Greenacre (1969). One is that she notes for some a persistence of early confusion between breast and penis, which makes me think of Mr. A's conviction that he had breasts (like a female), presumably as a result of his confusion about which body parts he did have. Only when, after years of treatment, his self-perceptions became more realistic, could he clearly acknowledge absence of enlarged breasts. The other important point from Greenacre (1969) is her description of the fetish as containing "congealed anger, born of castration panic ..." (p. 162). She states that "sadomasochistic fantasies and practices are quite commonly associated with fetishism ... [sometimes] rather slyly expressed [in the treatment] in the magic killings, or not looking, silence, and similar attacks by denial or deprivation" that are "clearly traceable to derivative repetitions of the original actual traumata [and] which contributed to the intensification of castration panic" (p. 163). Thus, we are considering a cluster of related phenomena which coalesce for the troubled adolescent that can include fetishistic behaviours, sadomasochistic fantasies and actions fueled by bodily confusion, as well as castration anxiety, and may repeat earlier, actual traumatic experiences.

Kohut, however, offers an alternative assessment. In *The Analysis of the Self* (1971), Kohut gives an example strikingly similar to Mr. A's that Kohut explains can be "understood not so much as sexual transgressions that are undertaken while external surveillance is lacking but rather as attempts to supply substitutes for the idealized parent imago and its functions ... [and arise] in the absence of the narcissistically invested self-object ... Perverse activities are thus attempts to re-establish the union with the narcissistically invested lost object through visual fusion and other archaic forms of identification" (pp. 98–99). Kohut, while acknowledging the perverse nature of the action, labels it as caused by early narcissistic deficits, not by instinctually induced anxiety and conflict. Rather than an either-or stance in this regard, I would not rule out the possibility that both factors could be at work.

Castration anxiety and oedipal paradox

Dr. Reichbart explains that he feels that the sadomasochism is a defence against Mr. A's anxiety. The anxiety may stem from the identity confusion, which leads to castration panic at a time when Mr. A is experiencing his own hormonal changes and upsurges of sexual tension. These changes occur along-side of the overstimulation from the mother and the shadowy sense of the father who fails to offer Mr. A protection from the overstimulation and provides a weakened male role model. The model that Mr. A seems to have adopted from his parents, typified by his pot smoking, only leads him into trouble (with the law)—which I see as a call for help on his part that seems to be ignored by the parents. To the extent that Mr. A does experience the capacity to be "like" the parents, he picks something not only destructive but blurring of ego capacities already compromised.

I would like to add a paradoxical oedipal influence. I say, paradoxical, in that the negative oedipal seems redolent with shame and disgust for his father and himself. At the same time, Mr. A is jealous of the father's privilege in the primal bedroom, a suggestion of his positive oedipal. He is also described as believing his mother prefers him to his weak father. He appears mixed up over whether he is his mother's lover and the oedipal victor, or her look-alike as a "castrated" male, or her infant to replace the sister as the baby getting "all the attention" and needing to be taught even the most basic of things. Parallel to Mr. A's own confusion, there is an implication that the mother, in switching roles with the father, is having her own identity crisis, driving a fantasy that she might replace the father, male, for which she might feel the need to "possess" her son's penis as her part object and her belonging. She cannot make up her own mind whether she wants to be the dominating seductress or the forever maternal nurturer to her "infant" son. Her availability to be the parent attending the son's athletic activities perhaps presages her wish for usurpation of her son's maleness for herself.

Sadomasochism

Now to turn specifically to the sadomasochism. The psychoanalytic definition of sadomasochism is somewhat illusive, as the term is often used to encompass a variety of meanings (See Chapters One and Two of this volume). For this discussion, I would include a conception of sadomasochism that is fairly broad. By sadomasochism I will be referring to behavioural action or fantasy that captures a sense of pleasure in hurting someone else (i.e., sadism) or in being hurt by someone else (i.e., masochism); the sexual or the aggressive component may be unconscious or conscious. In this case, however, I want to suggest, first, the possibility of an autoerotic form or meaning of the sadomasochistic ideation and action. Though played out with others, the sadomasochism might actually be thought of as an expression of a power struggle within Mr. A himself over his feeling of helplessness to resolve the major issues that had been triggered in him. It would be as if the sadistic side and the masochistic side represented an active and a passive alternative to his dilemma. He oscillated between whether he was to be the master of his fate, albeit riddled with sadism, revenge, haunting anxiety, and guilt, or to be the passive victim of his fate, punished, masochistic, and isolated from his objects. Caught in the excitement and terror of his form of "coping", I believe that he must eventually have felt at a hopeless impasse, unable to resolve the power struggle and beating himself (Freud, 1919) to the point of almost unrecognisability. Whatever allowed him to go for treatment at twenty-six years of age (thirteen long years after the Bar-Mitzvah), that act brought him to Dr. Reichbart, to psychoanalysis—and a chance at saving himself.

I find interesting the accidental repetition of numbers (give or take a little): the thirteen years to the Bar-Mitzvah, the thirteen years until he goes for help, the fourteen plus years of treatment, as if each segment of time were meaningful for how long he must suffer a particular state of mind. I admit that might be stretching credulity, but I am taking seriously the instruction to "free associate" to the material!

Treatment—locating the sadomasochism

There are many ways to think about and approach this topic. In thinking about the psychoanalytic experience, however, there is an assumption that many elements of relevance in a particular patient will emerge in the interaction with the analyst, not only as content to be discussed, but more particularly, in the actual fibre of the interaction—that is, in the transference and countertransference. Thus, the prediction would be that the central or core themes and conflicts will be reflected in the very fabric of that relationship as the treatment unfolds. Whether to think of this in terms of a one-person or two-person frame, however, could be argued either way. By that I mean that the one person, the patient, is present to get help with his problems, and in that sense, it is a one-person psychology; however, the assumption is that the analyst is drawn temporarily into the position of being the object and even, sometimes, the self of the patient. In that way the analyst participates in the dynamics of the patient as well as bringing his own capacity to make the patient his object and, at times, self—albeit in a more limited way. Thus, the interaction also embraces a two-person psychology, for limited times, with permeable boundaries. This phenomenon—the one-person, two-person experience—can best be studied by examining the transference and countertransference that provides the unique opportunity for thinking about what is happening in the treatment. In this case, we are discussing how sadomasochism plays a role in the analysis, and what we can come to understand about that.

Sadomasochistic ideation: arousal, revenge, and remorse

I have chosen to emphasise the distinction between fantasies of sado-masochistic ideation as content, like the telling of a story expressed to the analyst, and alternatively, as unfolding in the process of interaction with the analyst. In both forms, content and process, the transference and countertransference emerge. While not identified in that way, I believe that the analyst in writing his report may have envisioned such a distinction, since Dr. Reichbart recounted these fantasies in one section of his paper and statement of the analytic process in another. In volunteering that some of the fantasies might not be expected from the sense of the patient that the analyst was getting, perhaps the analyst was more shocked than he admits. If so, this possibly gives a window into his countertransference, which will be discussed further in the section centreing on countertransference below. With respect to the sado-masochistic fantasies (see pages of Dr. Reichbart's report), Dr. Reichbart understandably describes the sadism in these fantasies as unexpectedly brutal, interweaving a sense of grievance, injury, rage, and humiliation to the point of death, and always including an infantile sexual component.

The image of the chicken on fire caused Mr. A to laugh every time he recalled it. The laughing makes me think not only of his guilty, sadistic pleasure in being the doer rather than the one "done to," but also of it being a laugh of embarrassment and humiliation, since I believe he identifies with the "plucked" (my word) chicken. Nevertheless, the fact that the event is claimed to have actually happened may have added another dimension to his terror over his fantasy life, an **enacted** wish-fear. When a child's secretly wished for but disapproved and feared outcome actually occurs, that coincidental experience erroneously enhances the boy's feelings of grandiosity. The seeming confirmation of magical thinking can induce feelings of frightening power and can, in his mind, make his wish into an indelible crime. The image of the chicken on fire brings to mind a cowardly, defenseless being who is "on fire" with excitement. It would be difficult to work something like that through when the violence overpowers any possibility of repair.

The anger and aggression in the fantasies seem linked, as many analysts have discussed (Greenacre, 1953, 1969; Stoller, 1975; and many others), to early traumas. We only have hints of the traumas. One cannot help thinking, however, of the multi-determination of motives and confusion portrayed, for example, in his fantasy about his five-year-old daughter. It is a compromise formation that not only suggests sexual and aggressive wishes toward his own young daughter—fraught with anxiety, guilt, and shame—but in particular demonstrates an identification with her, of turning passive into active, an identification with the aggressor, as if this might reflect early trauma of an incestuous nature.

Dr. Reichbart uses the term "primitive" for the fantasies, and that seems right, especially if by primitive he means sounding like very early cognition. When he is mad at someone or excited by someone, Mr. A speaks in action, not feeling, language. For example, his references to dying and death sound like the kind of communication that young children use, in playing with a friend: "Bang, bang; you're dead. Oh, now I hear your mother calling that you have to come home. See you later." Thus, at the same time as something enacted in action may cement infantile grandiosity and magical thinking, so too can the opposite occur: that there are no real consequences to limit and contain one's wishes—a thought which may also be unbearably scary. In addition, Dr. Reichbart's comments on the black and white concreteness in the patient's understandings suggests a literalness that makes one thing as real or as likely as the next and, therefore, so difficult to differentiate.

Clearly, the ideas expressed in the fantasies have early oral, anal, and phallic sadism and masochism resonance. Mr. A oscillates between being now the sadist, and now the masochist. This idea recalls a statement in Dr. Reichbart's report that mentions Mr. A's struggles "with thoughts about his childhood masochistic friend Ralph". All the earlier descriptions of Mr. A's interactions with Ralph—including Dr. Reichbart's assessment: "He wants me [the analyst] to be a 'mean mother fucker' like Ralph"—suggest that Ralph is assigned the object relation of being the sadist, not the masochist. Whether this is a slip on Dr. Reichbart's part or on that of his patient, it does suggest how intertwined these two concepts are, two sides of the same constellation.

While I have not, by any means, covered all aspects of the sadomasochistic fantasy life as portrayed in Dr. Reichbart's report, several more bear mentioning. Echoes of oral masochism reside in the references to sucking and possibly incorporation, and oral sadism seems present, for example, in a biting, a cannibalistic, motif when Mr. A proposes he will "cut off [his analyst's] testicles" (a castration motif) "and eat them like franks and beans". Anal sadism seems most strikingly represented in the actual withholding and expulsion of the telling of his fantasies and providing information to Dr. Reichbart, which will be discussed below. An example in which the anal masochism also seems prominent is in the fantasy that the analyst would punish him by slowly beating him to death. This imagery so strongly conjures up Freud's beating fantasies (1919), in which the patient metaphorically submits masochistically to the father-figure out of sexual satisfaction as well as punishment, but expressed through an anal phase resolution. The phallic ideas seem to emerge in a variety of ways—in particular, fantasies focusing on activity to do with his or someone else's penis, with pleasure and castration, explicit or implicit.

There is also, however, a great deal of ideation that might be considered distorted and oedipal. For example, the idea that he himself wants to be "evil and a loser, the best loser there is" seems to turn competitiveness upside down. He makes reference to the woman he is attracted to at a party who reminds Mr. A of his mother and whose husband is present and therefore portrayed as a witness, not an actor. This reverses, in the fantasy, his own childhood role as witness and sounds like an oedipal wish. It quickly, however, turns from triumph to sexualised and exhibitionistic violence, when he shifts to the thought of "strangling the woman by the [phallic-like] neck and holding her up before everyone while doing that." Here the fantasy could be envisioned as encapsulating a complicated condensation of component instincts (Freud, 1905) and a primal scene creation: exhibitionism (perhaps to replace voyeurism) and addressing what he thinks the man (father) does to the woman (mother), perhaps including a picture of the neck/penis being squeezed (a fetishistic fantasy). It is as if, in the end, his only victory over his oedipal longings was revenge and the wish to make his mother suffer for humiliating him, thus claiming no oedipal victor here.

We see that Mr. A's inner life is in a state of constant turmoil, conflict, and intensity, and overwrought with the demands of the sadomasochistic fantasies. He tries to keep a lid on these emotions: "If I don't say, these terrible impulses are not mine" (denial of ownership) or "If I don't say, my shame will not engulf me" (his palpable feelings of shame and guilt, so well described by Wurmser, 2007), and "If I stay by myself away from others, I won't act to harm me or others." That last thought, even though not enacted, is a terrifying one for the patient and in his mind a "real" possibility because of his difficulties in reality testing, his lack of clarity over what is internal and what is external; his inability to distinguish between wishes and action; and his blurring of sexual differences, as well as the past and the present.

Transference

For Mr. A, the analyst seems to represent a combination of projections. First and foremost, the analyst is Mr. A's important object—for fifteen years. He is carried in Mr. A's mind well beyond the duration of the treatment signaling object permanence and object constancy—and gratitude. This is the glue that makes Mr. A attach and stay attached, even though at times he has such profound negative feelings. For much of the time, it is a sadomasochistic object relation. But it is a sadomasochistic relationship with a difference—the object, the analyst, does not fully engage in the relationship at the same sadomasochistic level as the patient. It is comparable, in a way, with the parent of the two-year-old or the parent of the adolescent who sidesteps the toddler's or adolescent's bid to get into a power struggle, always looking for solutions that are not confrontations; the parent who has patience to wait and help the struggling young person come to his own more successful solutions, no matter what the parent may be feeling inside.

The patient had what amounted to a ritual that he would state at each session: how much he did not want to be in treatment, how the analyst was out to hurt him, how he could not possibly say anything new, and how he wanted to leave. Strikingly, he needed to repeat this "mantra" for less and less of the session time as the years rolled on. It reminds me of the way a pre-adolescent might not want to "jinx" his luck when he has *something* good; or, of the idea, "[the patient] doth protest too much." At the same time, even as we know that the unconscious knows no "no", we are also aware that the patient was articulating, in this ritualised form, his obsessional masochistic attachment to his objects. He was rationalising why he could not proceed any less cautiously—that is, because of these dangers, these fears: his negativity would cause him to bolt and lose his analyst, but also his fear of being hurt making vulnerability to his analyst worrisome, and further his having to hold onto a belief that the analyst could not have good will toward him. Thus, he continually had to overcome his conviction that he dare not say anything "new". One might think of this as setting up the line in the sand for a power struggle over the contents in his mind. Apparently, the answer that he got to his challenge—that the analyst would wait, would listen with interest, would wait some more, and, most importantly, mostly would pay attention—were different enough or valuable enough for him to stick around and continue the process. So he came to understand that he *could* put his poop in the pot at his own body's rhythm. Mr. A was also testing the analyst, to see if the analyst would be able to tolerate Mr. A's separation anxiety. This could have been in identification with his mother's hysterical reactions to the father's absences that might have led him to believe that it was unbearable for him to be separate from his mother. At the end of early sessions, the patient would repeat a threat of suicide, even to the point of describing setting up a noose in the basement of his parent's home where he would routinely go. (I note again, an interest in something squeezing the neck—this time his own.) He apparently acknowledged deriving pleasure from this negativity about himself and the cruelty of the world. One wonders how the analyst would tolerate such perversity so triumphantly avowed. This masochistic provocation, again, could be considered a test of the resolve of the analyst.

Another interesting point: the analyst noted that the patient only noticed a large watercolour of tiger lilies on the far wall of his office after coming for fifteen years. He would look "sideways" at the analyst. Could such a furtive look at the analyst and lack of attention to his environment have reflected his thinking that his analyst (and his possessions) were "off limits"? I see this as indicative of his inhibition or his feeling of prohibition from "looking", an issue that seems to touch on his feelings of wish and fear to exhibit his own genitals and to look at those of his analyst.

Mr. A certainly saw his analyst as a superego incarnate who would be disgusted with him and disapproving of him, but also who might be a corrupter of conscience as well: exhorting against the analyst for tolerating his telling of his disturbing fantasies. Those two aspects— conscience and corrupter of propriety—seem to transferentially suggest Mr. A's complicated feelings toward his mother. Then, there were feelings toward the analyst that suggest a paternal transference in the form of the various homosexual (with himself as the "feminine" partner with the enlarged breasts) and sadomasochistic references to what he would "do" to the analyst and what the analyst would "do" to him.

The incidents described with the barber and with the Uncle who liked him and wanted to take him fly-fishing (fishing in the fly?), seem, in the displacements, evidence of his fears of his homosexual attraction to the analyst. With the barber, it seems, more blatantly, fear of his homosexual strivings. But, with the uncle in particular, it seems as if Mr. A is reaching for an identification—a mentor who can teach him how to be a man—and an aunt who accepts his manliness, perhaps in contrast to his conviction that his mother can only find him acceptable if he stays attached to her and to no one else, in a masochistic pseudo-oedipal way. This conviction seems matched by his own wish to possess his mother—in a regressed sadomasochistic translation of an oedipal striving—to brand her; to hurt her and prevent her from ever having sex with the father; to have her cry out in pain. Similar to the fantasy about strangling the woman by the neck, this could equal a child's listening at the primal scene door, hearing moaning while the parents are behind the closed door and interpreting the moaning as the woman being hurt and in pain.

This fantasy relating to his mother gets transferred on to the analyst— what he will do to the analyst reflects perhaps another iteration in his shifting identifications. He is now not identifying with the female, but treating the analyst as the masochistic female to his sadistic male self. He notices that his analyst is not aroused by his fantasy. He "realises" that the analyst is "a nice man and [is] not becoming aroused at his fantasies, which angers him." This fantasy, as riddled with sadomasochism as it sounds, could have been equal to his attempted overture to love-making to the analyst. That might explain why he would be angry at the analyst for not being aroused, even while the analyst's not becoming aroused protects the patient, something neither parent seemed to do.

Countertransference

The analyst's countertransference appears to show a split in the analyst's emotional stance to the patient, perhaps a little bit like the split that Sterba (1934) long ago spoke of as a desirable split between the observing and the experiencing ego. In this case, however, it seems more like levels of observing ego and levels of experiencing ego. Returning to my opening sentence to this discussion, I quoted Dr. Reichbart's phrasing that he often rolled his eyes, in particular while listening to the patient's repetitive and boring monologue, which I have labeled as an obsessional ritual. So how would I interpret the rolling of eyes? It is certainly some kind of reaction to the patient, a countertransferential response. Dr. Reichbart characterises his reaction as being bored to death. I would add to that description, incredulity, disbelief, and perhaps frustration. But by describing it as being bored to death, one might also include, torturous. My use of the adjective "torturous", moves the experience toward the sadomasochism spectrum. Dr. Reichbart explicitly states that "I experienced this as much more of a sadistic attack on me than any of his graphic depictions of sadism ... the wish to suck ... the enjoyment of life out of the envied, lively 'other' and to have the 'other' experience the same deadness that the patient experiences." Even though Dr. Reichbart obviously withstood the onslaught of unconscious sadism delivered to him via his patient's ruminations day after day and week after week until an eventual easing of that form of sadism occurred, we still could consider that while it was going on Dr. Reichbart was masochistically receiving and accepting it. Obviously, too, Dr. Reichbart was able to tolerate the way the patient was behaving toward him in the service of the treatment.

For Dr. Reichbart, the important point was that he was not influenced in any way that he was aware of by the more overt renditions of sadistic fantasies or reported behaviours that were historical. This was so, according to Dr. Reichbart, for several reasons. The first, he explained, was that the patient was—for the most part—telling him about fantasies as well as behaviours from much earlier times, like a story. Yet even as historical accounting, the analyst notices the patient's greater liveliness in the telling. When the patient spoke of sadistic behaviours toward his current family as opposed to his family of origin, however, Dr. Reichbart found himself—not without considerable internal conflict—educating the patient on the proper care of children in order to protect the patient's current objects. He explained that this approach was needed (as in, it was beyond psychoanalysis) on the basis of deficits in the patient, things the patient did not know. What seems particularly interesting, and confirmatory to me of the inherent twinship of sadism and masochism, is that I have noticed in myself and other analysts that when the patient induces in the analyst an identification with the patient's objects, there is a complicated shift that occurs. There is a kind of identification and disidentification with the aggressor in the patient in which the patient portrays himself as the aggressor, while the patient's objects stand in for the patient's self. Thus, in embracing a need to protect the masochistic objects of the patient and rejecting the patient's sadism, the analyst can inadvertently, but understandably, become allied with the masochistic part of the patient. If one considers the close relationship between external real objects and the internal objects in the patient's mind, the analyst can be thought of, in such moments, as identifying with the masochistic victim object inside the patient.

This phenomenon, as well as other factors, including the inevitable wish on the part of the analyst to protect a patient from harm to himself or others, may lead to a kind of countertransference different from one primarily of a sadomasochistic tenor being dominant in the analytic couple. It might be thought of as a kind of protective parental model, on the order of a corrective emotional experience in Bibring's (1954) positive use of the term that abjures the sadomasochistic.

Dr. Reichbart describes many internal issues that sustained him and permitted him to tolerate the power of the sadistic-masochistic pull. One was his joy at having the analytic case; thus, perhaps, the benefits outweighed the pain. It appears that Dr. Reichbart liked the patient, which provided an important balance to the situation. Another, as Dr. Reichbart described in discussing his transference to the patient, was a parallel to his own personal life experience. Dr. Reichbart empathised in a very intimate way with what he understood Mr. A had to endure based on Dr. Reichbart's experience with his own theatrical mother. Because of this, Dr. Reichbart considered that he was able to function toward the patient with the *"stalwartness"* that he had been able to exhibit with his own mother. Still another reason that Dr. Reichbart gives is that the sadism and masochism current to the treatment was not physical, so that the analyst could think about it for the most part as the workings in the mind rather than the patient's life.

Finally, although there were many years of work, the analyst may have been able to sustain his own liveliness and interest because, in fact, the patient did change. Ultimately, Dr. Reichbart was able to say to the patient, and the patient was able to hear, that "underlying his fantasies seems to be his wish that people notice his erection, and that he wants me to admire his erection. This need for this is a consequence, I say, of the fact that his mother denied that he had a penis, when she appeared to him in undress, as did his father." It is with the patient's recognition of this interpretation that the healing that needed to happen to the patient's sense of his male body image was contained, putting him on the road to recovery. No longer had he to be locked into the prison of believing that the only relationship he could have with another was a freakish sadomasochistic one. What a fine analytic outcome!

Summary

The drumbeat of this patient's sadomasochistic fantasy life must have been very absorbing, picturing violent, sexualised relations with his inner objects and making it difficult for him to attend to the outer world of reality. Up to the time of his treatment, this self-absorption may have functioned as a perverse (and perhaps addictive) adaptation. Yet, beginning with Dr. Reichbart, and seeing him day after day and year after year, may have been an effective invitation to work together to allow his mind to broaden his fantasies and inner life, and to include space for a more balanced view of himself and his objects. It seems as if he was able to rebuild and rebalance his identifications and consequently his relations to his objects to let the power of the earlier, sadomasochistic orientation recede into the background of his thinking.

I have followed the sadomasochistic coloration of Mr. A's thinking and object relations through attention to the transference, countertransference, and the process of the analysis. We owe a debt to Dr. Reichbart for his generosity in sharing this material that highlights sadomasochism so prominently.

References

Bibring, E. (1954). Psychoanalysis and the dynamic psychotherapies. *Journal of the American Psychoanalytic Association*, 2: 745–770.

Blos, P. (1962). *On Adolescence*. New York: The Free Press.

Freud, S. (1905). *Three Essays on The Theory of Sexuality*. *S. E.*, 7: 125–243. London: Hogarth.

Freud, S. (1919). 'A child is being beaten': A Contribution to the Study of the Origin of Sexual Perversion. *S. E.*, 17: 175–204.

Greenacre, P. (1953). Fetishism and body image. *Psychoanalytic Study of the Child*, 8: 79–98.

Greenacre, P. (1969). The fetish and the transitional object. *Psychoanalytic Study of the Child*, 24: pp. 144–164.

Kohut, H. (1971). *The Analysis of the Self. A Systematic Approach to the Psychoanalytic Treatment of Narcissistic Personality Disorders*.

Monograph #4 of the Monograph Series of the Psychoanalytic Study of the Child. New York: International Univ. Press.

Laufer, M. (1976). The central masturbation fantasy, the final sexual organization, and adolescence. *Psa. Study of the Child*, 31: 297–316.

Laufer, M. & Laufer, M. Egle. (1984). *Adolescence and Developmental Breakdown*. New Haven: Yale University Press.

Sterba, R. (1934). The fate of the ego in analytic therapy. *International Journal of Psycho-Analysis*, 15: 117–126.

Stoller, R. (1975). *Perversion*. New York: Pantheon.

Wurmser, L. (2007). *Torment Me, But Don't Abandon Me*. New York: Jason Aronson.

CHAPTER EIGHTEEN

Sadomasochism and aggression—clinical theory: discussion of the case of Mr. A

Leo Rangell

Sadomasochism and aggression

The choice of topic for this volume of the CIPS book series places the intrepid authors promptly at the head of a storm. Most psychoanalytic practitioners have pursued their craft for their lifetimes with assumptions of theoretical positions for various syndromes of different degrees of proof or conviction, never quite settling each issue in a totally satisfying way.

When I started to think about the theory of "S and M", I found myself searching around not in a theory about these specifically, but repeatedly on the psychoanalytic theory of aggression. The connection was promptly obvious. Does not the average analyst, confronted by any situation of "S and M", immediately think in terms of sadism being linked to aggression toward others, while in the opposite, masochism, the aggression is turned toward the self? The link seems automatic. So my focus was soon on aggression. What is it, psychoanalytically?

In keeping with my usual *modus operandi* in approaching any psychoanalytic subject for study, my way is to first identify and describe the phenomenology in question, then to delineate the relevant background theory, apply it to the presenting material, trace the developmental steps in the particular case history, and to attempt any generalisations that may be possible from such a combined approach and investigation.

Freud's (1930) theory of aggression, which is the supporting base of the clinical conditions under scrutiny, is half of Freud's famous dual instinct theory, but its locus and functions within the Freudian theoretical framework are of conflict and controversy. The call for clarity and definition in a murky area is a strong one.

Phenomenology

To focus first on the chosen topics, the data and clinical observations that one can consider coming under the aegis of sadism and masochism are themselves actually obscure and indistinct. It is difficult to definitively pin down observed data either at their periphery, to establish a border to other contiguous phenomena, or within their own psychic interior, to define a specific cluster of behaviour as coming under these two related concepts.

The same applies to the supporting, underlying theme of aggression in the body of psychoanalytic theory. The origins of this half of Freud's instinct theory, the variations it can assume during the course of any clinical material, and its general vicissitudes throughout life do not make for easy categorisation. The obscurity and fuzziness of the several possibilities, and the obstacles to arriving at a common scientific consensus have generally resulted in some kind of temporary bypassing of the problem by the average psychoanalyst, utilising in each case a formula that each feels serves him best.

Aggression is not synonymous with sadism, nor the opposite in masochism. The element of cruelty must be added—in one case the intent to hurt; in the other, to suffer or be hurt, to be treated unfairly. An action being aggressive, or forcefully executed, is not sufficient to be sadistic.

If this volume is an attempt, or possibly a hope, to improve on this less-than-settled scientific problem, we authors of its separate chapters have bitten off some difficult assignments. Each is stimulated to survey his life experience as a psychoanalytic clinician to see if any advance can be made in what have become the ongoing conceptualisations of this aspect of human life.

To do this in my own case, to see what I have been using as a working hypothesis in my psychoanalytic understanding of sadistic and masochistic behaviour, and whether this view can stand up to closer examination, I think back at a series of clinical experiences. Looking back where a psychoanalyst looks, to my actual practice, I can report that in a lifetime of clinical exposure, actually over seven decades, I cannot point to a long, accumulated list of patients but can remember only a few individuals to whom I would have applied the term "sadist"— perhaps more so to the "maso" variety. I remember one patient who played "the bad guy" in movies, and who looked and acted the part in life. I saw him after World War Two, where he suffered very traumatic near-death experiences, which increased his look and actions of badness. He was one of very few patients who scared me when he entered the consulting room. I cannot go into any biographic details for practical reasons.

Another was a man who was silent and sulky, near schizophrenic, malignant in his behaviour in many ways. He would extinguish a lit cigarette on his wife's abdomen. She tolerated it. He was "the black sheep" in a very accomplished family. His mother was actively seductive, his brother a national figure, his father an important scientist. He was a drifter, sullenly angry to an extreme. As a hobby, he raised wolves in a pen in his urban backyard. I can say more, but this would not lend itself to scientific answers to the many questions we are asking, except that I never felt that he was sadistic from birth.

A psychoanalytic practice, however, is hardly a place in which sadism would be prominent. I have been reminded that if any of us worked on death-row in a state prison, our impressions of statistics would be different. For a more fertile soil to witness large numbers within this syndrome, probably a broader, sociologic approach is a more logical path. There is hardly a daily newspaper without stories of rape, and its frequent even more terrible aftermaths. Or equivalents in the nonsexual sphere. Or we can look into shelters for abused women, or children, which abound in every urban population. Or in places which the homeless call home. In all of these, the outcomes have complex backgrounds, of individual inputs and society's roles. And the recipients are not always masochists but victims.

The sadistic components are often aspects minimised or eliminated from consciousness. Recently, a prisoner came up for parole (Los Angeles Times, 2011) who was one of three men who perpetrated the infamous "Chowchilla" crime (I can think of none more chilling). He had been a model prisoner for many decades. His attorney argued that he meant no hurt or pain to the victims. He and two other young men, all from wealthy families, did it for ransom, for money, he averred.

Still looking sociologically, there is also war, or a continuous series of the same. Here sadism is seen *en masse*, with no intimate contacts routinely visible to serve as the trigger points. National pride and identifications seem to also be sufficient reason to lead to a universal acquiescence to the regular sequence of war and peace throughout the history of man. Yet solitary incidents are not absent or difficult to find as starting points of such incendiary explosions. King Hussein himself has a secret arsenal of WMD, we were told as the country was led into a long, dubious war. Generations before, the First World War, the beginning of a new type of trench combat, was indeed ascribed to a single event, the murder of Franz Ferdinand, heir to the Austrian Empire, in Sarajevo, the capital of Bosnia, on 28 June 1914. Although long-term causes had been brewing for some time, this incident has been accepted by historians as the immediate cause of World War One. Following this tumultuous and multi-faceted event, although Franz Ferdinand was actually an unpopular leader, previous treaties and ententes were called into play, so that within weeks, most of the European countries were at war against each other. Here, in the trenches, participants, if not sadistic before, became so. The recipients were not masochists but victims. Sadistic acts were directed to others who would do the same in reverse.

While this type of individual entrance to war is not the rule, more and more are wars entered by presidents—cautious ones as well as the rash, in little Granada as in Vietnam—for constructed reasons, such as the presence of weapons of mass destruction, or the Bay of Pigs or the Gulf of Tonkin. Regression does seem rampant, universal, ready to explode, and regularly needs to be explained.

This "war to end war" was followed a short time later by the cataclysmic event of the 1930s and beyond, that encompassed the Holocaust, perhaps the greatest reservoir of mass sadism in human history. No history of violence will ever be able to be written again without a prominent role given to this period of mass group descent into the unthinkable.

The clinical case

At this point I will insert a discussion of the clinical case offered by the editors. As a start and summary, this is an excellent case to describe and understand (but in my opinion from an unexpected direction) not because it is a good example of the syndrome of sadomasochism, but because it is of a genre that is easily and commonly confused with that symptom complex. The patient, rather, and the analysis that he elicited, are good clinical examples of a complex, multi-layered chronic neurosis that is the prototype of the old-fashioned, long-term mental conflicts that were the analyst's fare routinely during the early period of psychoanalysis.

This analysis is a current example of that early period that is still vibrant and valid. It is a direct derivative of Freud's first theorising, his still-relevant instinct theory, the dominance of the sexual drive, reminiscences of Little Hans, the Wolfman, and the other great case histories, anxiety as a defence, and a strong repressive barrier to the conscious recognition of the patient's cluster of unconscious conflicts. This analysis could have been conducted, even in a much leaner way, by focusing on vicissitudes of the libidinal instinct alone, without any primary input from aggression or its derivatives.

The long, chronic, disabling neurosis of this patient centred around twists and turns and deviations of the patient's libidinal, erotic development, which met conflicts and dilemmas that were to him solvable only by the suspended state he worked himself into, to prevent either a fixation in a state of chronic anxiety, or the development of symptoms that would have been even more anxiety-producing. The symptomatology and character armour he adopted to direct his life were largely to protect himself from his fear of homosexuality; basically, his homosexual impulses, which produced anxiety, which prompted his defensive character armour. This was the underlying content behind his self-loathing and negation, his switch to new friends, the denial of his Jewishness, of his self or totality, as a person to be accepted and respected where it counted.

The turning point was the Bar-Mitzvah, becoming a man. The prelude was well described and credible, the seductive mother and weak (symbolically castrated) father. Each was extreme; a mother coming to the dining-room table in her underwear does not leave much doubt as to the correctness of the analytic thoughts and conclusions that follow. The patient, strongly identified with the wage-earning, all-powerful mother, while feeling distant, disappointed, almost phobic about his devalued father, slipped into a homosexual mode and a strong defence against this in turn. Various accompaniments and derivatives of this identification made their appearances: changing his friendships, his subservience to the more aggressive Ralph, aversion toward the female genitalia, a dip into secret transvestitism. One could have elicited sexual psychopathology wherever he explored.

Any attitudes or other clinical material looking sadistic or maso-chistic, however dramatically expressed, were a side issue, not the cen-tre, intellectual, not affective, empty boasting rather than substantial thoughts. The patient was grateful when these were not made too much of, and his real unconscious conflicts addressed. Recognition of this ena-bled the analyst to maintain the analytic attitude throughout, despite his being "bored to death". It was being met by this non-judgmental response on the part of the analyst time after time that enabled the patient to develop the trust that led to the series of exposures of the underlying conflicts, and ultimately the drastic positive changes that ensued.

For the analyst, his analytic role came from various sources. Besides his analytic goals and the gradual learning that came from this and other cases, and from training, there was the less-than-defensible real-ity of his needing the case and the patient. It was not the analyst's coun-tertransference that kept the boring analysis going so tenaciously and so long but at least partly his being "overjoyed" at the early analytic case and having a patient on the couch. Analytic candidates, as well as many analysts at various times, know this well. But to be complete without too much rationalisation, this did not harm the patient but did him a service, motivating him, and the analyst, to "hang in there" to a good ending.

But perhaps the main reason neither the analyst nor patient "gave up" at the boring repetitiveness of the early hours are stated near the end of the paper. Both knew, or felt, that the threats and whining and desperation expressed by the patient were quite empty gestures, rooted in fantasy life, far from any danger of reaching the border to the external world. The patient was well-defended against outer discharge. "I will do this and that to you, cut off your testicles and penis and eat them", etc., was nowhere near action. Such outbursts in fact sounded more like adolescent boasting than real threats. Both parties could relax.

Complications introduced by countertransference (i.e., in my understanding coming from the analyst's own unresolved past) were far from primary in the material reported, in spite of the analyst's few relevant references about his own mother which fortified his "stalwart" approach. His recognised boredom and discomfort were more related to the patient's manner of presenting and to the appropriate exasperation it produced after years of the same. What was slow in coming seems to have been the recognition of the unconscious psychopathological process, and the centrality of castration anxiety at the centre of his psychosexual development. This appeared from many directions, including his affectionate thinking of the analyst as "a dinosaur with a long tail".

When the interpretation of castration anxiety finally does come—not far from the end of the paper—it comes with a bang, and has a marked effect. Hearing that "he wished the analyst would acknowledge that he has a penis, which the behaviour of his mother toward him worked to deny", he becomes silent, tears streaming down his cheeks. He wishes he had a father like the analyst. The interpretation, not quite on target but somewhat inexact (Glover, 1955) was effective nevertheless. In today's climate, this moment of insight is actually one of the most touching understandings of castration anxiety I have heard in recent years (Rangell, 1991).

No doubt this interpretative event played a strong part in propelling the analysis toward its favourable end, enabling the patient to complete his object-choice that led to his marriage and fatherhood. This is also, incidentally, a brief commentary on unconscious object-choice in hetero and homosexuality, a subject of great conflict and disagreement in the modern sexual sphere. This patient demonstrated a bisexual disposition, was becoming uni-sexed as a compromise for strong conflictful reasons, gained some mastery over this basic conflict by the analysis, and was eventually able to exercise a satisfying and durable ego choice by the autonomous ego as a result of the security achieved.

Actually, political correctness aside, one would say that this patient's heterosexual choice, his natural aim during his developmental progression, was being pressured and compromised by his neurotic life, pushing him toward identification with his mother. The result was a surge of impulses as well as an accompanying fear (up to panic), of assuming an ego-dystonic feminine identity, which produced his chronic anxiety, which pressed him to reconsider his direction, from which path he came to make the heterosexual object-choice that characterised the rest of his life-span thus far, with a normal amount of contentment and psychic peace.

The word "natural" needs to be expanded, or it can today be the cause of much passion and conflict. The above statement was about a psychic situation occurring decades ago—and might not be the same today. Societal changes in attitudes and values in this area are in a constant state of flux.

I (2002) remember being the discussant to a paper by Charles Brenner which he gave at the New York Psychoanalytic Society, "Is psychoanalysis a natural science?" Not unexpectedly, Brenner's answer was in the positive: nature makes no exceptions, our discipline deals with the mind, the mind comes from the brain, the latter has no choice but to follow the rules of nature. Psychoanalysis is therefore an example of natural science.

On that occasion, as the discussant and responder, I concurred with this sequence of thought, and underwrote that author's conclusion (Brenner, 1999). In this paper, I look again, this time at a more specific aspect of the larger subject, and expect that I will come up with more complex reasoning.

Commenting on the same area today elicits another train of thought, with multiple paths to consider. First, nature does provide alternatives; if one is not available or does not work, another is there to be chosen. If not heterosexuality, there is a genetically-determined or influenced uni-sex direction to explore. Second, the external societal input is subject to rapid change. This patient came to his crossroads several decades ago. His choices were largely determined by the chosen path of his mother, transferred to the growing boy. Having the phallus in the family was crucial to power and dominance. Third, nature is not only what is present, or at least visible, at birth. Early environmental influences become part of a person, what I call his "second nature"! It can be as implacable as the first.

Nature is also one's potential, or timetable for the emergence of traits. One's "nature" can come out later. Typically, such later changes are in response to having experienced the "average expectable environment", Hartmann's (1939) felicitous phrase, which varies with cultures, geography, and group chronological age. For each culture, the accepted behaviour is its particular stamp of nature at that moment in time. And finally, even nature can change. In his book reviewing the history of revolutions, Robert Waelder (1967), speculating about whether or not aggression and despotism are inherent in the nature of man, writes, "Even if this condition were universal, however, it would not prove that man cannot alter it: for man, though rooted in nature, can transcend nature to a large degree." As Denis de Rougemont put it: "Man's nature is to pass beyond nature".

So much for one's "natural" choice. It is far from absolute.

Theory

The overall conclusion about the relevance of the clinical case presented for the study of the subject of this book is that it demonstrates not the syndrome to be explored but one with which it is commonly confused. It is of course clinically valuable to be able to recognise and distinguish pseudo-sadistic behaviour from contiguous states. Each calls for different approaches in an analysis.

Actually, the entire symptom constellation of the patient we have been attending derives from the twists of psychopathological development described rather than from any excessive presence or use of aggression in his psychic makeup, in spite of his complaints of internal suffering and his mode of resorting to aggressive but empty threats.

Nevertheless, since aggression is characteristically the base from which sadomasochism is executed when present, the theory to be understood behind the symptomatology—which is the central subject of this book—is still the theory of aggression and how this is utilised by the unconscious ego to bring about the compromise formations that constitute this symptom complex.

To begin therefore to fathom the theory or science behind two such opposite but joined clinical phenomena as sadism and masochism, I will turn as an opener to the subject from which both can be thought to derive: the theory of aggression, as this has occupied psychoanalytic theoreticians. Considering the fairly universal concurrence of analysts that both sadism and masochism are related to the course and direction of aggression in their developmental histories, it would be a quite rational move to examine closely the theory of aggression itself, to see whether this exploration would lead to agreement from the opposite direction: that is, starting from the original role of aggression and examining this element through its applied clinical phases and vicissitudes on its way to many different presenting syndromes.

Freud's theory of aggression did not become a part of his epoch-making new formulations until some two decades after his thinking was first introduced to the public at the end of the last century with *The Interpretation of Dreams* (Freud, 1900). This part of the general theory, moreover, was never assimilated in an equally global way as was the revolutionary sexual instinct, nor has it ever achieved the same intensity of interest, degree of reception, nor the clarity of its theoretical role as did the sexual half of Freud's instinct theory (in spite of the early huge rejection of Freud's sexual theories).

To mention some of the directions taken in various explanations of the vicissitudes of the phenomenon of aggression, the most frequent position described—which might mostly be in deference to the view of Freud himself—is that it is on a par with libido or love as a basic human instinct. In spite of its ubiquity, the fact that Freud was not moved to include this until his two sons were in the German army during World War Two did not speak for his objectivity as a scientific observer in this area as a base for the formulation. Not far behind as an explanation is the concept of aggression as a reaction and response to frustration, which is never absent, but present in every aspect of life from birth on. Other directions taken, such as aggression being the reaction to an underlying death wish or drive in keeping with the thrust of all living matter to return to the original inorganic state, I actually would prefer to leave more to philosophers of science than to psychoanalysts. Certainly, the nature of nature is an area for at least a combined approach. I am impressed and influenced by the fact that Otto Fenichel, whom I admire and respect, seemed to believe (1945) in the validity and veracity of this concept. So did an entire segment of analytic theorists at one point, around the views of Melanie Klein (King & Steiner, 1991). I am not sure whether it is still supported. The data and evidence seem problematic.

One colleague (Kalish-Weiss, 2011), who is a child analyst as well as an analyst of adults, suggested to me that a developmental line of understanding of aggression as an instinctual drive might have followed closely the theoretical history of its counterpart libidinal instinct. As an example, the idea was that this could have consisted of developmental phases based on forms of aggression analogous with the progressing libidinal organisation, such as biting, along with the oral phase of libido, pinching off, expelling, and separating, with the anal stage, and penetration, stabbing, injuring by invasive entry, with the phallic phase. But a detailed and authentically-presented proposal along these lines never came, nor was it ever widely suggested or recommended.

By serendipity, and independently related to this stream of thought, about half-way into that century of Freud, I attempted to highlight the aggressive aspect of human life by assigning that subject as the theme of the historic Vienna Congress in 1971. This was at the congress that marked the first return of a Freud to Vienna since the forced exile of the family to London concomitant with the history of horror in Austria, along with the rest of Europe, from the mid and late 1930s.

As my presidential address at the opening plenary session, I (Rangell, 1972) centred on the subject of aggression in psychoanalytic theory and the role this played in the progression of psychoanalytic thought. Not only did I feel that this general concept was exquisitely relevant to the circumstances of that historic congress, but that the concept was mired in many confusing areas of unclarity and subject to much misunderstanding.

Under the theme I chose as an umbrella for the congress, "Aggression, Oedipus, and Historical Perspective", I spoke on the pivotal role played by aggression in the unfolding of the Oedipus complex to illustrate the fusion of the two major developmental streams in which aggression mounts in centrality and intensity along with its counterpart, the libidinal instinct. As an ongoing side drama accompanying the fateful love elements, Oedipus mates with his mother, but is doomed also to murder his father Laius. He himself then penetrates his own eyes and pays with blindness—a symbol intended to conjure up a symbolic castration as punishment. Is any further demonstration of aggression necessary to include it in the theory? Aggression is as oedipal as libido and, being as centrally built-in to the symbolism of antiquity, enjoys an equally long history.

The next phase of this journey is to consider the links from aggression to sadomasochism, or the reverse, from the symptoms to the roots of aggression never found far behind the perversions of sadism and masochism. A home-run king of baseball is being charged with steroid use, which he denies. His ex-mistress testifies that when he told her to get lost, about five years after he married his second wife, during which time the affair had continued, he met her protests and disappointments by threatening to cut off her head, cut her breast implants, and burn her house (Bond, B., 2011). The confluence of the two—termination of a love relationship in its myriad forms and the appearance of hostility and viciousness of enormous degree—are not unusual, but too much the rule.

In ordinary inter-professional parlance referring to aggression in any clinical or applied discussion, the meaning and roles of the term have reached a complex level. There is no consistency or unanimity between the various connotations or meanings of the term. Nor can a consensus be expected to be arrived at in this collection of essays. That has not been the charge to the authors, nor is it the subject of this book. Each contributor has been left to describe and utilise his own definition or definitions in accordance with his personal use of the concept, or how it varies according to the larger subject or context in which the role of aggression is being called forth.

There is another issue I feel has been routinely underplayed in the literature of psychoanalysis generally and in certain central subjects within it (the present subject included) because it is usually regarded as unsolvable or too speculative. Whenever sadomasochism is mentioned, out comes the automatic thought or theory that sadism is aggression turned outward, while in masochism, the aggression is against the self. But does anyone ask "who, or what does the turning?" Who or what is the agent of "doing", or performing or setting any action in motion? This harks back to a subject I have been occupied with for over half this century: the matter of agency. Who "does", that is, anything mental, from directing traffic intrapsychically to executing actions or other perturbances into the outer world?

The large answer to this long enigma, in my (Rangell, 1989) view of a psychoanalytic theory of action, is that the agent of action is the system ego, the conscious ego at one end but also the active unconscious ego in the unconscious. Internal and external motion or movements are a mixture of conscious and unconscious direction and execution, of discharge which is at the same time automatic and directed, a fusion of psychic determinism and direction by the autonomous ego, acting together to bring about any stream of behavioural outcomes. I have described these states and moments in detail, imparting into analytic mental activity the factors of purpose, intention, and meaning, in my papers on "the unconscious intrapsychic process", "the executive functions of the ego" (1986), "a psychoanalytic theory of action", and a series of others, and will not repeat their contents here. "Free will", I have concluded (2009), is present but only partial. The ego is affected and limited by the determinism introduced by Freud, but also partially "free" to execute its own ends.

That is why in my book My Life in Theory (2004), the final sentence is, "Life is a combination of what has to be, and what we make of that."

And one more, perhaps the last enigma as to the "natural" characteristic of aggression, or even hostile aggression, en route to sadism: How can a concept of such multiple meanings become entrenched as one's nature in any guise in which it appears? How can it be that whether aggression is an instinct or a life force regulating all psychic phenomena, or even a link to or part of a death instinct, any of these roles can become part of a plan of "nature"?

Sadism and masochism are clinical phenomena, the carrying to an extreme the use of aggression in the service of administering pain or suffering, which in daily mental life is used in a more moderate and controlled fashion. However one conceives of aggression, whether as an economic force in the observance of all mental regulatory and directed activity, or a specific instinctual drive available for discharge on its own capabilities, these characteristics are at work in all cases. How can opposite or at least different meanings all be "natural"?

How can aggression as a response to frustration, which is sporadic, rather than as an instinctual drive, fit in with the natural course of mental life? In my thinking, there is no incompatibility. Frustration is also part of nature, and does not rule out aggression as being inborn, or having its own time-line for its emergence and for its occurrence being universal and predictable. Frustration, from birth onward, is part of Hartmann's (1939) "average expectable environment", which is also built-in to the expectable history of man, even though it is a different environment at every stage and phase of development of the individual as well as the group. An answer to the frequently asked question to psychoanalysis, "Is man good or evil?", is that he is both, depending on the circumstances or the provocation.

Freud's theory of the complementary series is the beginning of an explanation. Each of these two theories of anxiety contained partial understanding, one basically physiological, the other psychological (Rangell, 1955, 1968). If aggression in any form is adherent to a human life long enough, its permanence is accentuated, and vice versa. Here the long recognition of the link between Freud and Darwin (1859) is re-affirmed, as ontology and phylogeny mirror each other. As evolving cultures determine what is "natural" for each.

Evolutionary era—so does what is "normal" evolve and change with advancing age in an individual with each move to the next developmental stage? Both change and evolve with advancing history. Analysis can help the process of gaining some control over the automatic process, with a diminution or perhaps a delay in its inevitability.

A pride of lions—licking their chops, feasting on the carcass of a large animal one of them has just felled—bears more similarities than differences to a human dinner party consuming a supply of decapitated chickens. Yet "*homo sapiens*" has added motivations to the interpersonal human world—cruelty, revenge fantasies, inflicting punishment, and enjoying making others suffer—that we do not know existed in prehistoric or even more modern times. It is the combined genius of Freud and Darwin (1859) that explains how these forces gradually become built-in to the evolutionary scale in the service of natural adaptation. One thinks of both together in these connections.

Sadomasochism represents two poles of a dichotomy, which, as all such pairs, contains most instances not at the extremes but at various points in the centre. The more of one, the less of the other. There are probably none who are entirely free of its operations, at least in the unconscious, since what they are composed of are universal experiences. Every person wants to be treated fairly every moment of his/ her life, and there are not likely any who achieve this perfectly. Deep fantasies—evening the score, making an offender or neglector feel the same lack, disappointment or humiliation—stimulates at least nascent forms of unconscious fantasies carrying out such a wish.

At the extremes of the perverse and persistent presence of these characteristics, individuals afflicted with such obsessions can be quite maladaptive and come to represent significant danger to themselves or others. Ignoring their potentialities and tenacity can be at the peril of severely destructive consequences, whether to an individual or a large group. Now that terrorism has become an additional issue of universal concern, the ubiquity and spread of the results of sadistic behaviour can never be discounted. The same holds for the other end of the spectrum, guilt or anxiety over actions toward others. There is no one who cannot feel the pull of the need for atonement, for what he did to or failed to do in the social world. Otherwise we would not have the regular and recurring setting aside of the day of Yom Kippur.

References

Bond, B. (2011). Ex-mistress testifies. *Los Angeles Times*, 29 April.
Brenner, C. (1999). Reflections on psychoanalysis. Paper delivered to The New York Psychoanalytic Society, 13 June.
Chowchilla. In: Kidnap memories won't be buried, *Los Angeles Times*, 4 April 2011.
Darwin, C. (1859). *The Origin of Species*. Oxford: Oxford University Press.
Fenichel, O. (1945). *The Psychoanalytic Theory of Neurosis*. New York: Norton.

Freud, S. (1900). The interpretation of dreams. *S. E., 4 & 5*. London: Hogarth.

Freud, S. (1930). *Civilization and its discontents. S. E., 21.*

Glover, E. (1955). The therapeutic effect of inexact interpretation: A contribution to the theory of suggestion. In: *The Technique of Psychoanalysis* (pp. 353–366). New York: Int. Univ. Press.

Hartmann, H. (1939). *Ego Psychology and the Problem of Adaptation.* Trans. by David Rapaport. New York: Int. Univ. Press, 1958.

Kalish-Weiss, B. (2011). Personal communication.

King, P. & Steiner, R. (Eds.) (1991). *The Freud–Klein Controversies 1941–45.* London: The New Library of Psychoanalysis.

Rangell, L. (1955). On the psychoanalytic theory of anxiety: A statement of a unitary theory. *Journal of the American Psychoanalytic Association*, 3: 389–414.

Rangell, L. (1968). A further attempt to resolve the "problem of anxiety". *Journal of the American Psychoanalytic Association*, 16: 371–404.

Rangell, L.(1972). Aggression, Oedipus, and historical perspective. (Presidential Address to the 27th International Psychoanalytical Congress, Vienna, Austria, 26 July 1971.) *International Journal of Psychoanalysis*, 53: 3–11.

Rangell, L. (1986). The executive functions of the ego. An extension of the concept of ego autonomy. *Psychoanalytic Study of the Child*, 41: 1–37.

Rangell, L. (1989). Action theory within the structural view. *International Journal of Psychoanalysis*, 70: 189–203.

Rangell, L. (1991). Castration. *Journal of the American Psychoanalytic Association*, 39: 3–23.

Rangell, L. (2002). Discussion of Brenner: "Reflections on Psychoanalysis" and parallel reflections. Presented at the New York Psychoanalytic Society, 13 April 1999. *Journal of Clinical Psychiatry.*, 11: 96–114.

Rangell, L. (2004). *My Life in Theory.* New York: Other Press.

Rangell, L. (2009). Discourse on free will: Psychoanalysis and the soul. International Psychoanalysis website.

Waelder, R. (1967). *Progress and Revolution.* New York: Int. Univ. Press.

INDEX

adaptive assumption 187–188
adolescence 230–233
affect flooding 219
affect regression 222
affect regulation 219
affective development 218
affective interpenetration, in analytic
    dyad 184
aggression 283
aggressive or sexual desires 234
alexithymia, concept of 146
anal character, building of 16
anal sphincter 17–18
anality, and sadomasochism 16–18
analytic sex 112
analytic trust, concept of 183–185
annihilation anxiety 124, 132, 140
annihilation fear 18, 249
anti-shame-hero 222
anxiety, depressive position and 49
archaic defences 221

archaic superego 220–221
arousal 237–238
articulated sadomasochistic thoughts
    240
Austrian Empire 276

Bach, Sheldon (1994, 2001, 2006) 11,
    214, 247–253
Bass, Alan 8–9, 45–61
Basseches, Harriet 1–14, 255–272
beating fantasy
    and sadomasochism 20–21
    Freud on 55
    in children 67
    in women 50
Beyond the Pleasure Principle (Freud)
    49, 56
Bird, Brian 192
Blos, Peter 258
"borderland" 67
Brouček, Francis (1991) 216

case study
    of Diane by Paula Ellman
        (*see* Ellman, Dr. Paula, case
        study by)
    of Mariah by Andrea Greenman
        (*see* Greenman, Dr. Andrea,
        case study by)
    of Mr. A by Richard Reichbart
        (*see* Reichbart, Dr. Richard,
        case study by)
    of Mr. B by Nancy Goodman
        (*see* Goodman, Dr. Nancy,
        case study by)
castration anxiety 129, 131, 259
childhood
    chronic and severe
        traumatisation 220, 222
    countertransference 243
    recurrent traumatisation 218–219
Chowchilla 275
claustrophobic anxiety 117–118
consistent and utilisable transference
    184
contingency, concept of 118
countertransference 1–14, 242–246,
    268–271
    boredom in 248

Darwin, Freud 286
death drive 56
death instincts 5
deep fantasies 286
defensive cycles 193
defensive splitting of self-
    preservation and sexuality 58
denigration, togetherness and 2
depersonalization 213–214
depressive anxiety 83
destructive consequences 286
destructiveness, instinct of 48–49
developmental images 73–74
"dilettantish adventure" 202
direct transference interpretations 216

disavowal in transference/
    countertransference 21
disidentification 202
disintegration anxiety 124
dominance-submission
    and dependence-independence
    250
    and pain-pleasure 250

ego
    passivity 223
    restrictive defences 182
Ellman, Dr. Paula, case study by 8,
    29–44
    Bass discussion on 8–9, 45–61
    case presentation 29–34
    Novicks discussion on 9, 63–78
    process material 35–44
    Robinson discussion on 9, 79–92
Ellman, Steven 10–11, 179–193, 250
emotional anxiety 199
emotional communication, and
    change ins psychic functioning
    133
emotional involvement, of analytic
    couple 112
emotional vacancy 213
empathy, advantages and limitations
    of 73
Eros 56–57
erotic sadomasochism 5
erotic sex 115
evaluation phase, of treatment
    69–72
evolutionary era 285

fantasy 80
    beating (*see* beating fantasy)
    unconscious 80
Fenichel, Otto 282
Fischer, G. 216
Freud 1, 3, 5–6, 49–50, 54–55, 63, 117,
    192, 209

Freud's theory of component drives
    of infantile sexuality 55, 285
frustration tolerance, individual
    level of 82

Gergely, G., (2000) 250
German army 282
Goodman, Dr. Nancy, case study by
    9, 95–110
    case presentation in beginning
        96–98
    countertransference in 101–102
    Grotstein discussion on 9–10,
        111–119
    Hanly discussion on 10, 123–135
    McBride discussion on 10,
        137–151
    pain and collapse in 105–107
    rejecting thoughts and
        behaviours in 99–100
    sado/masochistic representation
        in analytic room 100–101
    searching for relationship in
        98–99
    shock of difference in 103–105
    stormy phase of work 107–110
Greenman, Dr. Andrea, case study
    by 10, 157–177
    case history 158–159
    Ellman discussion on 10–11,
        179–193
    Rockwell discussion on 11,
        197–210
    treatment process 159–177
    Wurmser discussion on 11, 213–226
Grotstein, James S. 9–10, 111–119
Grubrich-Simitis, I., (2007, 2008)
    223–224

hands-off psychoanalytic approach
    245
Hanly, Margaret Ann 10, 123–135
hateful love 113

homophobia 51
homosexual mode 277
hurting love 9, 95, 112, 118–119, 141.
    see also Goodman, Dr. Nancy,
    case study by
hyper-sexuality 251

identification 207–209
illusion of oneness 18
infantile psychosexual
    development 1
infantile sadism 18
infant-mother interactions, early
    18, 46
inner continuity 214
innerego-passivity 223
instinctual anxiety 124
intense anxiety 149
"internalised homophobia" 51
inter-professional parlance 283
intrapsychic passivity 223
Ives, David 2

Joseph, Betty 58

Kilborne, Benjamin (2002) 215
Klein, Melanie 209, 282
Kohut, H., (1971) 249

Lacan, J., (2002) 252
life instincts 5

malapropisms 237
manic defence 89, 113, 118
Masoch, Leopold von Sacher 2
masochism proper 55
masochism. see also sadomasochism
    derivation of term 2
    Freud on 52, 54–56
    Novicks on 47–48, 50
    primary 54
masochistic remorse 229
massive shaming 221–222

masturbation, maternal prohibition
    of 50
masturbatory activity 259
McBride, Terrence 10, 137–151
McDougall, Joyce 46
mirroring 184
momentary self-defence 248
movements regressions 193
mutual painfulness 252–253

narcissistic rage 182
narcissistic vulnerabilities, and
    growth of sadomasochism 15
narcissistic wounds, and
    sadomasochism 18
negative transference states 189
New York Psychoanalytic Society
    280
non-metabolised destructiveness 53
non-self-disclosure, frame of 49
Novick, Jack 9, 63–78
Novick, Kerry Kelly 9, 63–78

"objective love" 64–65, 72
objectification 217–218
obligatory time 229
observable parallelism 214–215
oedipal paradox 260–261
oedipal period, developmental task
    of 138
oedipal, triad of 20–21
omnipotence 68–69
omnipotent beliefs 64
one-person field 180
oscillation in sadomasochistic
    relationships, phenomenon of
    144
outer victimhood 223
oversexualised 257
overstimulating, exhibitionistic 257
overweening superego 221

pain. see also specific case study
    oedipal phase and 20
    pleasure and 22, 52
    togetherness and 2
passion play, analytic 116–117
penis envy 50
perverse entrapment 22
perversion 21–22, 55
pleasure
    in cruelty 56
    in pain 52
    principle 54
preoedipal period, characteristic of
    138–139
"prey-predator instinct" 113
primary masochism 56
primary masochism, Freud idea of 54
primitive superego 229
Prince of Tides (movie) 203
priori assumption 224
priori presupposition 224
projective identification 84–85, 116,
    128, 146–148, 182, 199, 202, 206
"psychosomatosis" 46
psychic sadomasochism 5–7, 23
psychic space, destruction of 22
psychoanalysis 280
psychoanalytic sex 10, 112
psychoanalytic theory 274
psychosis 230
psychotic anxiety 124
psychotraumatology 216
puberty/adolescence 258

Rapaport, David (1953) 223
Rangell, Leo x–xxiii, 273–287
reflective self-awareness 249
regression 258
Reichbart, Dr. Richard, case study
    by 229–246
    Bach discussion 247–253

Basseches discussion 255–272
Rangell discussion 273–287
remorse 237–238
repeated traumatisation 218
repression, Fairbairn's view on
    146
revenge 237–238
revenge, desire for 125
Riedesser, P. 216
Robinson, Marianne 9, 79–92
Rockwell, Shelley 11, 197–210
Rosenfeld, Henry 207–208

Sade, Marquis de 2
sadism
    components of 113
    and masochism 252, 285
    and primitiveness 244
sadism/sadist, derivation of term 2
sadistic acts 276
sadistic ideation
    and wishes 242
sadomasochism 1–2, 5–6, 140, 255,
    261–262, 286
    anal phase of development in
        15–18
    and transference/
        countertransference 4
    case studies on (*see* case study)
    development of 15–23
    erotic 5
    genital/oedipal and 19–21
    growth of 15
    ideation 263–266
    imaginary scene related to 2
    in clinical work 15
    in plays 2–3
    narcissism and 18–19
    pain in (*see specific case study*)
    perversion and disavowal of
        difference and 21–23

pleasure and pain in, co-existence
    of 5, 22
psychic 5
relationships 258
trauma and 18–19
unrecognised 4
sadomasochism and aggression
    clinical case 276–280
    phenomenology 274–276
    theory 281–286
sadomasochistic
    arousal 251
    behaviour 233
    desires 234
    dynamics 182
    fantasies 217, 250–251
    ideation 237–238
    modality 250
schizoid anxiety 124
self-abasement 216
self-degradation 216
self destructiveness, increase in 49
self-object transference 184
self-punitive masochism 238
self-regulation and conflict
    resolution, systems of 64–67
    closed system 64–65
    open system 64–65
separation anxiety 140, 252
separation guilt 67
sex and erotism, distinction between
    115
sexual
    desires 236
    excitement 242–243
    fantasies 236
sexual arousal, by pain 52
sexualisation 219
sexuality and self-preservation 56–58
sexuality, masochistic nature of 55
sexual pleasure 22

sexual sadist 55
shame, masochism, and
    homophobia, links between 51
Shengold, L. (1989) 218
Sodre, Ignes 207
Sohn, Leslie 198, 207–209
soul blindness 215, 217
sphincter, in sadomasochistic mind
    17–18
split-off traumatic experience 128
splitting, as defensive structure
    182–183
"stalwartness 270
subjective object 113
superego command, sadistic 51
"symbiotic circle" 67
symbolisation and desymbolisation
    126–127

terror of twoness 124
Theaters of the Mind (Joyce
    McDougall), 46
therapeutic alliance tasks 65
Three Essays (Freud) 17
togetherness, ingredients of 2
"tolerate ambivalence" 130
"toomuchness" sense of 19
Torok, Maria 50
transference cycles 189–190
transference interpretations 216
transference 1–14, 266–268
transference/countertransference
    1–14. see also specific case studies
    interaction 255
trauma
    and perverse fantasies, link
        between 124–125

definition 217
narcissistic 19
on psychosexual development,
    impact of (see Goodman,
    Dr. Nancy, case study by)
and sadomasochism 18–19
"trauma of Eros" 57–58
    at beginning 72–74
traumatic anxiety 124
traumatic shame 216
traumatisation 217
traumatizing humiliation 216
traumatogenic shame 216
treatment 262–263
twinship transference 188
two-person field 180

unconscious fantasies 80, 83
unconscious guilt 84
unconscious sexualised scenes 2
unthinkable anxiety 124

Venus in Furs (Leopold von Sacher
    Masoch) 2
vertical splitting 185–186
Vienna Congress 282

Who's Afraid of Virginia Wolf (Edward
    Albee) 3
whole-object relationships 252
Winnicott, D. W. 72, 113–114, 140,
    150, 183, 185, 193
Winnicott, D. W. (1953, 1958, 1971)
    249–250
woman's work 256
World War Two 275
Wurmser, Léon 11, 213–226